Isaac Basier

The History of the English and Scotch Presbytery

Wherein is discovered their designs and practises for the subversion of government

in church and state

Isaac Basier

The History of the English and Scotch Presbytery
Wherein is discovered their designs and practises for the subversion of government in church and state

ISBN/EAN: 9783337410780

Printed in Europe, USA, Canada, Australia, Japan

Cover: Foto ©ninafisch / pixelio.de

More available books at **www.hansebooks.com**

THE HISTORY OF THE ENGLISH & SCOTCH Presbytery.

Wherein is discovered their Designs and Practises for the Subversion of Government in CHURCH and STATE.

Written in *French*, by an Eminent Divine of the REFORMED CHURCH, and now Englished.

The Second Edition Corrected and Enlarged.

EPIPHANIUS, Lib. 1. Hæres. 27.

Quod hominum Genus ad Ecclesiæ Dei probrum & Scandalum adornasse & submisisse Satanas videtur, quippe qui Christianorum sibi nomen indiderint, ut prop er eos offensæ Gentes à sanctæ Ecclesiæ utilitate abhorreant, nunquamq; veritatem, ob immania illorum facinora & incredibilem nequitiam, repudicut; ut inquam frequentibus illorum sceleribus animadversis, eos quoque, quia Sancta Dei Ecclesia sunt, tales esse sibi persuadeant, atque ita a verissima Dei Doctrina aures avertant, ut certe paucorum improbitate, conspecta in universos eadem Maledicta conjiciant.

Printed in Villa Franca, *Anno Dom.* 1660.

THE PREFACE.

WE will take our first rise from that Royal Declaration or Manifesto which his Majesty of great Britain, Cha. the I. commanded to be exposed to the world, for the satisfaction, not only of his own people, but of the Reformed Churches abroad, at that time when the differences were at the highest, 'twixt him and his Par-

Parliament-Subjects, who practised all the artifices that could be, (by making use of Press and Pulpit for that purpose) to make him not onely odious at home, but sent clandestine Agents, and intelligence abroad, to traduce him among the Reformed Princes and States, that He was branling in his belief, and had a design to re-introduce the Roman Religion into his Dominions, which was the motive of publishing this Manifesto hereunto annext.

       Carolus

CAROLUS, *singulari Omnipotentis Dei providentia* Angliæ, Scotiæ, Franciæ & Hiberniæ *Rex, Fidei Defensor,* &c. *Universis & singulis qui præsens hoc scriptum ceu protestationem inspexerint, potissimum Reformatæ Religionis, cultoribus cujuscunque sint gentis, gradus, aut conditionis salutem,* &c.

CUM ad aures nostras non ita pridem fama pervenerit, sinistros quosdam rumores, literasq; *politica* vel *perniciosa* potius quorundam industriâ sparsas esse, & nonnullis protestantium ecclesiis in exteris partibus emissas, nobis esse animum & consilium ab illa Orthodoxa Religione quam ab incunabilis imbibimus, & ad hoc usque momentum per integrum vitæ nostræ curriculum amplexi sumus recedendi; & Papismum in hæc Regna iterum introducendi, Quæ conjectura, ceu nefanda potius calumnia nullo prorsus nixa vel imaginabili fundamento horrendos hosce tumultus, & rabiem plusquàm belluinam in Anglia suscitavit sub prætextu cujusdam (chimericæ) Reformationis regimini legibusque hujus Dominii non solum incongruæ, sed incompatibilis: VOLUMUS, ut toti Christiano Orbi innotescat, ne minimam quidem animum nostrum incidisse cogitatiunculam hoc aggrediendi, aut transversum unguem ab illa Religione discedendi quam cum corona, sceptroque hujus regni solemni, & sacramentali juramento tenemur profiteri, protegere & propugnare. Nec tantum constantissima nostra praxis, & quotidiana in exercitiis præfatæ Religionis præsentia cum crebris in facie nostrorum agminum asseverationibus, publicisque procerum hujus Regni testimoniis, & sedula in regiam nostram sobolem educando circumspectione (omissis plurimis aliis argumentis) luculen-

luculentiſsimè hoc demonſtrat, ſed etiam fæliciſsimum illud matrimonium quod inter noſtram primogenitam, & illuſtriſsimũ principem *Auriacum* ſponte contraximus, idem fortiſsimè atteſtatur: Quo nuptiali fœdere inſuper conſtat, nobis non eſſe propoſitũ illã profiteri ſolummodo, ſed expandere, & corroborare quantum in nobis ſitum eſt.

Hanc ſacroſanctam Anglicanæ Chriſti Eccleſiæ Religionem, tot Theologorum convocationibus ſancitam, tot comitiorum edictis confirmatam tot Regiis Diplomatibus ſtabilitam, una cum regimine Eccleſiaſtico, & Liturgia ei annexa, quam liturgiam, regimenq; celebriores proteſtantium Authores tam *Germani,* quam *Galli,* tam *Dani* quam *Helvetici,* tam *Batavi,* quam *Bohemi* multis elogiis nec ſine quadam invidia in ſuis publicis ſcriptis comprobant & applaudunt, ut in tranſactionibus *Dordrechtanæ Synodus,* cui nonnulli noſtrorum *præſulum,* quorum
Dig-

Dignitati debita preſtita fuit reverentia (interfuerunt, apparet Iſtam, inquimus, Religionem quam Regius noſter pater (beatiſsimæ memoriæ) in illa celeberrima fidei ſuæ *Confeſsione* omnibus Chriſtianis principibus (ut & hæc præſens noſtra *proteſtatio* exhibita, publicè aſſerit : Iſtam, iſtam Religionem ſolenniter proteſtamur, Nos integram, ſartam tectam, & inviolabilem conſervaturos, & pro virili noſtro (divino adjuvante Numine) uſque ad extremã vitæ noſtræ periodũ protecturos, & omnibus noſtris Eccleſiaſticis pro muneris noſtri, & ſupradicti ſacro-ſancti juramenti ratione doceri, & prædicari curaturos. Quapropter injungimus & in mandatis damus Omnibus miniſtris noſtris in exteris partibus tam Legatis, quam Reſidentibus, Agentibuſque & nunciis, reliquiſque noſtris ſubditis ubicunque Orbis Chriſtiani terrarum aut curioſitatis aut comercii gratia degentibus hanc ſolennem & ſinceram noſtram

noſtram proteſtationem quandocunque ſeſe obtulerit loci & temporis opportunitas, communicare, aſſerere, aſſeverare.

Dat. in Academia & Civitate noſtra Oxonienſi pridei Idus Maii, 1644.

CHARLES by the Providence of Almighty God, King of *England, Scotland, France,* and *Ireland*, Defender of the Faith, &c. To all who profeſs the true Reformed Proteſtant Religion, of what Nation, degree, and condition ſoever they be to whom this preſent Declaration ſhall come, Greeting.

Whereas *We are given to underſtand, That many falſe Rumors, and ſcandalous Letters, are ſpread up and down amongſt the Reformed Churches in forreign Parts, by the* Pollitick, *or rather the pernitious induſtry of ſome ill affected perſons, that we have an inclination to recede from that Orthodox Religion, which we were born, baptized, and bred in, and which We have firmly profeſſed and practiſed throughout the whole courſe of our life to this moment, and that We intend*

intend to give way to the Introduction and publick exercise of Popery again in Our Dominions: Which conjecture or rather most detestable calumny, being grounded upon no imaginable foundation, hath raised these horrid Tumults, and more then barbarous Wars throughout this flourishing Island, under pretext of a kind of Reformation, which would not only prove incongruous, but incompatible with the fundamental Laws and government of this Kingdom. We desire that the whole Christian World should take notice, and rest assured, that We never entertained in Our imagination the least thought to attempt such a thing, or to depart a jot from that holy Religion, which when we received the Crown and Scepter of this Kingdom, We took a most solemn Sacramental Oath to profess and protect. Nor doth Our most constant practice and quotidian visible presence in the exercise of this sole Religion, with so many Asseverations in the head of Our Armies, and the publick Attestation of our Barons, with the circumspection used in the education of our Royal Off-spring, besides divers other undeniable Arguments, onely demonstrate this; but also that happy Alliance of Marriage, We contracted twixt Our eldest Daughter, and the Illustrious Prince of Orenge, most clearly confirms the reallity of Our intentions herein; by which Nuptial ingagement it appears further, that Our endeavours are not only to make a bare profession thereof in Our own Dominions, but to inlarge and corroborate it abroad as much as lieth in our Power: This most
-holy

holy Religion of the Anglican Church, ordained by so many Convocations of learned Divines, confirmed by so many Acts of National Parliaments; and strengthened by so many Royal Proclamations, together with the Ecclesiastick Discipline and Liturgy thereunto appertaining, which Liturgy and Discipline, the most eminent of Protestant Authors, as well Germans as French; as well Danes as Swedes and Switzens; as well Belgians, as Bohemians, do with many Elogies (and not without a kind of Envy) approve and applaud in their publick Writings, particularly in the transactions of the Synod of Dort, wherein besides other of Our Divines (who afterwards were Prelates) one of Our Bishops assisted, to whose dignity all due respects and precedency was given: This Religion We say, which Our Royal Father of blessed memory doth publickly assert in that His famous Confession address'd, as we also do this our Protestation, to all Christian Princes; This, this most holy Religion, with the Hierarchy and Liturgy therof. We solemnly protest, that by the help of Almighty God, we will endeavour to our utmost power, and last period of our life, to keep intire and inviolable, and will be careful, according to our duty to Heaven, and the tenor of the foresaid most sacred Oath at Our Coronation, that all our Ecclesiasticks in their several degrees and Incumbences shall preach and practise the same. Wherefore we enjoyn and command all our Ministers of State beyond the Seas, as well

Ambas-

Ambassadors, as Residents, Agents and Messengers; And We desire all the rest of Our loving Subjects, that sojourn either for curiosity or commerce in any forraign Parts, to communicate, uphold, and assert this Our solemn and sincere Protestation, when opportunity of time and place shall be offered.

This *Royal Declaration* or *Manifesto* was committed to the management and care of *James Howel* Esq; Clerk of His Majesties Privie Council (who though then Prisoner in the Fleet) performed the business very worthily and like himself.

Charles

CHARLES, par la Providence de Dieu Roy de la grand' Bretagne, de France, & d' Irlande, Defenseur de la Foy, &c. A tous ceux qui ceste presente Declaration verront, particulierement a Ceux de la Religion Reformee de quelque Nation, degre ou condition qu'ils soient, Salut.

Yant receu advis de bonne main que plusieurs faux rapports & lettres sont esparses parmi les Eglises, Reformees de là la mer, par la *politique*, ou plustost la *pernicieuse* industrie de personnes mal affectionnes a nostre governement, que nous auons dessein a receder de celle Religion que Nous auons professè & pratiquè tout le temps de nostre vie iusques a present; & de vouloir introduire la papautè derechef en nos Dominions, Laquelle conjecture, ou *calumnie* plustost, appuyee sur nul fundement imaginable, a suscitè ces horribles tumultes & allumè le feu d' une d'une tres sanglante guerre en tous les quatre coins de ceste fleurissante Monarchie, soubs pretexte d'une (*chymerique*) Reformation, la quelle seroit incompatible avec le governement, & les loix fondementales de ce Royaume.

Nous Desirons, quil soit notoire a tout le monde, que la moindre pensee de ce faire n'a pas entree en nostre imagination, de departir ancunement de cell' Orthodoxe Religion, qu'auec la Couronne & le sceptre de ce Royaume Nous sommes tenus par un serment solennel & sacramentaire a proteger & defendre. Ce qu'appert non seulement par nostre quotidienne presence es Exercies de la dite Religion, avec, tant d'asseverations a la teste de nos Armees & la publicque Attestation de nos Barons, avec le soin que nous tenons en la nourriture des Princes & Princesses nos enfans, Mais le tres-heureux mariage que nous avons conclu entre la nostre plus aisnee, & le tres-illustrie Prince d'*Orenge* en est encore un tres-évident tesmoignage, par la quell' alliance il appert aussy que nostre desir est de n'en faire pas vne nue profession seulement dicelle, mais de la vouloir estendre & corroberer autant qu'il nous est possible: Cest' Orthodoxe Religion de leglise *Anglicane* Ordonnee par tant de Conventione de Teologues, confirmee par tant de arrests d'Parlement, & fortifie par tant d'Edicts royaux auec la discipline & la Lyturgie a elle appartenant, laquelle discipline & Lyturgie les plus celebres Autheurs Protestants,

tant

tant *Francois*, qu' *Allemands*, tant *Seudois* que *Suisses*, tant *Belgiens*, que *Bohemiens* approuent entierement & non sans quelqu envie en leur escrits particulierement en la Synode de *Dort*; ou un de nos Euesques assistoit, & la Reverence & precedence deue a sa dignite Ecclesiastique luy fut exactement rendue : Ceste tres-sainte Religion que nostre feu *pere* de tres-heureuse memoire aduoue en sa celebre *Confession* de la Foy addressee come nous faisons ceste *Declaration* a tous Princes Chrestiens; Nous Protestons que moyennant la grace de Dieu, nous tascherone de conseruer ceste Religion inviolable, & en son entier selon la mesure de puissance que Dieu a mis entre nos mains; Et nous requerons & commandons a tous nos ministres d'estat tant Ambassadeurs, que Residens, Agens ou messagers, & a tous autres nos subjects qui font leur seiour es pays estrangers de communiquer, maintenir & aduouer ceste nostre solennelle Protestation toutes fois & quantes que l'occasion se presentera.

TO THE
MINISTERS
OF THE
REFORMED CHURCH
AT
PARIS.

Gentlemen,

Aving to contend with them who invite you to uphold their disloyalty by your example, nothing can be more to our purpose, then to prefix your example in the front of this work to teach them Loyalty. During the Agitations of the State, your Church, as the Needle in the Marriners Compaß, kept steady upon the point of rest, which is God and the King: And your obedience served as an Enſign on a hill to France, to guide the people to their duty. Whereby you have justified the holineſs of your profeſſion, making the world know, the Religion you teach binds you to be good ſubjects, and that you honour the King, becauſe ye fear God.

There-

Therefore the English Covenanters did very ill to address themselves to you, since they hold a method quite contrary, for they dishonour and massacre their King, under a colour of devotion to God, and undertake to set up the Kingdome of Jesus Christ, by the ruine of the Kingdome of their Soveraign; which is as if they would build the Temple of God with Cannon shot, and defend Religion in violating it.

The truth of the Gospel was never advanced by these wayes, but the patience, and even the sufferings of the Christians, was it which propagated the Christian Religion, and rendered the Church mighty and glorious. Those who suffered under the Pagan and Arian Emperours, conquered both the Empire and Emperours; and the Champions of truth purchased a Kingdome to Jesus Christ, not in shedding the blood of their Soveraigns, but in pouring forth their own for righteousness, by a voluntary submission to their judgement.

He who cannot frame himself to this Doctrine, doth not so much as God requires of him, if he makes profession of Christianity; for Christ tells us in calling us, that whosoever taketh not up his Cross, and cometh not after me, cannot be my Disciple; and commands him who would imbrace the Gospel, to set down before and calculate the expence, as if he were about to build. Certainly he that cannot resolve to subject himself to his Soveraign for the love of God, and never draw his sword against him to whom God hath committed it, made an ill calculation before he dedicated himself to Jesus Christ, for he ought not to take upon him Christianity, if he were not able to go through with it, and was not resolved rather to suffer then resist, and to spend his goods and life to preserve himself in that subjection, commanded by the Word of God.

For maintaining this holy Doctrine, we have been banished and pursued with Armes, and after we had defended our Soveraign with more fidelity then success, we have been constrained to forsake our dear Country; driven from our houses,

houses, and spoiled of our revenues, but yet we praise God for giving them, since he hath done us the honour that we should lose them for his service; and we ought this to our King, of whom our lands held, to abandon them for love of him: For to enter into a Covenant against him peaceably to enjoy his, and the Kings his Predecessors bounty, and to betray the truth, and our consciences, to save our moneys, we could never resolve.

Now since those who have done the evil, began first to cry out, and have spread their unjust clamours through all the Reformed Churches, we'll make the same journey with our just complaints, and after the example of the abased Levite, by the Sonnes of Jemini, we send this recital of our grievances through all the quarters of Israel; Judg. 19. 30. Consider of it, take advice, and speak your minds.

The injury which doth touch us nearest, is not our Exile, nor the loss of our goods, nor theirs of our nearest Relations, but the extreme wrong done to the Gospel, and the Reformed Churches, to whom these new Reformers falsly impute their Maximes of Rebellion, and hereby render our most holy profession suspected and hateful to Princes of a contrary Religion.

This (Gentlemen) toucheth you very near, considering your condition, and the Summons the Assembly at Westminster, made to you to covenant with them, or to make a covenant like theirs. The Epistle was addressed to the Church of Paris, in the name of all the Reformed Churches of France, and with the Epistle they sent the Oath of their Covenant, which concludes with an Exhortation in form of a prayer to God, That it would please him to stir up by their example, other Churches who live under the Tyranny of Antichrist, to swear this Covenant, or one like it.

This same Epistle, together with the Oath, being sent to the Ministers of the Church of Genevah, stirred up in them

them a holy jealousie, and drew from that excellent person, Monsieur Diodati, *who is now in glory, an answer worthy of him in the name of all the Church*: Repell this horrible scandal, which so extremely wrongs Christianity in general; wash and cleanse this filthy attempt of the blackest oppression, which above all is imputed to the most pure profession of the Gospel, as if the Gospel opposed, and affronted by a kind of antipathy and secret hatred, all Royal Power of Soveraign Authority. Pacifie the exasperated spirit, and too much provoked of your King, and drive him not upon Pinacles and Precipices.

Blessed be God who touched the heart of this great person, whose memory shall be for ever precious for rendring so open a testimony to the truth; *And because he have not suffered himself to be flattered and perswaded by the complements of these enemies to his aMjesty, to applaud them in their evil actions, such are these Refiners of Reformation, as not content by their factious zeal to set their own country on fire, but they labour also to cast the fire into their neighbours, and to blow Rebellion through all* Europe.

And of late the most enormous actions of the English *drew from Master* Salmasius, *Prince of Letters, and the Honour of* France, *a defence of the Right of Kings*; *God was so pleased to raise up the Learnedst pen of these times to defend the best cause of the world, in which this great person hath highly honoured his country*; *But to speak right, he more honoured himself, and the Church wherein he was educated. For if hereafter these malefactors dare be so bold, as to say the Reformed Churches approved their actions, they shall produce this book which condemns them, and defends the Royal cause with such wisdome, and efficacy of spirit, suitable to the dignity of the subject, and shall require them to produce, if they can, any one of the Reformed Churches who have in the least manner written in favour of their proceedings*: *It should have been a strange and shamefull* thing, if there were none found amongst the Reformed Churches who should not disown their wicked Doctrines, and cause all Princes and people of the world to know that the Reformed Churches are very far from following their counsels, and abhor their seductions to disloyalty, from what part soever they come.

Heretofore indeed it was accounted the duty of charity and prudence, to cover the faults of this faction, and if corruption enter into Israel, not to publish it in Gath; but when the Doctrine of Rebellion disputed in corners, ascends the Pulpit, hold assizes in open Court, sends forth Ambassadors, invites the Reformed Churches to their party, and imploy the Gospel, Piety, zeal of Gods Glory, to raise subjects against their Soveraigns; now 'tis time or never to pluck off their mask of hypocrisie, and shew where the evil lies, and discover the wickedness of a party, to preserve from shame and disgrace the general; and the rather since the Aphorismes of Rebellion, and seducing people to sedition, are reproached to the Protestants, and imployed by the enemies of our holy Religion to stir up Princes against the Church, and the pure profession of the Gospel. Tis the duty of the Reformed Churches to speak aloud, that 'tis not we that teach the people are above their King, and that endeavour by Letters and Intelligences a general rising, but that it's the Covenanters of England, who attempting to cut off their King and Monarchy by the sword, labour in vain to seduce their neighbours, to encrease their party, thereby to hide themselves in the multitude of their complices, they came forth of us long since, but were not of us, and for their Doctrines and actions (which are the only things evil in their Reformation) they never received any countenance or incouragement from us.

We assure our selves Gentlemen, in that Divine assistance which hath to this present upheld you, that ye will never be seduced to defend evil, neither by complacency nor contradiction, but will follow the precept of the Apostle Saint James,

Jam.

Jam. 2. 1. My Brethren have not the Faith of our Lord Jesus Christ, the Lord of Glory with respect of persons. *Ye will consider that those who chase us, seek not your alliance, but to strengthen their separation from us, and not to imbrace good Doctrine, or follow your councel, which if they had asked and followed, the one had never sold their King, nor the other ever massacred him.*

Believe it (Sirs) they are your best friends at distance rather then neer, and if ye never converse with them, ye will never be weary of their company.

Your free, meek and solid piety, which feeds it self simply upon the substance of Religion, without picking quarrels at the shell, is very far from sordid superstition, and the Hypocondriak and bloody zeal of these Covenanters, who pretend to advance the Kingdome of Jesus Christ, by cutting the throats of his Disciples, and cementing his Temple with blood instead of the cement of charity; and in the mean while, make some petty circumstances, the principals of Religion, and cut out their holy Doctrine according to the Discipline which they are forging, as he that cuts his flesh to make his doublet fit for his body.

By how much more these are wicked, by so much the more are they worthy of compassion, whom we must behold as people drunken with the Wine of Astonishment, *which they themselves confess in their Epistle they sent unto you, they shall find the rest of their description in that place, where they borrowed those words, and shall there behold themselves set forth,* as a wild Bull in a net, they are full of the fury of the Lord, Isa. 51. 20. *For as the wild Bull rageth when he feels himself intangled, and intangleth, and insnares himself more by raging; so these miserable people, who by an impetuosity without reason rid themselves out of all Laws, Ecclesiastical and Civil, are insnared in stronger bonds then before, and by their bruitish fury are more and more intangled. These, these are the sad effects of the just wrath of God, who hath smote those with blindness, who have*

abused

abused the light of the Gospel, and have given them the heart of a beast, Dan. 4. 16. as he did to Nebuchadnezzar, who have cast off all humanity. God by his mercy reduce to their senses, and guide them and us in his paths, and grant his peace to them that are far off, and to them that are near, Isa. 57. 19. For in civil wars, that party that is neerest to God, and right, is yet very far from his duty.

Your wisdome will instruct you to profit by the folly of your neighbours, and their evil actions teach you to do well, they will let you see that to destroy the Ecclesiastical and Political Order, by a bloody war to reform Religion, is to commit the fault in the vulgar Latine Translation, Evertit domum, instead of Everrit, Luke 15. 8. That is to overthrow the house in stead of sweeping it; the folly is the greater, when its only to find a trifle, and that they overthrow both Church and State, for some particularity, which were it good, cannot recompence the general destruction.

You will also learn by the proceedings of these Covenanters, that its impossible to alter the foundation of Church and State, without pulling down the house, which is the work of the blind, as Sampson, to over-turn the Pillars of the publick building, that those that thrust them down might be crushed to pieces under the fall; that those that take the Church and State apieces to cleanse it, have not the power to put it together and in order again when they please, and that all violent changes in a State, as in an old body, are alwayes for the worst.

We hope also that our good God, beholding us with pity, in this our weak condition, will give you somewhat to observe and learn from us, as that a Rebellion which pulls down Monarchy, without thinking so, lifts it up, and fortifie't, as a violent Crisis, which if it takes not away the Patient, contributes to his recovery. For the insolence of the new masters, doth mind the people of their duty to their lawful Prince, and the unlooked for success of a new Obligarchy, sowes dissention amongst the Usurpers. The conduct of the Providence

of

of God in the movings of States teacheth us, that in chasti-
sing Kings by the rebellion of their subjects, hereby he punisheth the people more then their Kings, and those very
Kings that God gives people in his wrath, Hose 13. 11.
are not taken away without his fury, and the publick ruine,
which is then greatest, when he takes from an ungrateful people, a King whom he have given in his mercy; the wise,
and fearing God, should consider their sufferings under their
Soveraigns, as sinister influences of celestial bodies, against
which no man in his wits will draw his sword, for both the
one and the other comes from heaven, and cannot be remedied
but by humility, prayers, and veneration, all other remedies
are worse then the evil.

Also amidst your grief to behold the ruine of our not long
since flourishing Churches, you may comfort your selves in
the weakness of our condition, which now renders us less subject to the like dangers; for as full and sanguine bodies, are
most subject to violent feavers and sharp diseases, which those
of weaker complexions are ordinarily free from, so those
persons who have power in their hands, and are puffed up with
a long prosperity, ordinarily fall into most violent evils,
which seiseth not upon them, but with too much strength:
Then when the Church hath the least lustre, she oft times is
neerest to God, as the Moon is never neerer the Sun then when
she is in the lowest degree of her declension, and without light
to our regard. The Power of God is made perfect in our
weakness, and we hope to behold you subsist, yea encrease and
grow in bowing down under the storm, whilst those that have
so striven and contended against their Soveraigns shall be
rooted out by their arrogancy.

By humility and submission under the mighty hand
of God, which leads his Church through waies he knows
safest for them, and stopping the ear to all factious Councils cloathed with the zeal of Religion, ye will at last obtain that testimony of God which he gives to the Church
of Ephesus; I know thy works, and thy labour,
and

and thy patience, and how thou canst not bear them which are evil, and thou hast tried them which say they are Apostles, and are not, and hast found them liars, and hast borne, and hast patience, and hast not fainted, *Rev.* 2.2. *and thus ye shall surely obtain the promised reward following*, To him that overcometh, will I give to eate of the tree of life, which is in the midst of the paradise of God, *v.*7.

This hope is our support in the depth of our afflictions, for under that terrible weight of publick and particular miseries, capable to bear down the strongest and firmest spirits, we are raised and kept up by this consolation, that we serve a good Master, who will never forsake them who forsake all which is most dear to them to follow him. What though our sufferings be the effects of our sinnes, yet are they also honourable markes of our loyalty, both to God and our King, and though we have left our estates a little before death would have taken them away, yet God hath by his grace preserved in us a good conscience, riches which is not subject to sequestration, but dying we shall carry away with us.

In these great tryalls of our faith and patience, whilst we seek ease in pouring forth our griefs into the bosome of our brethren, behold yet another encrease of affliction, upon affliction; for we find to our great regret, that the subtilty of our enemies have begotten an evil understanding between you and some of ours, to which some have much contributed, if the complaints we bear be true, that they have manifested and declared themselves contrary to the Doctrine of the Reformed Churches, and that they have despised your assemblies, as not being Churches, and maintained that there could be no Church where there was no Bishop.

As for their Doctrine, if it be divers from our publick Confession, they are no more of our Church then of yours;

yours; and to satisfie you upon this point, we have joyned the Confession of the Church of England, which all those who have been received into holy Orders, sware to defend at their reception, and all who were to be admitted into Churches were injoyned at their entrance, publickly to read, and to professe thereupon, their consent to them, under pain of losing their Benefices. If any have departed from that profession, which they did so solemnly make, the body of the Church which maintains that holy Doctrine, is no way responsible for their erring. If the Rebels had not prevented the King from assembling a nationall Synod, to which his Majesty purposed to invite other Reformed Churches, your Judgments would have been heard for the purging our Churches of all new Doctrines, which without all comparison are worse, and in a farre greater number amongst our enemies, then amongst the Royall party.

As for this position, that there cannot be a Church without a Bishop, we account it full of rashnesse and void of Charity; It's indeed a cruel sentence to deprive of the benefit of the Gospel, and of their union with Christ, all those Churches which live under the Crosse, and cannot enjoy the Episcopal Order. That Famous Dr. Andrews Bishop of Winchester, was not of this opinion, for in one of his Epistles touching Episcopacy, He (saith he) should be harder than Iron, who would not acknowledge that there are holy Churches that subsist and flourish without Bishops; and with what respect our Bishops speak of your Church, you shall read in this ensuing Treatise.

It's easie to see that the Episcopal Order is wholly incompatible with the present condition of the Reformed Churches of France, for if there were twenty or thirty Bishops amongst you, that should Govern all the other Churches, it would be easie for those of the contrary Religion under whom you live, to fil up those places with some persons who should be at their devotion; whence would follow, either

ther a seduction, or an oppression of the other Pastors: But whilst the Gentlemen of the Clergy in the Court behold all Pastors equal, they will lose their cunning in this multitude, and although they be excellent in playing on the Organs, yet they have not fingers enough to touch every Key.

If your Order of equality might or ought to be conserved, if it should please God the French Monarchy should embrace the Reformation, its a thing we will not touch, but if that only were the obstruction, we account you too wise and good Christians, and such as would not hinder the setling of the holy Doctrine, for maintaining a point of Discipline.

You then (Gentlemen) joyning to your Christian charity, the French courtesie, pardon our English Schollers, who peradventure have brought with them from the University, an humour a little affirmative, and from the fresh remembrance of their Glorious Church, retain yet an admiration of home things, which is an humour Neighbour Nations observe in the English, and which those that heretofore have known England, will easily pardon.

Consider on the other side, whether some of yours have not given them just occasion to be so sharp and bitter, and to passe their limits in their affirmations; it cannot be denied but we have met with spirits possessed with the reports of our adversaries, who have been more ready to court you than we, as alwaies those that have an evil cause, are ever more diligent to gain by faction that which they want, and cannot obtain by right. It may be also that your people have manifested themselves too rigid in their Opinions, as well as some of ours, upon points which touch not the principles of Religion; and as it is ordinary for humane infirmity to turn custom into necessity, you may not wonder that if some of yours maintain as necessary and perpetual, which your wise Reformers established as arbitrary, and for the present necessity, as it is formally declared by the last Article of your Disciplins.

We

We have placed in the Front of this work, the Manifesto of the Late King Charles the First, of Blessed and Glorious Memory, in which he takes a religious care to satisfie you, touching his Constancy in the Reformed Religion, and of his Resolution to enlarge and strengthen it in all forraign Countries to the utmost of his power, he could no more to manifest how much he valued your affection and good opinion, and we following the example of our holy and Glorious Martyr, labour here to knit with you a holy union, which our enemies have so vigorously laboured to break, and in these our great afflictions do take care to prevent your, and to give you saving Conncell.

Know then, Gentlemen, that your most holy Religion is much defamed by the Actions of these paracide Zealots, who have particularly courted and invited you to Covenant with them, and that your Churches are blemished in reputation, onely because these men have dared to addresse their infamous complements to you, a thing neverthelesse which ye could not prevent how great soever your aversion were from their wicked actions; wherefore we beseech you, as you love your subsistance and the honour of the Gospel, which ought to be dearer to you then your lives, that you exhort the general of your Churches to declare readily and vigorously by a publick Act against these false brethren and their pernicious Maximes, for fear least the crime of men, be imputed to Religion, and that the innocent suffer not for the guilty. Let it appear to the State under which ye live, that the Reformed Religion for conscience sake upheld Kingly Authority, and that it is the true Doctrine that maintains subjects in their duty, and a Kingdome in peace.

You may also boldly advise the Gentlemen at Court to beware of them, and that they give order to prevent that inundation, that is threatned from our Ilands, and let them be most assured that the Independent Armies, have not lesse ambition to cause all people to rise, and overthrow

throw all the Monarchs of Christendom, & that to this effect Cr——have often declared his intentions: all the popular tumults in France are the productions of this Artist, ever in motion, infatigable, swoln with successe, who hath his eyes and hands every where, and gains in all places either by the sword or gold; now in all changes of the State whosoever gains, the Church loseth, and the filth in all inundations resteth upon the vallies.

We are so near neighbours that the contagion of our evils cannot but passe to you, therefore ye shall do prudently and Christianly to keep your selves from the contagion of our evils, and since those of the Reformed Religion are better instructed, then the other, it is therefore for them first to begin to do their duty.

And to this the considerations in this ensuing Treatise will encourage you, and our adversities will furnish you with better Counsels then the prosperity of our persecutors, Agræ Fortunæ sana Concilia, we hope that this true and lively pourtraiture of their Rebellious Covenant that we present unto you, will so strike the spectators with horror that they will become good Christians, and good subjects by Antiperistisis.

THE

THE ARTICLES OF RELIGION of the CHURCH OF ENGLAND.

I.

There is but one living and true God, everlasting, without body, parts, or passions; of infinite power, wisdom and goodnesse, the Maker and preserver of all things both visible and invisible. And in unity of this Godhead there be three persons, of one substance, power, and eternity; the Father, the Son, and holy Ghost.

II.

II.

The Sonne, which is the Word of the Father, begotten from everlasting of the Father, the very and eternall God of one substance with the Father, took mans nature in the womb of the blessed Virgine, of her substance: so that two whole and perfect natures, that is to say, the Godhead and manhood, were joyned together in one person, never to be divided, whereof is one Christ, very God and very man who truly suffered, was crucified, dead, and buried, to reconcile his Father to us, and to be a sacrifice, not onely for Originall guilt, but also for actuall sinnes of men.

III.

As Christ died for us, and was buried: so also is it to be beleeved, that he went down into hell.

IV.

Christ did truly rise again from death, and took again his body, with flesh, bones, and all things appertaining to the perfection of mans nature, wherewith he ascended into heaven, and there sitteth untill he return to judge all men at the last day.

V.

The holy Ghost proceeding from the Father and the Sonne, is of one Substance, majesty and glory, with the Father and the Son, very and eternall God.

VI.

Holy Scripture containeth all things necessary to salvation: so that whatsoever is not read therein, nor may be proved thereby, is not to be required of any man, that it should be beleeved as an Article of the faith, or be thought requisite or necessary to salvation. In the name of the holy Scripture, we do understand those Canonicall Books of the Old & New Testament, of whose authority was never any doubt in the Church.

Of

Of the Names and Number of the *Canonical Books.*

Genesis.
Exodus.
Leviticus.
Numeri.
Deuteronomium.
Josue.
Judges.
Ruth.
The 1. Book of Samuel.
The 2. Book of Samuel.
The 1. Book of Kings.
The 2. Book of Kings.
The 1. Book of Chronicles.
The 2. Book of Chronicles.
The 1. Book of Esdras.
The 2. Book of Esdras.
The Book of Hester.
The Book of Job.
The Psalmes.
The Proverbs.
Ecclesiastes or Preacher.
Cantica, or Songs of Solomon.
4. Prophets the greater.
12. Prophets the lesse.

And the other Books (as Hierome saith) the Church doth read for example of life and instruction of manners: but yet doth it not apply them to establish any doctrine; Such are these following.

The 3. Book of Esdras.
The 4. Book of Esdras.
The Book of Tobias.

The Book of Judeth.
The rest of the Book of Hester.
The Book of Wisdom.
Jesus the son of Sirach.
Baruch the Prophet.
The song of the three Children.
The Story of Susanna.
Of Bell and the Dragon.
The Prayer of Manasses.
The 1. Book of Maccabees.
The 2. Book of Maccabees.

All the Bookes of the New Testament, as they are commonly received, we do receive and account them Canonicall.

VII.

The Old Testament is not contrary to the New, for both in the Old and New Testament, everlasting life is offered to mankind by Christ, who is the onely Mediator between God and man, being both God and man. Wherefore they are not to be heard which feign that the old fathers did look only for transitory promises. Although the Law given from God by Moses, as touching Ceremonies and Rites, do not bind Christian men, nor the civil precepts thereof ought of necessity to bee received in any Commonwealth; yet notwithstanding, no Christian man whatsoever is free from the obedience of the Commandments, which are called Morall.

VIII.

The three Creeds, Nice Creed, Athanasius Creed, and that which is commonly called the Apostles Creed, ought throughly to be received and beleeved: for they may be proved by most certain warrants of holy Scripture.

IX.

Originall sin standeth not in the following of Adam (as the Pelagians do vainly talk) but it is the fault and corruption of the nature of every man, that
naturally

naturally is ingendred of the off-spring of Adam, whereby man is very far gone from originall righteousnesse, and is of his own nature inclined to evil, so that the flesh lusteth alwaies contrary to the spirit, and therefore in every person born into this world, it deserveth Gods wrath and damnation. And this infection of nature doth remain, yea, in them that are regenerated, whereby the lust of the flesh, called in Greek ϕρόνημα σαρκὸς, which some do expound the wisdome, some sensuallity, some the affection, some the desire of the flesh, is not subject to the Law of God. And although there is no condemnation for them that beleeve and are baptized, yet the Apostle doth confesse, that concupiscence and lust, hath of it self the nature of sinne.

X.

The condition of man after the fall of Adam, is such, that he cannot turn and prepare himself by his own natural strength and good works to faith and calling upon God: Wherefore we have no power to do good works pleasant and acceptable to God, without the grace of God by Christ preventing us, that we may have a good will, and working with us, when we have that good will.

XI.

VVE are accounted righteous before God, only for the merit of our Lord and Saviour Jesus Christ by faith, and not for our own works, or deservings. Wherefore, that we are justified by faith onely, is a most wholesome Doctrine, and very full of comfort, as more largely is expressed in the Homily of Justification.

XII.

Albeit that good works, which are the fruits of faith, and follow after Justification, cannot put away our sinnes, and endure the severity of Gods judgement, yet are they pleasing and acceptable to God in Christ, and do spring out necessarily of a true and lively faith, in so much that by them a lively faith may be as evidently knowen, as a tree discerned by the fruit.

XIII.

Works done before the grace of Christ, and the inspiration of his Spirit are not pleasant to God, forasmuch as they spring not of faith in Jesu Christ, neither do they make men meet to receive grace, or (as the School-Authors say) deserve grace of congruity: yea, rather for that they are not done as God hath willed and commanded them to be done, we doubt not but they have the nature of sinne.

XIV.

Voluntary Works, besides, over and above Gods Commandments, which they call works of Supererogation, cannot be taught without arrogancy and impiety. For by them men do declare that they do not onely render unto God as much as they are bound to do, but that they do more for his sake then of bounden duty is required: Wheras Christ saith plainly, When ye have done all that are commanded to you, say, We are unprofitable servants.

XV.

Christ in the truth of our nature, was made like unto us in all things (sinne onely except) from which he was clearly void, both in his flesh, and in his Spirit. He came to be a Lamb without spot, who by sacrifice of himself once made, should take away the sinnes of the world: and sinne (as Saint John saith) was not in him. But all we the rest, (although baptized and born again in Christ) yet offend in many things, and if we say we have no sinne, we deceive our selves, and the truth is not in us.

XVI.

Not every deadly sinne willingly committed after Baptisme, is sinne against the holy Ghost, and unpardonable. Wherefore, the grant of repentance is not to be denied to such as fall into sinne after Baptisme. After we have received the holy Ghost, we may depart from grace given, and fall into sinne, and by the grace of God (we may) arise again, and amend our lives. And therefore, they are to be condemned, which say they can no more sinne as long as they live here,

here, to deny the place of forgivenesse to such as truly repent.

XVII.

PRedestination to life, is the everlasting purpose of God, whereby (before the foundations of the world were laid) he hath constantly decreed by his counsel, secret to us, to deliver from curse and damnation, those whom he hath chosen in Christ out of mankind, & to bring them by Christ to everlasting salvation, as vessels made to honour. Wherefore they which be indued with so excellent a benefit of God, be called according to Gods purpose by his Spirit working in due season: they through grace obey the calling, they be justified freely: they be made Sons of God by adoption: they be made like the Image of his onely begotten Sonne Jesus Christ: they walk religiously in good works, and at length by Gods mercy they attain to everlasting felicity.

As the godly consideration of Predestination and our Election in Christ, is full of sweet, pleasant, and unspeakable comfort to godly persons, and such as feel in themselves the working of the Spirit of Christ, mortifying the works of the flesh, and their earthly members, and drawing up their mind to high and heavenly things, as well because it doth greatly establish and confirm their faith of eternall salvation, to be enjoyed through Christ, as because it doth fervently kindle their love towards God: So, for curious and carnall persons, lacking the Spirit of Christ, to have continually before their eyes the sentence of Gods predestination, is a most dangerous down fall, whereby the devil doth thrust them either into desparation or into retchlessenesse of most unclean living, no lesse perilous then desparation.

Furthermore, we must receive Gods promises in such wise as they be generally set forth to us in holy Scripture: and in our doings, that will of God is to be followed, which we have expresly declared unto us in the Word of God.

C 3   XVIII.

XVIII.

They also are to be had accursed, that presume to say that every man shall be saved by the Law or sect which he professeth, so that he be diligent to frame his life according to that law, and the light of nature. For holy Scripture doth set out unto us only the Name of Iesus Christ, whereby men must be saved.

XIX.

The visible Church of Christ, is a congregation of faithfull men, in the which the pure Word of God is preached, and the Sacraments be duely ministred, according to Christs Ordinance, in all those things that of necessity are requisite to the same.

As the Church of Hierusalem, Alexandria, and Antioch have erred: So also the Church of Rome hath erred, not onely in their living and manner of ceremonies, but also in matters of faith.

XX.

The Church hath power to decree Rites or Ceremonies, and authority in controversies of faith: And yet it is not lawfull for the Church to ordain any thing that is contrary to Gods Word written, neither may it so expound one place of Scripture, that it be repugnant to another. Wherefore although the Church be a witnesse and a keeper of holy Writ: yet as it ought not to decree any thing against the same, so besides the same ought it not to inforce any thing to be beleeved for necessity of salvation.

XXI.

Generall Councels may not be gathered together without the commandment and will of Princes. And when they be gathered together (forasmuch as they be an assembly of men, whereof all be not governed with the Spirit and Word of God) they may erre, and sometime have erred, even in things pertaining unto God. Wherefore things ordained by them as necessary to salvation, have neither strength nor authority, unlesse it may be declared that they be taken out of holy Scripture.

XXII.

The Romish doctrine concerning Purgatory, Pardons, worshiping and adoration as well of Images as of Relicks, and also invocation of Saints, is a fond thing, vainly invented, and grounded upon no warranty of Scripture, but rather repugnant to the Word of God.

XXIII.

It is not lawfull for any man to take upon him the office of publick preaching, or ministring the Sacraments in the Congregation, before he be lawfully called, and sent to execute the same. And those we ought to judge lawfully called & sent, which be chosen & called to this work by men, who have publick authority given unto them in the Congregation, to call and send Ministers into the Lords vineyard.

XXIV.

It is a thing plainly repugnant to the Word of God, and the custome of the Primitive Church, to have publick prayer in the Church, or to minister the Sacraments in a tongue not understanded of the people.

XXV.

Sacraments ordained of Christ be not onely badges or tokens of Christian mens profession: but rather they be certain sure witnesses, and effectuall signes of grace and Gods good will towards us, by the which he doth work invisibly in us, and doth not onely quicken, but also strengthen and confirm our faith in him.

There are two Sacraments ordained of Christ our Lord in the Gospel, that is to say, Baptisme and the Supper of the Lord.

Those five commonly called Sacraments, that is to say, Confirmation, Penance, Orders, Matrimony, and extream Unction, are not to be counted for Sacraments of the Gospel, being such as have grown, partly of the corrupt following of the Apostles, partly are states of life allowed in the Scriptures: but yet have not like nature of Sacraments with Baptisme and the Lords Supper, for that they have not any visible sign or ceremony ordained of God.

The Sacraments were not ordained of Christ to be gazed upon, or to be carried about, but that we should duely use them. And in such onely, as worthily receive the same, they have a wholsome effect or operation: But they that receive them unworthily, purchase to themselves damnation, as S. Paul saith.

XXVI.

Although in the visible Church the evil be ever mingled with the good, and sometime the evil have chief authority in the ministration of the Word and Sacraments: yet forasmuch as they do not the same in their own name, but in Christs, and doe minister by his commission and authority, we may use their ministry, both in hearing the Word of God, and in the receiving of the Sacraments. Neither is the effect of Christs ordinance taken away by their wickednesse, nor the grace of Gods gifts diminished from such, as by faith, and rightly do receive the Sacraments ministred unto them, which be effectuall, because of Christs institution and promise, although they be ministred by evil men.

Neverthelesse, it appertaineth to the discipline of the Church, that inquiry be made of evil Ministers, and that they be accused by those that have knowledge of their offences: and finally being found guilty, by just judgement be deposed.

XXVII.

Baptisme is not onely a sign of profession, and mark of difference, whereby Christian men are discerned from others that be not Christned: but it is also a sign of Regeneration or new birth, whereby, as by an instrument, they that receive Baptisme rightly, are grafted into the Church: the promises of the forgivenesse of sinne, and of our adoption to be the Sonnes of God, by the holy Ghost, are visibly signed and sealed: faith is confirmed: and grace increased by virtue of prayer unto God. The Baptisme of young children is in any wise to be retained in the Church, as most agreeable with the institution of Christ.

XXVIII.

XXVIII.

The Supper of the Lord is not onely a sign of the love that Christians ought to have among themselves one to another: but rather it is a Sacrament of our redemption by Christs death. Insomuch that to such as rightly, worthily, and with faith receive the same, the bread which we break, is a partaking of the Body of Christ: and likewise the Cup of blessing is a partaking of the blood of Christ.

Transubstantiation (or the change of the substance of Bread and Wine) in the Supper of the Lord, cannot be prooved by holy Writ: but it is repugnant to the plain words of Scripture, overthroweth the nature of a Sacrament, and hath given occasion to many superstitions.

The body of Christ is given, taken, and eaten in the Supper onely after an heavenly and spirituall manner. And the mean whereby the Body of Christ is received and eaten in the Supper, is Faith.

The Sacrament of the Lords Supper was not by Christs ordinance reserved, caried about, lifted up, or worshipped.

XXIX.

The wicked, and such as be void of a lively faith, although they do carnally and visibly presse with their teeth (as S. Augustine saith) the Sacrament of the body and blood of Christ: yet in no wise are they partakers of Christ, but rather to their condemnation do eat and drink the signe or Sacrament of so great a thing.

XXX.

The Cup of the Lord is not to be denied to the Lay people. For both the parts of the Lords Sacrament, by Christs ordinance and commandement ought to be ministred to all Christian men alike.

XXXI.

The offering of Christ once made, is that perfect redemption, propitiation, and satisfaction for all the sins of the whole world, both originall and actuall and there is none other satisfaction for sin, but that alone.

Wher-

Wherefore the sacrifices of Masses, in the which it was commonly said, that the Priests did offer Christ for the quick and the dead, to have remission of pain or guilt, were blasphemous fables, and dangerous deceits.

XXXII.

Bishops, Priests, and Deacons, are not commanded by Gods Law, either to vow the estate of single life, or to abstain from marriage: Therefore it is lawfull also for them, as for all other Christian men to marry at their own discretion, as they shall judge the same to serve better to Godlinesse.

XXXIII.

That person which by open denunciation of the Church, is rightly cut off from the unity of the Church, and excommunicated, ought to be taken of the whole multitude of the faithfull as an heathen & Publican, untill he be openly reconciled by Penance, and received into the Church by a Judge that hath authority thereunto.

XXXIV.

It is not necessary that Traditions and Ceremonies be in all places one, or utterly like, for at all times they have been divers, and may be changed, according to the diversitie of Countries, times, and mens manners, so that nothing be ordained against Gods Word. Whosoever through his private judgement, willingly and purposely doth openly break the Traditions and Ceremonies of the Church, which be not repugnant to the Word of God, and be ordained and approved by common authority, ought to be rebuked openly, (that other may fear to do the like) as he that offendeth against the common Order of the Church, and hurteth the authority of the Magistrate, and woundeth the Consciences of the weak brethren.

Every particular or nationall Church, hath authoritie to ordaine, change, and abolish Ceremonies or Rites of the Church, ordained onely by mans authoritie, so that all things be done to edifying.

XXXV.

XXXV.

The second Book of Homilies, the severall titles whereof we have joyned under this Article, doth contain a godly and wholsome Doctrine and necessary for these times, as doth the former book of Homilies, which were set forth in the time of Edward the sixth: and therefore we judge them to be read in Churches by the Ministers diligently and distinctly, that they may be understanded of the people.

Of the Names of the Homilies.

1. Of the right use of the Church.
2. Against peril of Idolatry.
3. Of repairing and keeping clean of Churches.
4. Of good works, first of Fasting.
5. Against Gluttony and Drunkennesse.
6. Against Excesse of Apparel.
7. Of Prayer.
8. Of the Place and Time of Prayer.
9. That Common Prayers and Sacraments ought to be ministred in a known Tongue.
10. Of the reverent estimation of Gods Word.
11. Of Alms doing.
12. Of the Nativity of Christ.
13. Of the passion of Christ.
14. Of the Resurrection of Christ.
15. Of the worthy receiving of the Sacrament of the Body and Bloud of Christ.
16. Of the Gifts of the holy Ghost.
17. For the Rogation daies.
18. Of the State of Matrimony.
19. Of Repentance.
20. Against Idlenesse.
21. Against Rebellion.

XXXVI.

The Book of Consecration of Archbishops, and Bishops, and ordering of Priests and Deacons, lately set forth in the time of Edward the sixth, and confirmed at the same time by authority of Parliament, doth contain all things necessary to such Consecration and ordering: neither hath it any thing, that of it selfe is superstittious and ungodly. And therefore, whosoever are consecrated or ordered according to the Rites of that Book, since the second year of the aforenamed King Edward, unto this time, or hereafter shall be consecrated or ordered according to the same Rites, we decree all such to be rightly, orderly, and lawfully consecrated and ordered.

XXXVII.

The Queens Majestie hath the chief power in this Realm of England, and other her Dominions, unto whom the chief government of all estates of this Realm, whether they be Ecclesiasticall or Civil in all causes doth appertain, and is not, nor ought to be subject to any forreign Jurisdiction.

Where wee attribute to the Queenes Majestie the chiefe government, by which titles we understand the mindes of some slanderous folkes to be offended: we give not to our Princes the ministring, either of Gods word, or of the Sacraments, the which thing the Injunctions also lately set forth by Elizabeth our Queen do most plainly testifie: but that only prerogative which we see to have been given alwaies to all godly Princes in holy Scriptures by God himself, that is, that they should rule all estates and degrees committed to their charge by God, whether they be Ecclesiasticall or Temporall, and restraine with the Civil sword the stubborne and evil doers.

The Bishop of Rome hath no Jurisdiction in this Realm of England.

The Lawes of the Realm may punish Christian men with death, for heinous and grievous offences.

It

It is lawful for Christian men, at the Commandment of the Magistrate, to weare weapons, and serve in the warres.

XXXVIII.

The Riches and goods of Christians are not common, as touching the right title and possession of the same, as certain Anabaptists do falsly boast. Notwithstanding, every man ought of such things as he possesseth, liberally to give almes to the poore, according to his ability.

XXXIX.

As we confesse that vaine and rash swearing is forbidden Christian men by our Lord Jesus Christ, and James his Apostle: So we judge that Christian Religion doth not prohibite, but that a man may sweare when the Magistrate requireth, in a cause of faith and charitie, so it be done according to the Prophets teaching, in justice, judgment, and truth.

The

The Contents.

Chap. 1. Of the Seditious Liberty of the new Doctrines which hath been the principal means of the Covenant, p. 1.

Chap. 2. That the Covenanters are destitute of all Proofs for their war made against the King, p. 12.

Chap. 3. Express Texts of Scripture which commands Obedience, and forbids Resistance to Soverigns, p. 23.

Chap. 4. The Evasions of the Covenanters upon the Texts of Saint Paul, Rom. 13. and how in time they refuse the judgment of Scripture, p. 28.

Chap. 5. What Constitution of State the Covenanters forge, and how they refuse the judgment of the Laws of the Kingdom, p. 40.

Chap. 6. What Examples in the Histories of England, the Covenanters make use of to authorize their actions, p. 46.

Chap. 7. Declaring wherein the Legislative power of Parliament consists, p. 50.

Chap. 8. How the Covenanters will be Judges in their own cause, p. 63.

Chap. 9. That the most noble and best part of the Parliament retired to the King, being driven away by the worser, p. 65.

Chap.

Chap. 10. *A Parallel of the Covenant with the holy League of* France, *under* Henry *the Third,* Pag. 71.

Chap. 11. *The Doctrine of the* English *Covenanters parallel'd with the Doctrine of the Jesuits,* p. 72.

Chap. 12. *How the Covenanters wrong the Reformed Churches, in inviting them to joyn with them: with an Answer for the Churches of* France, p. 81.

Chap. 13. *The preceding Answer confirmed by Divines of the Reformed Religion, with an Answer to some Objections of the Covenanters upon this Subject,* p. 101.

Chap. 14. *How the Covenanters have no reason to invite the Reformed Churches to their Alliance, since they differ from them in many things of great importance,* p. 115.

Chap. 15. *Of abolishing the Lyturgy, in doing of which the Covenanters oppose the Reformed Churches,* p. 122.

Chap. 16. *Of the great prudence and wisdom of the first* English *Reformers, and of the Fool hardinesse of these at present,* p. 132.

Chap. 17. *How the Covenanters labour in vain to sow Sedition between the Churches of* England *and* France, *upon the point of Discipline: Of the Christian prudence of the* French *Reformers, and of the nature of Discipline in general,* p. 145.

Chap. 18. *How the Discipline of the Covenanters is far from the practise of other Churches,* p. 156.

Chap.

Chap. 19. *That the Covenanters ruine the Ministers of the Gospel under colour of Reformation,*
p. 163.

Chap. 20. *Of the Corruption of Religion objected to the English Clergy, and the waies that the Covenanters took to remedy them,* Pag. 167.

Chap. 21. *An Answer to the Objection, That the King made War against the Parliament,* p. 176.

Chap. 22. *Of the Depraved and Evil Faith of the Covenanters.* p. 184.

Chap. 23. *Of the Instruments both Parties made use of, and of the Irish Affairs.* p. 207

Chap. 24. *How the different Factions of the Covenant agreed to ruine the King, and contributed to put him to death,* p. 226.

Chap. 25. *Of the cruelty of the Covenanters towards the good Subjects of the King,* p. 232.

CHAP.

CHAP. I.

Of the seditious Liberty of New Doctrines, which hath been the principal means of the Covenant.

Complear History of our Affairs since the beginning of these Commotions, would be the best Apology for the Justice of our Cause; but this let some brave Spirits labour that are furnished with Records and Intelligences, and who are indued with a judicious Candor, which may leave to after Ages an accomplished portraicture of the wickednesse of this last Age; but that we shall not undertake here: Yet neverthelesse, since the Question of Right depends upon that of Fact, and that to judge of a Different, we must know who began the Quarrel, it is necessary that something be said of the occasions and beginning of this here; for in regard of the progresse, it is so notoriously and prodigiously wicked on our Enemies side, that their neighbours that formerly had too good an opinion of their Cause, acknowledge now that they have rendred it very evil.

It shall be our Task then to let the world see that it hath been Evil from the very beginning, and that their first proceedings were contrary to the Word of God, to the constitution of the Kingdom, and to natural Equity; Yea, that all those fearfull prodigies of Iniquity

quity which the world beholds with a just execration, are the necessary consequences of their first avowed and published principles.

Ye must therefore know, that the Parliament assembled in *Novemb.*1640, was composed for the most part of Persons of Honour, affectious to their Religion, King and Country, and of some others also, whose designes aimed at a general overthrow of all things: These finding themselves to be few in number, labour to joyn to their Faction the numerous and meaner sort of people of *London*, who being kept under a just and gracious Soveraign in their duty, and in happy subjection, could not be induced to mutiny by no other motive then that of Religion, which is the handle by which the Politicians in all times have wound and turned about the Spirits of the people.

We will not neverthelesse deprive them of this Glory, that it was they that first brought the Reformation of Religion upon the Stage, but the Honour is due to them who since have suffered for their Loyalty towards God and the King; that in this holy enterprise they only carried themselves vigorously and sincerely, but their good Zeal by the Cunning of the Party was driven so far, that labouring to reform the Clergie, they served, without thinking, the design of them that would destroy them, and to cause afterward Monarchy to stumble upon the Ruines of the Church.

This profession of the Parliament to Reform the Church, fils the hearts of all good men with joy and hope; for although that the excellent Order in the *English* Church deserves highly to be respected and admired; the purity of the Gospel there being clothed with Honour, and defended by an Episcopal Gravity, yet is it of our Government, and of all other in the world, be they Ecclesiastical or Civil, as with Watches, that how good and excellent soever they be, length of
time

time disorders them, that ever and anon they have need of mending and making clean.

It is almost an Age since the Doctrine and Discipline of our Church hath been renewed, and it is a wonder both the one and the other have been so well conserved in so long a space: Nevertheless, the faults of some Particulars ought not to be imputed to the General. The Church hath flourished under our Discipline, and the Truth hath been preserved, and the Good being put in the Ballance against the Evil, the people had far more cause to glorifie God, than to complain; but we have to do with Spirits whose nature is like Lapwings, which in a Garden full of fruits, feed only on the Caterpillars.

There is nothing so well done, that doth not displease some, even the works of God displease the Devil, because they are well done; and in all those works wherein the spirit of man hath a part, there is nothing so perfect which may not be amended. Our Lyturgie, so holy, and so highly esteemed in all the Reformed Churches, hath nevertheless given offence to many persons amongst us. And although it was for a very small matter, yet those who were affectionate to peace, were content to change somthing, and so to purchase Concord with their Dissenting Brethren at that price.

Whence this overture of Reformation opened a gate to the Liberty of them that desired a change, and the Parliament being composed of persons of different inclinations, in matters of Religion, every one had liberty to say and write what he pleased, and had a Party in the Assembly of Estates, that protected and encouraged them: The *Germans* never wrote so much upon Logick in a hundred years, as the *English* wrote of the Designs of their Ecclesiastical Discipline in three moneths; every week brought forth a thousand seditious

A 2 pamphlets,

pamphlets, which supplied the scarcity of Coals; every writer made a Platform of Reformation according to his humour, and in this new building none would content himself to be a Mason, but every one would be Architect; and there was none of them who called not his reformation the only Kingdom of Jesus Christ, out of which there was no salvation: But these Kingdoms of Jesus Christ agreed one with another, and with the nature of the thing, as the Titles and Chapters of *Montagues Essays*: The people are called a Beast with many Heads, and when all these heads shall cry out at one time, and every one with a different cry, I leave you to guesse what an odious discord they make in the ears both of God and man.

In the midst of this universal distraction, it was appointed that a certain number of Divines, differing in the point of Discipline, should meet together to confer about Religion, as well for the interiour as the exteriour part, where many Bishops and other of the chief of the Clergy met; the Bishop of *Lincolne* (who afterward was Arch-Bishop of *York*) made this Proposition to them, That the Divines should in no wise touch upon the point of Discipline, until such time as they were agreed about the points of Doctrine, hoping thereby that their spirits being united by the bond of one common, but holy Faith, they would easily accord about the exteriour Government or Discipline.

This Counsel was embraced by all, and so wisely managed by that great Person, that in three Meetings, the Divines accorded upon all the substance of Religion, and formed hereupon divers Articles, and with one consent condemned divers opinions: This general consent in Doctrine filled them with hope, that the points of Discipline would pass with the like sweetness; and indeed there wanted not much to have made us happy.

But

But before the report of this good Agreement could be published abroad, the Factious party of the State, fearing above all things this accord in Religion, suddenly raised a strong Quarrel against the Degree of Bishops, as an appurtenance of Antichrist; and another, about their sitting in Parliament; and did so exasperate the people against the Prelates, that in stead of pursuing their design of Reformation, they were constrained to provide for the safety of their own lives. After this, there was no more speech of the Agreement in Religion, for that would utterly have spoiled their work, for it had never been possible to have raised the people against the King, if the conclusion of this conference had been made known to the world, that the King, the Court, and the Bishops, made profession of the sincere reformed Religion. Now, because all the Lies and Subtilties of the Devil were not capable to impute unto them another Confession of Faith, but that which they maintain, which was Holy and Orthodox, known every where, and confirmed by the Confessions of all the reformed Churches of *Europe*; the Factious perswaded the people, both by their Sermons and seditious Libels, that the degree of Bishops was an essential Branch and Mark of Antichrist, and that to pull them down, was to do the work of the Lord, and to ruine Antichrist; and that if the King would maintain them, he would be destroyed with them, as being one of those Kings who gave his power to the Beast.

And besides the destruction of Bishops, they openly demanded the Abolition of the Divine Service received in the Church of *England*, condemning the use of all other prayers, yea even of the *Lords Prayer*; quarrelling with the Apostles *Creed*, denied the necessity of the Sacraments, boasted of a new Light that had apreared to them from Heaven to draw them out of Popish Darkness; and all that was not compatible with their

extra-

extravagant Illuminations, they called Popery; and the Ministers that disobeyed them, *Baal*'s Priests, and the supporters of Antichrist.

By such kind of people were the great multitudes stirred, who came crying at the Gates of the King and Parliament for Reformation, threatning with fire and sword all those that should oppose it: Of these Assemblies, we may speak what is spoken of the uproar at *Ephesus*, Acts 19.32. The Assembly was confused, and the more part knew not wherefore they were come together, for those that called for Reformation, understood not one another, and their opinions were different in Religion, as appears at this day; agreeing only in this, to pull down the Ecclesiastical Government; and what New Government they will build upon the Ruines of the Old, we shall know, when the sword hath decided the controversie; but whilst the Mariners strive, the Ship sinks. The Lord behold his poor Church in compassion.

We have great hope now, beholding the diversity of Opinions and Inclinations, that these evil ingredients will together make a good Temperature, and that the disorder, yea, even the Licentiousness it self will inforce order, as commonly evil Manners beget good Laws; but to attain this, it's required in this general confusion, that those of clear and sound judgments, who see the bottom of the evil, and know the Remedy of it: But having considered them that walk before in the design of Reformation, we find that they are such that neither know the Remedy nor the Evil.

As for the Evil, in stead of having their eyes upon the errors of particulars, against the principal points of Faith, and Confession of the *English* Church; they grew obstinate against certain small and indifferent Ceremonies which the King had many times offered to change by a Synod lawfully assembled; and cast all the

Fire

Fire of their paſſion upon the Epiſcopal preheminence, a Surpliſs, a Feſtival, Forms of Prayer, Painted windows; and condemning many good things amongſt the evil.

And as for the Remedy, we have here whereat to admire, that ſtriking at ſo ſmall and light evils, they would employ ſuch extream Remedies, nothing being able to ſerve but general deſtruction, as if to heal the pain of the Teeth, they would cut off the Head, in ſtead of proceeding by an amiable conference, appointing a deputation of the Clergy of the Kingdom to aſſemble in a Synod to calm the fiery ſpirits, and to keep the people in obedience to their Soveraign, and to faſten the building that ſhaked, by the Ciment of Charity; they made open profeſſion that the Reformation could not be effected but by blood, that they would have no peace with the Biſhops and their Clergy, that they muſt deſtroy before they build, raze *Babylon* (as they called our Diſcipline) even to the very foundations, overthrow the Altars of *Baal*, and ſacrifice all his Prieſts; that now the time was come, that the *Iſrael* of God ought to pillage the *Egyptians*. And that now the juſt ſhould waſh their footſteps in the blood of the ungodly, for ſuch they accounted us; and thus they did us the honour to plunder and kill us in Scripture Language.

And with this Divinity the Pulpits ſounded aloud, and the people publickly exhorted to take up Arms againſt the King, and to deſtroy all Miniſters both of Church and State, that ſhould joyn with him; and for this effect, theſe following Texts of Scripture were preſſed by their zealous Preachers, *Luke* 19.27. *Thoſe mine enemies which would not that I ſhould reign over them, bring hither, and ſlay them before me.* Judg. 5.23. *Curſe ye* Meroz, *curſe ye bitterly the Inhabitants thereof, becauſe they came not to the help of the Lord, to help the Lord againſt the mighty.* Jer. 48.10. *Curſed be he that doth the work*

work of the Lord deceitfully, and *cursed be he that keepeth back his sword from bloud*; and these they appropriated to their war against their King and Clergy of *England*, and all that adhered unto them; there being no way of Reformation in these mens accounts but to kill us for the Love of God, and the Advancement of his Kingdom.

Now being exceedingly astonished, how men of Learning could possibly be so bewitched with a furious and foolish zeal; we found at length, having sounded the depth of their opinions, that their Brains were troubled with Prophesies and Revelations, that their principal reading was in Commentaries upon the *Revelation*, which they interpreted according to their fancies; and that they had studied more, what God would do hereafter, than what their Duty was to do for the present; that they made no Conscience to transgress the declared Will of God in his Commands, to accomplish the secret will of his Decree. That they were Millenaries, expecting a Temporal Kingdom of Jesus Christ, believing that the time of that Kingdom was now come; and to establish that Kingdom, they were to pluck down that of Antichrist (as they understood) the ancient Ecclesiastical Order, and to dispossess Kings, drive away the wicked, dash the children of *Babel* against the stones, tread the winepress of the wrath of God, till the Blood rose to their Bridle reins, that thereby Christ alone may reign in the world, and the meek inherit the earth: We have since enough tasted of the fruits of their meekness: All this is drawn from the model of the Common-wealth of *John a Leyden*, and the Prophets of *Munster*.

But if any of the Covenanters shall disavow these opinions, they cannot deny but they were preached publickly and ordinarily; neither can they deny but the defenders of this pernicious Doctrine were the chief of
their

their New Reformation, and the Authors of the war; people whose Counsels were applauded as Oracles, and who drew after them their party by the repetition of their sanctified strength of zeal; those who dared to contradict them, did it very fearfully, and kissing their hands before they spake, but they themselves carried all before them, acting with a prophetick liberty and boldness; also, after all, they only were the men to be trusted, and who were put upon all great designs and employments; for they feared that they who are less governed by Enthusiasms, might at last so far forget themselves, as to be faithful to their Sovereign, and yield to a peaceable accomodation.

Behold here then, wherefore we would not joyn our selves with these Reformers, because we see that even they themselves have the greatest need of Reformation, being far gone from the Doctrine of the reformed Churches, erring in the Faith, but yet more in Charity; It's they would sweep the Church, as God swept *Babylon*, with the Beesom of destruction: They speak not of reforming neither Doctrines nor Manners, but to ruine the Persons: They account the most part of the Clergy of the Kingdom unworthy to be corrected, but altogether to be rooted out; that one part of the Reformation was to ruine the King, and to take the sword from his side to cut off his head; the favourers of tumults were the only persons that were caressed, they lent their ears to the popular tumults, whilst they shut the mouths and bound the hands of the Magistrates: It was they taught that the people were above the King, and that the Command of Saint *Paul*, that every one should be subject to the higher Powers, obligeth the King for to obey the People; it was they that upheld, yea, favoured and courted all sorts of pernicious Sects, provided that they would bandy with them against their King: It was they that suffered to

go

go unpunished the Blasphemies in the Pulpits, the Insolencies, Sacriledges and horrible profanations of the Service of God, and permitted all things to those who were of the zealous party.

We beheld on the other side, that the King took knowledge of the grievances of his people, as well for the spiritual as temporal, and laboured sincerely to remedy them; that he consented to the alteration of offensive things in Religion, and to the punishment of those who were accused as troublers of the Church, provided that the things and persons were examined by regular and lawful waies of a general Synod, which he offered to assemble; he also was pleased to yield of his own right to augment the rights of his Subjects, and daily multiplied acts of favour, capable to convert the most alienated spirits, passed by the many and great affronts that were done to his authority, and endeavoured by all waies possible to overcome evil with good.

But the more the King yielded, the more insolent were the factious against him; he offered to reform both the State and Church, but they would not permit him, they themselves would do that work without him. The King sent divers messages to know of them what things they would reform, but to this they answered only with complaints. Neither could he obtain any declaration of that which they desired, until that his Forts, Magazines, Ships and Revenues were taken from him; the reason of which hath since been given by one of their principal Champions.

Fuller Anf. p.7.

Having to sow the Lords Field, they had need to make a fence about it before they begin, that the work-men might labour without interruption; and that to lance the Apostume of a sick State, they must first bind the Patient.

Our Conscience could not accomodate it self to this prudence, neither ever expect any good from such a way of Reformation, which would bind the Royal hands and feet of Majesty, before they would declare what they desired of his Favour; and cut asunder the Nerves of his Authority and subsistance, under colour to establish the Kingdom of Jesus Christ.

A strange proceeding to us that have learned of S*t* *Paul, that a Prince beareth not the sword in vain*, Rom. 13. 4. But in that is the Minister of God to execute wrath; and that to resist him, yea, when he should make use of the sword to commit injustice, is to resist the Ordinance of God: But if he use it well or ill, that ought to be left to him who gave it him, and to whom only he ought to render account; his Subjects ought to counsel him, if he did ill, and refuse to assist him in evil doing, and not repress him by Arms: That if this Command of S*t* *Paul* obliged the *Romans* to obey a cruel vicious Prince, and enemy to God, we should account our selves much more bound to obey a just, merciful, religious Prince, whose life was a rare example of piety and sanctity, and his Government so just and peaceable, that he might well be called the Father of his Subjects; who wanted nothing to make them happy, but to know their happiness.

CHAP.

CHAP. II.

That the Covenanters are destitute of all Proofs from Holy Scripture for their War made against the King.

THese violent beginnings of the Covenanters, and their Progress also, which overthrows all humane Authority, had great need to strengthen it self by Divine Authority, to satisfie the Conscience; whence is it that they made a great noise of it in their Pulpits, but not in their Disputes; for those that exhorted the people in Scripture-term to War against the King, hang down the head, when in conference their Proofs are demanded, saying; that, It is not for Divines but Lawyers to decide the present quarrel; Whence it appears that there is a great difference betwixt the terms and proofs of Scripture, and that many that have the voice of the Lamb, speak as the Dragon.

But fearing lest they should accuse us, that we suppress their proofs, behold here all that they make use of, both in their Books and Sermons, part borrowed from the writings of the Jesuites, and part from * two Books which are Printed with Machiavels Prince, and not without great reason, for there are three wicked Books together, and its a wonder how that in threescore years their Books have not been burnt for company by the hands of the common Executioner.

* *Vindiciæ contra Tirannos, & De jure Magistratus.*

They alledge the example of *David*, who had six hundred men for his guard when he was pursued by *Saul*, 1 *Sam.* 22. 2.

The example of the Army of *Israel*, which saved *Jonathan*,

nathan, when *Saul* would have put him to death, 1 *Sam.* 14. 45.

Of *Ehud*, who slew *Eglon* King of *Moab*, an Oppressor of the *Israelites*, Judg. 3. 21.

The example of the Town of *Libnah*, which revolted from the obedience of *Jehoram*, because he had forsaken the Lord God of his Fathers, 2 *Chr.* 21. 10.

Of *Jehu*, that cut off the House of *Ahab*, 2 *Kings* 9.

The example of *Jehojadah* the High Priest, who commanded *Athaliah* the Queen to be put to death, 2 *Kings* 11. 15.

Of the Priests of *Jerusalem*, who resisted *Uzziah* the King, when he would have exercised the Priests Office, 2 *Chron.* 26. 18.

The example of *Elisha* who caused the door to be shut, when *Joram* the King of *Israel* sent a messenger to cut off his head, 2 *Kings* 6. 13.

And also the malediction that *Deborah* gave to the Inhabitants of *Meroz*, because they came not to the help of the Lord, when *Barak* fought against *Sisera*, *Iudges* 5. 23.

Likewise the malediction pronounced by *Jeremy* against him that should do the work of the Lord deceitfully, and that should keep his sword from shedding the blood of the *Moabites*, Jer. 48. 10.

The Idols of *Laban*, and the Genealogies of the Patriarchs might also have been brought to this purpose; it must needs be, that the Spirit of Error and of Lies, have a great power upon the understanding of these people, for to perswade them by such reasons to hazard their Goods, and Lives, and Consciences in an open War against their Soveraign.

All these passages of Scripture are Examples and particular Cases, and all except one far from the point in controversie; but in a matter of such importance as the resisting of the King, which is so expresly forbidden,

bidden, and under pain of damnation, there is need of a formal command, or of a permission expressed, that exempts Christians; at least in some certain cases, for the crime of resisting the higher powers, which is to resist God, and from the punishment of eternal damnation; without this all the Examples of Subjects rising up against their Princes from the very Creation of the World cannot, nor is able to put Conscience into a quiet condition: He hath but small knowledge that knows not that Examples prove nothing, but that such a thing hath been done, and is possible; not that it ought to be done, or that it is lawful to be done; if there be not a Law built upon the Example, and a Soveraign Authority given to it, that it may be a pattern for the future; and then its not the Example, but the Law that we are bound to follow, which cannot be said of the Examples before alledged, which beside the general insufficiency of Examples in matter of proof touch not the point of Resistance in question, except the first, which is wholly contrary to it.

Which is the Example of *David*, who being persecuted by *Saul*, took six hundred men for his Guard; this might suffice for Answer, That this action is not recommended by the Word of God, nor proposed as an example for us to follow; Christian piety and prudence, may imitate many actions of holy persons, which are not formally recommended in the word of God; but the question being to exempt us from a prohibition, and a formal threatning, *Rom.*13.2. one of the most considerable and penal in all the Scripture, we may receive no example to the contrary, if it be not expresly recommended and turned into a command; and besides the last command ought to have the advantage, and to be obeyed before the first.

Moreover, extraordinary Cases in Scripture, wherein there is a Miraculous and Prophetick Conduct, cannot

not serve for a pattern in ordinary cases: *David* was Anointed King over *Israel*, by a special command of God, and in all the List of the Kings of *Judah*, there were none but *Saul* and *David* called to the Kingdom in this manner. And this holy Unction gave them priviledges in *Israel* which were onely proper to them, and which the Gentlemen of the Covenant have not in *England*, for ordinary cases there are perpetual and inviolable precepts, and these precepts are wholly contrary to the resisting of Soveraigns by Arms.

Our Enemies nevertheless challenge a particular Interest in this example of *David*, because they account themselves the anointed of the Lord, but deny this Title to their *King, if he be not one of the Elect of God; but let them learn, that that which renders Kings the anointed of the Lord, is not true Faith, nor the Gifts of the Spirit, but that Soveraign power which they have from on high.

And therefore *Cyrus* a Pagan King is called by God himself, his anointed, and his Shepherd, *Isai.*45.1. If then Kings are the anointed of the Lord, without consideration of their Religion or vertue, it follows then that they lose not their unction, neither by their Errors nor their Vices; and that falling from the grace of God, yet they fall not from that power which they held of him. This is spoken of by the way against the Heresie of most part of the Covenanters, who deny the divine Unction of Kings, and fasten it to their fantasies in Religion.

And we have cause to give thanks to these men who alledge to us the example of *David*, there being nothing in all the Scripture more contrary to them; for in stead of that they pursued the King with weapons in their hands, and gave him Battel; *David* fled continually from place to place, and never struck one stroke nor drew his Sword against his King. Twice he let him

him escape when he had him in his power, and having taken away his spear, restored it to him again; and having but cut off the Lap of his garment, his heart smote him for it; and when one counselled him to dispatch him, then when he was in his hands, he said, *The Lord forbid that I should do this thing unto my Master, the Lords anointed, to stretch forth my hand against him, seeing he is the Anointed of the Lord,* 1 Sam. 24. 6. And when his servants would have slain him, he saith, *Destroy him not: for who can stretch forth his hand against the Lords Anointed, and be guiltless,* 1 Sam. 26. 9. This Divine Title bound his hands, and possessed his spirit with fear and astonishment.

And since our Enemies make him to say that he would not stretch forth his hand against the King, if he descended not in Battel against him; let them well read the Text, but especially in the Original, and they shall find no such thing; *David* doth rather put *Saul* wholly into the hands of God, *Vers.* 10. *The Lord shall smite him, or his day shall come to die, or he shall descend into the battel and perish; The Lord forbid that I should stretch forth my hand against the Lords Anointed*: He doth not say that he will not stretch forth his hand against him, unless that the Lord smite him; for if God smite him, what need had *David* to smite him? He doth not say he would descend into Battel against him, for then his Actions would have contradicted his Words, for he always fled from him; the Event proved that his words were Prophetical, and that he waited whilest *Saul* should be slain in a strange War, and that the hand of the Lord should be upon him.

And if *David* never gave him Battel, we cannot impute it to his weakness; for he might as well have defeated the Army of *Saul*, as that of the *Philistines* before *Keilah*, with his small number; if God who guided him in all his ways had found it good, since it had been

been easie for him to have raised mighty Armies, being designed the Successor of *Saul* in the Kingdom; for people naturally adore the Rising Sun.

David retired into *Keilah*, and having heard that *Saul* had an intention to come thither to take him, enquired of the Lord, if those in the City would deliver him up to *Saul*, and God having answered him, that they would deliver him, fled from thence; the Ministers therefore of the Covenant infer, that *David* had a desire to fortifie *Keilah*, and to endure a siege. But all which they can gather from that Passage is, that *David* was not safe in that retreat, and that God advised him to seek another, for the Inhabitants of *Keilah* might have delivered him to *Saul* without attending a siege; but when they shall have proved that *David* would have fortified *Keilah*, it makes nothing for them, since God declares by his Answer, that it was not pleasing to him.

We would beseech the Gentlemen of the Covenant to hold themselves to this example which they have chosen, that they would cashier their great Armies, for *David* had but a few people with them, 1 *Sam.* 25. 16. that they would not rob the Subjects of their King, of their Goods; but imitate the Souldiers of *David*, who were a wall both by night and day to the Flocks and Herds of *Nabal*; That having seized upon the Arms of the King, let them peaceably restore them again as *David*, and not with the points forward. Let their Conscience strike them, and make them cry out, *The Lord forbid that I should do this thing against my Master the Lords Anointed, for who can stretch forth his hand against him and be guiltless?* Words which beside the example carry with them a perpetual and express command, and shall one day be produced in judgment against those that defend the late Commotions by the example of *David*; and if

their

their continuance in the Kingdoms of his Majesty, is either displeasing or dangerous to them, instead of opposing him, let them retire into some strange Country, as *David* did to King *Achis*; let them also imitate his sincerity in making use of strangers onely for his protection, and not to invade his Country, and raise his Subjects against their King, which is that use the Covenanters imployed the Scots; In one point onely they imitate and surpass *David*, in that he fained himself a Fool, for they indeed act the Fools in good earnest.

In brief, the Example of *David* which they alledge, is so contrary to the Actions of the Covenanters, that they have great reason to fear least God alledge this at the dreadful day of Judgement against them, saying, *Out of thy own mouth will I judge thee, thou wicked servant*, Luke 19.22. The other passages of Scripture are most ridiculously alledged, and serve only to shew their great weakness.

They bring the action of the Army of *Saul*, that saved *Jonathan* against the Oath of his Father, 1 *Sam*. 14. 45. but to what purpose is this? Doth this Army draw their sword against the King? Use they any violence either against his Person or Estate? If a King would put to death his Innocent Son, those faithful Subjects whom the King employs in this Execution do well not to do it, and to refuse giving obedience to so unjust a command.

They make use also of the example of *Ehud*, who slew *Eglon* King of *Moab*, who kept the Israelites in slavery, *Judg*. 3.21. we have often heard this example pressed with much vehemency in Pulpits. The Preachers compared *Eglon* to the King, affirming that *Eglon* was the lawful King of *Israel*, and that it is lawful to kill a legitimate King, if he oppress the people of God; all this is false, and proper to be refuted only by the Hangman, to whom we leave them.

The

The Example follows of the City of *Libnah*, which appertained to the *Levites*, which revolted from the obedience of *Jehoram, because* (saith the Text) *he had forsaken the Lord God of his Fathers*; the Covenanters apply the word *Because* to the intention of the Inhabitants of *Libnah*, and not to the judgement of God; whence these Gentlemen conclude, That it is lawful for the people to shake off the yoke of their Prince, when the Prince forsakes God, of which they will be Judges. Although *Libnah* should revolt for this reason, yet it follows not that the reason is of strength, or that it ought to be turned into example; a thing which requires a new proof of Scripture; but the drift of the Text is, to assign the cause of this revolt to the Justice of God, and not to that of men: Take the whole Text, 2 *Chron.* 21. 10. *So the Edomites revolted from under the hand of Judah unto this day. The same time also did* Libnah *revolt from under his hand, because he had forsaken the Lord God of his Fathers*. Having consulted with the Original, we find that the revolt of *Edom* and of *Libnah* were both together, without the least distinction; but between the discourse of these two Revolts, and the reason adjoyned, there is * there the usual mark for the distinction of half periods: which shews that this reason serves equally for both the Revolts, and the sense of the Text carries it evidently, that the *Idumeans*, and those of *Libnah* revolted for the same cause, and that these *Idumeans* which were Idolaters, had no ground to revolt from the King of *Judah*, because at that time he was also fallen into Idolatry; its therefore the Divine justice that the Text regards, and not the Motives of second Causes.

* *Accentus Athuath.*

Also the same Author saith, that *Pekah* the Son of *Remaliah* slew in *Judah* 120000 in one day, which were all valiant men, *because they had forsaken the Lord God*

B 2 *of*

of their Fathers. In these two passages the sense is alike, and the reason of the punishment couched in the same terms; now its most evident that the *Syrians* had no Quarrel against the *Jews* for forsaking God, because they did not believe in him, wherefore we are to look to Justice of the King of Kings, who for the sins of Princes suffers them to lose the obedience of their Subjects; for God serves himself of the wickedness of men, whereof he is not the cause, for to execute his just judgments; but that excuseth not the Rebellion of Subjects, for it is their part to consider what they owe to their King, and not what their King deserves of the Justice of God. They add the example of *Jehu*, who exterminated the King of *Israel*, and all the posterity of *Ahab*, 2 *Kings* 9. in which without doubt he did very well, because God commanded him, but the Covenanters did very ill in persecuting their King, because God had forbidden them: After this they bring the Execution of the Queen *Athaliah*, by the Command of *Jehojadah* the High Priest, 2 *Chron.* 26. 18. which no more then the former toucheth the Question; for not only *Jehojadah*, but all other people might have done as much, because there was a lawful King, whom they ought to defend and maintain against a stranger usurping, and that had murthered the Royal Family; and here the Maxime is valid, *That against a publike enemy, every one hath right to take up Arms*: But what conclude they from these two last examples, they would have been ashamed to have named them before the death of their King, but since they have explained themselves, God defend the holiness of his Word, and confound this Divelish Divinity.

Those that follow are not much better; they alledge the example of the Priests, who resisted King *Uzziah*, when he would have exercised the Priests Office, so ought the Ministers of the Gospel to resist the King, if he would administer the Sacraments; but this resistance

ance ought to be done by humble admonitions, and as refusing to serve him in his design, not by way of Arms: In the matter of *Uzziah*, the Priests used not any violence, it is said indeed they caused him to go out of the Temple, because God had smitten him with the Leprosie; but that was done without force, for the Text saith, *verf.* 20. he himself also hasted to go out, because *the Lord had smitten him*: This serves nothing for their Subject, they have no other reason to alledge this, but because having quarrelled against all Kings, they take delight to blast their Dignity. The like is the example of *Elisha*, who commanded the door to be shut against the messenger that was sent from *Ioram* to cut off his head, 2 *Kings* 2. 32. If *Elisha* had sent a Messenger to cut off the Kings Head, the example had been to the purpose, for this is our case at this day; but to shut the door against an Officer of the Kings to save his life, being condemned to die wrongfully, and without force of Justice, is very far from attempting either against the Person or Authority of the King: The English Law in many Cases gives to every one his house for a place of safety, neither is there any Law either Divine or Humane, that forbids us to defend a blow from what part soever it comes; if the Covenanters had done no other thing, there never had been a War, but they proceeded further then defence; Was there ever a more important Action upon so small a foundation, to persecute their King by Sea and Land, destroy his Estate, plant their Cannon against his Person, imprison him, and at last cut off his head, because *Elisha* caused the door to be shut against the Messenger of *Joram*.

But in recompense, behold here two proofs, wherein there is as much piety as reason, *Judg.* 5. 23. *Deborah* cursed the Inhabitants of *Meroz*, because they came not forth to help the Lord against *Jabin* and *Sifera*; and *Jer.* 48. 10. *Jeremy* cursed them that kept their sword from

from shedding the blood of the *Moabites, Ergo,* Cursed are all they that came not to help the Covenanters against the King: For these rare consequences they deserve a bundle of Thistles, such as Asses feed on, and to be driven from the society of men, as being deprived both of Reason and Humanity; who hath given them power to stretch to the King either by words or actions, the judgements pronounced against the enemies of God, and which are restrained to certain Nations and Persons: The King, was he a *Moabite*? Was he a Pagan? or an Usurper of a Kingdom, as *Jabin*? Are you Prophets as *Deborah* and *Jeremy*, to curse with Authority? If ye be not Prophets, ye are Sacrilegious, for cursing is a Fire that appertains only to God to cast forth, they who are so bold to take it into their hands without Authority burn them, and hurt none but themselves, but oftentimes doth good to them whom they would hurt; *for this Rashness moves God to jealousie, and provokes him to do the contrary,* according to the Psalmist, *Psal.* 109. *Let them curse, but do thou bless;* we have great hopes that our enemies shall be the Occasion of the blessing of God upon us, since they take such pains to curse us; it is the constant Argument of their Sermons and publike Prayers; to it they employ the vehemency of their Eloquence and fervour of their Devotion; Let us then say with *David,* 2 *Sam.* 16. 12. *It may be the Lord will look upon our affliction, and that the Lord will requite good for their cursing;* but let us bless them that persecute us, and despitefully use us: O our God! turn their Hearts, and bless their persons, and as our Lord Jesus by his Prayer on the Cross saved them which crucified him, save we beseech thee all those that crucifie him in his Members, and those who killing us think they do God service.

CHAP.

Expreß Texts of Scripture which Commands Obedience, and forbids Resistance to Soveraigns.

FOr to draw them from Examples and particular Cases, which is their retreat, to general Precepts, we beseech them as they love God and their own salvation, to review their proofs, and consider that in all the Scripture there is neither Precepts nor Permission that authorizeth the taking up of Arms against their Soveraign, but there are very many formal Commands to the contrary.

The first Commandment, *Honour thy Father and thy Mother*, binds us to honour the King; for in the beginning Soveraignty appertained to Fathers, and is derived of the paternal power, *Deut.* 13.6, &c. Now it is impossible to honour the King, and draw your sword against him; upon which we observe that in case of Idolatry, the Father was commanded by the King to accuse his Son and Daughter, and the Husband his Wife, and to stretch forth first his hand against them to slay them; but neither the Son nor the Daughter ought to accuse the Father, nor the Wife the Husband, much less to put forth their hand against them: Whence we learn, that neither Children nor Subjects ought to rise up against their Fathers or their Kings, which have in them the Paternal Character, no, not for the service of God; and that their Persons ought to be inviolable; those who confess this Truth, and yet in the mean while separate the Authority of the King from his Person, deny that which they have confessed, and expose the Person of the King to violence, for it is the Authority that renders the Persons of Kings unviolable.

Therefore among so many Reprehensions and Judgments

ments against Idolatrous Kings, whereof the holy History is full, ye shall in no place nor part find that the people are reproved for not depressing or deposing their King; ordinarily the punishment that God sent upon them, came immediatly from himself, or out of the Kingdome, not by their own Subjects: Before God would employ *Jehu*, who was a Subject, to destroy the Kings of *Israel* and *Judah*, he anointed him King, and besides, gave him a special and extraordinary Command.

We say the like of *Jeroboam*, whose Example is very ill alledged to defend Rebellion, for *Jeroboam* was sent of God to take the Kingdom from *Rehoboam*, and was authorized by a formal donation. The sentence of *David* before mentioned, 1 *Sam*. 26.9. is of very great weight: *Who can stretch forth his hand against the Lords Anointed, and be guiltless?*

And this other of him, *Touch not mine Anointed, and do my Prophets no harm*, Psal. 109.19. But the Covenanters have violently and cruelly proceeded against both.

God speaking under the name of Soveraign Wisdom, saith, *By me Kings reign, and Princes decree Justice: By me Princes rule, and Nobles, even all the Judges of the earth*, Prov. 8.15,16. If it be by him that Kings reign, they should be respected for love of him, and he that resists them makes against God.

To this purpose also tends that excellent scripture, *Prov*. 24.21,22. *My Son, fear thou the Lord and the King, and meddle not with them that are given to change: For their calamity shall rise suddenly, and who knoweth the ruine of them both?* A Scripture which shews, that the fear of the King, is a part of the fear of God, and that those that rise up against him, are reserved of God for a sudden calamity.

And this is also of him, *Eccles*. 8.2. *I counsel you to*
keep

keep the Kings Commandment, and that in regard of the Oath of God. A passage that binds us to keep the Commandment of the King, for the Love of God, and the Oath of Allegiance, under which all Subjects are born, and many have actually taken; for every Oath is a contract made with God.

And a little after, *Eccles.* 8.14. *Where the word of the King is, there is power; and who may say unto him, what dost thou?* But we have to do with those, who make this Question to their King, and care neither for his word nor power.

The Law speaks expresly, *Exod.* 22.28. *Thou shalt not revile the Judges, nor curse the Ruler of thy people.* Yea, it restrains the thoughts as well as actions, *Eccles.* 10. 20. *Curse not the King, no, not in thy thoughts.* If we are not to speak nor think ill of the King, much less should do ill to him; the violation of these Commands by the Covenanters, are too enormous, and cry aloud to Heaven for vengeance.

Our Lord Jesus Chist himself commands us, *to render to Cesar the things which are Cesars, and to God the things that are Gods,* Mat. 22.21. He himself would pay Tribute to *Cesar,* although of right he should have made *Cesar* Tributary to him? and not having money, he caused it to be brought to him by a Miracle, rather than he would be wanting in this duty; this is far from taking the Kings Revenues from him, and employing the Tribute due to him, to raise a war against him.

When the Officers of Justice *came to take him, he rebuked his Disciple who had drawn his sword against them, and healed the wound that he had made,* Mat. 26. He suffered himself peaceably to be led before *Herod* and *Pilate,* whom he might have as easily destroyed, as make them fall down backward who came to apprehend him; but he submitted to the Divine Authority that
shined

shined in the Person of the Governour, yea even to death; openly professing that the power which he had, was from above, *John* 19.11. If the power of Kings depended upon the gift of their Subjects, as the Covenanters held, Jesus Christ should have said that the power that he had was from below; but this Divinity proceeds from another Doctor than the Son of God.

Saint *Paul* is marvellous express and full upon this point, *Rom.* 13.1, &c. *Let every soul be subject unto the higher Powers, for there is no Power but of God: The Powers that be, are ordained of God. Whosoever therefore resisteth the Power, resisteth the Ordinance of God, and they that resist, shall receive to themselves damnation. For Rulers are not a terrour to good works, but to the evil. Wilt thou then not be afraid of the Power? Do that which is good, and thou shalt have praise of the same. For he is the Minister of God to thee for good; but if thou do that which is evil, be afraid: for he beareth not the sword in vain; for he is the Minister of God, a revenger to execute wrath upon him that doth evil: Wherefore ye must needs be subject, not only for wrath, but also for Conscience sake. For, for this cause pay you tribute also, for they are Gods Ministers, attending continually upon this very thing. Render therefore to all their dues, Tribute to whom Tribute is due, Custome to whom Custome, Fear to whom Fear, Honour to whom Honour.*

Oh! behold with what vigour of spirit and power the Apostle presseth Obedience, and condemns resistance of Soveraign Powers; Is there any thing in the world so strong and pressing as this Divine Lesson? the authority alone had been sufficient, but over and above he adds threatnings, promises reason upon reason; they who shall well consider the Text, will learn; That it is impossible to be a good Christian, without being a good Subject, and that they cannot resist the King without resisting God; also that terrible threatning of damnation

on should retain men in their duty: Let every one (in the fear of God) that have born Arms against their King, think well of this, and repent: Oh! it is a dangerous thing to resist God, he must be very imprudent that will hazard the damnation of his soul, so formally denounced against Rebels, upon distinctions and good intentions, at the great day of account they will find these very light things. The Divines of the Covenant labour with might and main to elude the force of this Scripture, which plucks them by the throat, they change themselves into many contrary forms to escape it, as we shall see hereafter.

Saint *Paul* recommends this Doctrine to *Titus*, Tit.3.1,2. *Put them in mind to be subject to Principalities and Powers, to obey Magistrates, to be ready to every good work; to speak evil of no man, to be no brawlers, shewing all meekness to all men.* A dangerous Scripture; to teach subjection and meekness, is to strike the Covenanter at the heart.

Saint *Peter* speaks in the same stile, 1 *Pet*.2.13, &c. *Submit your selves to every Ordinance of man for the Lords sake, whether it be to the King as supream; or unto Governours, as unto them that are sent by him for the punishment of evil doers, and the praise of them that do well, for so is the will of God, that with well doing ye may put to silence the ignorance of foolish men: As free, and not using your liberty for a cloak of maliciousnesse, but as the Servants of God. Honour all men, Love the Brotherhood, Fear God, Honour the King.* The rest of the Chapter is employed in teaching Christians to submit to their Superiours, and to suffer for righteousness: Behold truly the Doctrine of Christ, it's thus that the Apostles planted the Church, it's thus that they fought the good fight, not in killing Kings, but in bearing the Cross for the Gospel.

One of ours, having requested a Learned Divine that
followed

followed the party of the Covenanters, that he would give him a precept of Scripture, where it's commanded for Subjects to take up Arms for Religion against their Soveraign: He returned this Scripture, *Stand fast therefore in the Liberty wherewith Christ hath made us free*, Gal. 5. 1. But we maintain against him, that both Saint *Peter* and Saint *Paul* preserved themselves more stedfast in their Christian Liberty in suffering death, than all the Armies of the Covenanters in fighting; and that they take the waies not to establish, but to shake and overthrow their liberty in Christ: We need not prove that Saint *Paul* in this Scripture, never meant to speak of fighting, but to preserve the spirit free from superstition. Christian Liberty consists not in shaking off the yoke of Superiour Powers, but of that of Error and vice; and that liberty which our enemies have assumed, to present their Petitions to their King, upon their Pikes point, and in the end to kill him, was not the liberty from which Christ had made them free: Let them learn the Lesson of Saint *Peter*, to carry themselves as free, and not using their Liberty for a Cloak of Maliciousness.

CHAP. IV.

The Evasions of the Covenanters upon the Texts of Saint Paul, Rom. 13. *And how in Fine they refuse the Judgment of Scripture.*

THE Apostle commands, *Rom.* 13. 1. *That every Soul be subject to the higher Powers, for there is no power but of God. The Powers that be, are ordained of God.*

To this Scripture, some of them answer, that evil
Kings

Kings are not ordained of God, having learned this Doctrine of *Goodman*; but therein they directly contradict Saint *Paul*, who spake of the Powers then in being; they that were then when Saint *Paul* wrote this Epistle, were one of the three *Nero*'s Successors of *Tyberius*, the best of them were nothing worth; a child is capable to distinguish betwixt the wickedness of a Prince, and his authority; the first whereof is of himself, the second is of God, and it's of the power that Saint *Paul* speaks of, without distinction of persons.

Goodman of Obedience.
'Αἱ ἐοαι ἐξουσίαι.

As for the following verse, where Saint *Paul* infers thus, *Whosoever therefore resisteth the Power, resisteth the Ordinance of God, and they that resist, shall receive to themselves damnation.* Buchanan and his followers answer, that this Command was but for a time, whilst the Church was in it's Infancy weak, and under the Cross, incapable to resist their Prince; but if Saint *Paul* had lived now, and were to write a body of Commonwealth, he would speak far otherwise, and would leave Kings to be punished of their Subjects, and this is that *Buchanan* assures us upon his word.

Buchanan de Jure Reg. p. 56, 57.

Likewise one of the best writers of the Covenanters affirms, that Saint *Paul* spake to some particulars dispersed in the condition of the Primitive Church, who had not means to provide for their safety; if this Licence were lawful, men might reject all the Doctrines of Saint *Paul*'s Epistles, as written to particulars, and the Masters of the Covenant would make a way to exempt themselves from many duties commanded by Saint *Paul*, which would very ill accord with their intentions: So when the Apostle saith, *Rom.* 12. 9, 10. *Let Love be without dissimulation, abhor that which is evil cleave*

Observator defended, p. 8.

cleave to that which is good, be kindly affectionate one to another, with brotherly love preferring one another, there is some appearance that they take this Command addressed to some particulars, and not to them, since they give themselves the liberty to do the quite contrary: There is in these Epistles some Commands provisional, moveable according to the times and persons, as those which concern the outward Order; others which are purely personal, as the Command made to *Timothy*, to come to him before Winter; but the Moral Doctrines are immoveable, and vary not according to the Times, since that reason of Saint *Paul* given, *that the Powers that be, are ordained of God,* is a Truth perpetual and universal, and the Command not to resist the Powers, ought also to be general for all Ages and all people; so likewise this reason is perpetual, *That the Magistrate beareth not the sword in vain, but to do justice;* and this other, ye must needs be subject, *not only for wrath, but also for Conscience sake*: Wherefore the Command grounded hereon to be subject to the higher Powers, & not resist them, is of perpetual necessity and obligation. And since to resist the powers, is *to resist the Ordinance of God*, may we not ask of our new Divines, why the strong and not the weak are permitted to resist *the Ordinance of God? It's enough to have a good sword to exempt a man from the Commands of the Gospel.*

Bellar. de Pont. l.5. Cap. 7.

The Covenanters might defend this interpretation of the Text of Saint *Paul*, by the authority of Cardinal *Bellarmine*, who saith, that if the Christians long since did not depose *Dioclesian, Julian,* the Apostate *Valens* the *Arrian*, and others, it was because they wanted temporal forces, otherwise of right they might, which is the language of our Covenanters; but this opinion draws along with it three inconveniencies.

First, That it blasts the primitive Church, and deprives

prives the Martyrs of their honour; for it's little worth praise to suffer for the Gospel, when a man hath a will without means to rebel; their obedience to their Soveraigns was then nothing worth, since it was forced, and all their protestations of subjection in the writings of the Fathers, of which they are full, ought to be imputed to weaknes and hypocrisie.

This likewise is to accuse Saint *Paul* of want of sincerity, as if he taught patience and obedience to Kings, only to accomodate himself to the Times, and not to obey God; but he clears himself sufficiently of this accusation, saying, that we must not only be *subject for wrath*, that is to say, *for fear of punishment, but also for Conscience*.

Moreover this Doctrine is pernicious to the Church, for if it were embraced, it would render Christians suspected, and hateful to their Soveraigns; as persons who would subject the Conscience of their Prince to theirs, and submits to them only out of weaknes, and wait only an occasion to cast off their yoke; which would oblige Kings ever to keep them weak, and to impose heavy burdens upon them, and so prevent their rising.

Also this Doctrine is pernicious to the profession of the Gospel, for it would much hinder the conversion of Pagan Kings, since that turning Christians, according to the Mode, they should lose their authority, there being no Pagan Religion, which teacheth Subjects to resist their Prince by Arms; which would also induce Christian Kings of a diverse Religion, to hinder with all their might the Conversion of their Subjects: Blessed be God that there are none but the *Jesuits* and *Covenanters* that maintain so destructive an Opinion: The Reformed Churches, and the most part of the *Roman* Church give no jealousie to their Princes hereupon.

The

The holy prudence of the Apostles saw well, that even besides Conscience, the Counsel, the most profitable for the conservation of the Church, and the propagation of the Gospel, was to subject themselves wholly to their Soveraigns, and without any reservation, but *to suffer for righteousnesse sake*, rather than disobey God; for hereby the principal hinderance was removed, namely, that shadow, which the enemies of the Gospel made the Emperors to apprehend that this Doctrine which spread so fast, would bring along with it an alteration in their Estates, and that the Christians waited but the coming of a King, that would break in pieces all other Kings, and have for his possession the ends of the earth; it's that which Saint *Peter* had regard unto, where he exhorteth Believers, 1 *Pet.*2.13,15. *To submit themselves to every Ordinance of man for the Lords sake, that in all well-doing ye may put to silence the Ignorance of foolish men.* By this manner of subjection whole States were converted, and in the end patience overcame: For the Christians of the first Ages have made appear by their piety and moderation, that the Kingdom whither they aspired was not of this world, neither did in any thing diminish the rights of *Monarchs*, but rather strengthened their authority, binding their Subjects anew by Conscience, yea so far as to make whole Armies of valiant men that had power in their hands, to lay down their necks rather than to draw their swords against their Emperor; so did the Christian Souldiers under *Maximinian*, who would have constrained them to sacrifice to his Idols.

The Armies of the *English* and *Scottish* Covenanters are not capable of this Doctrine; these Northern people are impatient Libertines and haughty, they will form a Gospel according to the Ayr of their Climate.

Their other crafty Evasion is not much better, that
Saint

Saint *Paul* forbids to disobey the power of the King, but not to his person; but the Text is formally against this, for the Apostle by Power doth not understand a Quality without a Subject, but fastens it to the Person, saying in *vers.*6. That the Prince is the Minister of God, *and that he bears not the sword in vain, and that they are ordained of God to do Justice.* And he speaks, *vers.* 6. *of Princes in the plural number, they are Gods Ministers, attending continually upon this very thing.*

'Tis the style of Saint *Paul* to call the Angels, who excel in power, Principalities and Powers: When he speaks, *Eph.*3.10. *That the manifold wisdom of God might be known to Principalities and Powers in heavenly places:* It appears that he speaks not of Accidents, but of Persons, for they are the Persons, and not the Titles, that are capable of knowledge.

Now I would fain know of these men, what this Person is that it is lawful to resist? If it be the person of the King or supream Magistrate, whilst it is joyned to his power, they resist the power in the person; and if it be the person separated from the power, they must needs before resist either the one or the other for to make this violent separation.

And seeing that the Covenanters maintain that the authority of the King resides in their Chief, those that draw the sword against them, may return the same answer, and say, that they resist not their authority, but their Persons; but the Oath of Allegiance, and that of supremacy, which are imposed by Act of Parliament, cause all these subtilties to vanish, for men take these Oaths to the person of the King, and not to his power, or to his supremacy separated from him.

Moreover this distinction is contradicted by another, which hath been frequent a long time in their mouths, that they resisted not the King, but his Armies, which signifies in effect, that they resisted not the person of

G   King,

King, but his power; for his power laid in his Armies, and as it is the nature of a lie to enter far, these people who say they are licensed by Saint *Paul* to oppose the person of the King, and not his power, were marvellously impatient when they were told they fought against the King, and affirmed that they fought for him and defended his person, which doubtless seems to be spoken to move laughter and indignation; but God cannot be mocked, nor Conscience wholly blinded, by their impatience; hereupon they testifie that their Conscience makes their process, and dictates to them within, that to bear Arms against the King, is to sin against God and Nature.

It's a notable Symptome of a desperate sick State, where the reason of a people is smitten with astonishment, whereof we have a most lamentable example, for was there ever such a capricious madness, to accuse the Royal Majesty of Treason, to make Edicts by the King against the King, to swear a Covenant for defence of the King, which nevertheless obligeth them to make war against him, and the King being alive, to forge a Platonick Idea of the same King, residing fifty miles from himself, that so they might fight against the Person of the King. There is no *Cymera*, nor fantastical humour like this! Behold the work of the Spirit that now works efficaciously in the children of disobedience! Behold another Evasion! The Apostle (say they) doth not teach us who is the Superiour Power, but that it is the Superiour Power that we must obey, and therefore they strive to form in the Kingdom a Superiour Power above the King, a thing contrary to the Constitution of this Monarchy, as I hope to make appear.

It was declared by the two Houses that the Kings coming to the House of Commons was Treason

It's easie to gather which is the Superiour Power, which

which Saint *Paul* underſtands, for he expreſſes it himſelf, *Its the Power which bears the Sword*, ver. 3. And *he to whom Tribute is paid*, Pſal. 7. Rights that appertain to the King alone, and which were actually poſſeſſed by the Emperor, where Saint *Paul* wrote this Epiſtle: That which they alledge againſt this; that the Emperor then was more abſolute than the Kings at preſent, is falſe, but he was much more limited: *Suetonius* that lived under *Trajan*, puts amongſt the enormities of *Caligula*, to have been very near changing the form of Government (which was a Principality) into a Kingdom, and to place the Diadem upon his head. *Caligula parum abfuit quin Speciem Principatus in Regnum converteret & capiti diadema circumponeret.* And the Learned called not the power of theſe Emperors *Regnum* but *Principatus*; and were this allegation true, yet it would be far from the purpoſe; for be it that the Emperor ſhould be more or leſs abſolute than our Kings, the command of Saint *Paul* is alwaies the ſame, *That we muſt not reſiſt him that bears the Sword, and to whom Cuſtome is due, becauſe his Authority is of God.*

This other ſtarting hole is of the ſame ſtuffe, they ſay that the defence not to reſiſt Supream Powers, obligeth only Particulars, and not the States of a Kingdom; this is to make another Goſpel for the General than for the Particulars; as if they ſhould ſay, the Commandments of God are directed to every one, but not to all, which is to overthrow common Senſe, ſince the Oaths of Allegiance and Supremacy are impoſed upon all the States of *England*, whereby they are bound alſo in General; none ſit in Parliament that takes not their Oaths at his entrance, neither is it in their power to overthrow without and againſt the King that which is eſtabliſhed by the King ſitting in Parliament.

Alſo this is a thing that never entred into the ſpirits

of the *English* before the times of this epidemical phrensie, that the Kings Writs which makes the Estates to assemble, and the deputation of the people that sends them, should exempt their Deputies or Parliament men from the duty of Subjects, and absolve them of their Oath of Allegiance and St. *Pauls* Command. The Text of St. *Paul* according to the *Greek* requires that every Soul should be subject; If so be then that their Deputies or Parliament men have no souls, they are not bound to give obedience to the King.

When we reason thus, our adversaries are extraordinarily moved, and would take this matter out of the hands of the Clergy, saying, that the Lawyers, & not the Divines are to decide where the Supream Power of the State rests, whether it be in the person of the King or the people, and with what limitations the King ought to be obeyed, and that the Apostle requiring an obedience to supream Powers, intends an obedience according to the Laws, and the Laws are every where different, and that one and the same Rule of Scripture cannot serve for all Kingdoms; that the Kingdom of *England* not being formed as the Kingdom of *Israel*, or the *Roman* Empire, the Commands of the Old and New Testament alledged, toucheth not the present Quarrel.

Now are they not ashamed to forbid our Clergy to discourse of Political affairs (whilst the Gentlemen of the Bar take upon them to teach Divinity to the Clergy, and by infinite Books, as processes, stir up the people to Rebellion by Reasons of Religion) and to uphold staggering Consciences in the duty of Obedience and Christian Concord, and to defend the Truth of God by our sufferances, as we have endeavoured to do; It's not to meddle in the affairs of State, but to discharge our Consciences, and to keep that good thing which God hath committed unto us. We cannot be accused to intrude our selves into the Civil Government, as their Mini-

Ministers, who serve as Agents and Factors in publick affairs. Its henceforth the duty of Divines to handle this point of State, for the Lawyers and States-men of the Covenant, who having lately built their New Policy upon a New Divinity of their fashion, have forced the Divines to become Politicians, at least so far as to defend true Divinity from the crime of Disobedience; since they press us for Conscience to joyn with them to resist the King, they must satisfie our Consciences that the fundamental Laws of the Kingdom require us so to do. But if they would that Divines rest themselves upon the faith of the Lawyers in the point of resistance, upon which there is no less penalty than damnation, it is to press an implicit Faith, and blind obedience upon those that preach the contrary.

Without exceeding then the limits of our vocation, we do acknowledg that the Apostle requires an obedience, according to the Laws of the State, not only of the State of *Rome*, but of every other form of Government; and we deny, that there may not be found in Scripture a Rule of Obedience, which serves for all sorts of Estates, for such is that of the present Text, *That every Soul should be subject to the Higher Powers*, and that *he that resisteth the Powers, resisteth the Ordinance of God, and thereby shall receive to himself damnation*; the reason inserted between these two sentences do manifestly regard all forms of States, that *there are no powers but they be of God, and the powers that are, are ordained of God*; therefore the Command that goes before and after, appertains to all sorts of Government: Let every one be subject to the power, and let none resist the power and threatnings; also which is the terriblest of all threatnings, that those that resist the Powers, shall *receive to themselves damnation*.

Saint *Peter* wills us *to be subject to every Ordinance of man for the Lords sake*, that is, we are to subject our selves

selves to every form of Government lawfully established, and to perswade our selves that that Ordinance is of God: Generally the Scriptures before alledged, oblige all persons of all Estates to yield Obedience to him, and those in whom the Supream Power resides; and there cannot be brought any valuable reason why it is more lawful to resist the Supream Power in *England*, than in *Israel* or in *Rome*.

Indeed if they could produce a fundamental Law of the Kingdom, that did permit the people of *England* in certain cases to take up Arms against the King, they had some reason then to say that Saint *Paul* did not forbid the *English* to resist their Prince, beyond the nature of their Laws, as the Princes of *Germany*, when they took up Arms against the Emperor, produced the Golden Bull of *Charles* the fourth, and the Emperial Capitulation, for by it they were expresly permitted to make war against him, if he attempted any thing against their ancient composition; although I account that this Capitulation could not be made without contradicting the Command of the Apostle, for Histories mention that the Emperour was reduced to it by the threatnings and Menaces of the Pope; but now by long prescription, the Empire is not that it was, and it's a point disputable what is the Supream Power in divers States of *Germany*.

Melchior Golodast. Tom.3.p.124.

'Tis that which but of late hath been put to the Question in *England*, and was never disputed before the year 1642. where the Supream Power of the Kingdom resides, unless when the Crown was in dispute between two Princes: The Kings enemies employed all their forces to prove that the Soveraign Authority appertained to the people, to evade the Text of Saint *Paul* and other Texts of Scripture, which did marvellously incommode their affairs, imitating those that al-

ter

ter the Lock of their doors, when the Key is in possession of their Adversary; for beholding to their great regret, that the Scripture is wholly ours, commanding obedience, and strictly forbidding resistance to Soveraigns, *yea under pain of damnation*, they labour with all their might to change the nature of the State, that thereby the rules of subjection contained in the Scripture might be of no use.

One of their Authors, of whom they make great account, affirms boldly, that the passages in Scripture against resisting the Supream Power are of no force, but in simple and absolute Monarchies, as that of the *Jews* and *Romans*, and do no waies touch ours: This is a clean shaver, who cuts the knot that he cannot untie; wherein he imitates the ingenuity of *Buchanan*, who having taught Subjects to punish their King, and feeling himself pressed by Conscience, which suggested to him, that the Scripture was wholly contrary to it, prevents the Objection that might be made, by maintaining, that it's ill inferred to say that the thing is unlawful, because there is no such thing or the like found in Scripture. *Fuller Ans. p. 21.* *Buchanan de Jure Reg. p. 57.*

These their Confessions are very remarkable, and indeed most strange, coming from Christians, who should rather frame their policy to Scripture, than reject the Scripture, because it contradicts the policy they would establish: They have found out an invention to cast off the yoke of their King, which is to cast off that of the Word of God. After this so open a profession, it's against all equity they should make use of Scripture for their cause, either in their Writings or Sermons: They alledg nothing but examples, but there is no reason that the examples should be made use of by them who reject the Commands, but after they have turned themselves into as many postures as a Fencer, to defend

C 4

themselves againſt the invincible Text of the Apoſtle; in the end, hither they are driven, to refuſe wholly to debate the difference touching their duty to their King by the Commands of Scripture. The laſt Figure of *Proteus* is the Natural, and after all their tricks of Lying and Hypocriſie, at laſt their Nature ſhews it ſelf. In fine, when all is ſaid, this is the only anſwer on which they reſt, that the Commands of Scripture cannot determine the point of their reſiſtance, and that we muſt have recourſe to the Lawyers. This ſpeech is commonly in the mouths of all the wiſeſt of their party, and let all Chriſtian Churches take notice of this their moſt ſhameful Evaſion.

 The Covenanters of *England*, who pretend to eſtabliſh the Kingdom of Chriſt according to the Word of God, refuſe to be judged by the Commands of Scripture, touching the War made againſt their Soveraign.

CHAP. V.

What Conſtitution of State the Covenanters forge, and how they refuſe the Judgment of the Laws of the Kingdom.

TO elude the ſtrength of humane Laws as well as divine, they forge a primitive and fundamental Conſtitution of this Eſtate, deſtitute of all authority both of God or man.

 And here we muſt diſtinguiſh between their doctrine they taught in the beginning of their Covenant, and that

that which they taught afterwards; for then when they were to fight with the King in the field, and were not yet capable of so high hopes as afterwards they effected; they forged a form of State suitable to their possibility then, which was to constrain the King by the Terror of their Arms to accord to all that should please them, and wholly to put the Government into their hands; notwithstanding their Principles then led them to those Conclusions which since followed, for they supposed that the Soveraign Power was inherent in the People, that the People elected the King, and had committed to him the Authority that he exercised, reserving to themselves the Power to assume it again when the State should judge it most convenient; and to take away the sword of Justice and the *Militia*, to make use of it against him if there were need. That the King had not the Supream Power but by Paction, which being once broke by him, the Subjects were exempted from their Obedience, That he was onely Depository of the Supremacy, but when the Estates were assembled, the Supremacy was joyntly possessed by him and the two Houses; so that the King had but the thirds, and that but very hardly, for they held that the States had a Negative voice, and the King could do nothing without their consent; and whether the King had the Negative Voice of right they were not agreed, but all accorded to take it away from him in effect; that is to say, after their account, That the People might refuse the King what displeased them; but if the King denyed what the People propounded to him, they esteemed that the two Houses might and ought to do it without him, and force him to it by Arms; and this Doctrine hath been confirmed by their practise, or to speak the truth, this their practise hath occasioned this Doctrine.

Now since God through his secret and incomprehensible Judgments, hath suffered the wickedness of this

this Age to have success above their desires, they built upon these principles this Conclusion, that the People may judge and execute their King, dissolve the Monarchie for ever, and turn it into an Aristocracy or Popular Government: for yet they cannot agree to which they should hold themselves; since then they would perswade us that the Constitution of the *English* Government, exempts us from these two great dangers; Disobedience to God, and damning our Souls in resisting the King; and since they would oblige us for Conscience sake to oppose the King in obedience to God and the higher Powers; and that our Clergie are commanded to exhort the people, that God hath commanded them to draw their Swords against their Soveraign; there is a necessity to satisfie our Reason, and resolve our Consciences hereupon, to enquire whether the Nature of the State be such as they have painted it out to us.

And for this we have not referred our selves to those of the Royal party, but have consulted with the most Judicious Writers of the Covenanters, who pass amongst them as Oracles of the State, expecting that for proof of this form of Government, they would have produced the old Records of the Kingdom, which are now in their Custodie, the ancient Statutes of Parliaments, and the Testimony of their old Historians; but they alledge no such things, though much pressed thereunto by their Adversaries, onely they make a Discourse in the Air upon the Law of Nature, that hath given to every person, and by consequent to every Estate, a power for his preservation; troubling the Ignorant Readers brains with barbarous terms, and thorny distincti-

Fullers Answer. ons, and extracting the Quintessence of the State into an invisible substance: They tell us that the Parliament was coordinate, and not subordinate to the King; That the three Estates of Parliament, whereof the King made one, being

ing fundamental, admitted not of the difference of Higher or Lower: That the power of the King in Parliament was not Royal but Political: That this Fundamental Law of the kingdom was not written, for if it were it should be superstructive, and therefore Mutable, and not Fundamental: That the mixture of the three Estates in Government was not Personal but Incorporate.

Those that understand not these Mystical sentences, ought to be neverthelefs content; it being not reasonable that they should understand them better then the Authors themselves. An affected obscurity amongst Ideots passeth for knowledge; and ye shall find that the Discourses that have least reason in them are most difficult, like Olive stones which are very hard, because there is nothing in them.

Now is it not requisite to subtilize upon the virtuality and actuality of the Peoples power, for to inform the Conscience of the Subject, touching the Justice of his Arms against his King; but for that there is indeed need both of Divine and Humane Authority, and such as is easie, and to be understood of all. But the observation of Mr. *du Moulin* is very true, that ordinarily Lying arms its weaknesse with thorns, like Lizards, who save themselves by running into Bushes.

Above all in a point where the Question of Right is founded upon that of Fact; as this Question now, whether it be lawful for the *English* to take up Arms against their Prince, here to go about to satisfie Reason and Conscience with political and metaphisical Contemplations is not to purpose, they should (besides Divine Authority which should ever march before) enquire whether the Laws and Constitutions of the Country authorize this War.

The Question being not to dispute which is the best Form of Government, but to preserve the Form to
which

which God hath subjected us, and to observe the Laws of the Kingdom, and after many Moral and Political Discourses (for our Adversaries pay us with no other) those that have any Honesty or Understanding come always to this, that they would shew us by what Law of *England* it is permitted the Subjects to take up Arms without the Kings permission, and against him: When did the people ever make this Election? Where is it that they have reserved the liberty to resume the Supreme Authority when they shall please? Is there any Statute made during the Ages that this Monarchy hath continued, that prefers or equals the two Houses to the King, or doth authorize them to ratifie any thing without him? Where is the Articles of that Capitulation which in some certain cases dissolves the Subjects Oath of Allegiance? Is there any Case in the Law in which it should be lawful for Subjects to take from their King or Supreme Magistrate, his Forts, Navies, and Magazines, and to take into their hands the sole Administration of Justice, and the *Militia*, to confer the great Offices of the Crown, to receive Ambassadors, to treat with Forreign Nations, and to dispose of the Goods and Lives of the Kings Subjects.

To these so important Questions, for the duty and happiness of all the members of an Estate, and the eternal salvation of their Souls and Bodies, to answer with Platonick considerations, and in stead of producing the Laws of the Kingdom, to Philosophy upon the Law of Nature, and form an appeal from Authentical and known Laws to a Word not written, made at pleasure; This is to mock God and men, this is to insult upon the Brutality of the people, and to take a wicked advantage from the wine of Astonishment or Senselesness, which God in his just wrath hath poured forth upon this miserable Nation; for if they did beleeve there remained any common sense in this blind and mad people, durst they

they so boldly return so ridiculous an Answer to those that demand where are those Fundamen- *Full. Ans.p. 6.* tal Laws written, that now make all other *l. 12.* Laws bow to them, namely, that the Fundamental Laws are not written, and that if they were, they should be superstructive, and not fundamental; after this account the command to love God with all our heart, and our Neighbour as our self, is not fundamental, because it is written; it were to profane Reason to imploy it to refute a reasoning so unreasonable; it must needs be that these people know they have to do with Persons of great credulity, since they dare give them for a Fundamental Law, a Fantasie which they never heard before spoken of, and whereof no Writings nor Histories make mention, and this is to fight against their King, overthrow the State, lose their goods, hazard their Lives and Consciences: But what should I say? There is no reason but is perswasive when the Conclusions are taken, and there is strength to maintain them.

Christendome which have now their eyes upon our Broils, will take notice of the open confession of the Troubles of this State; That for the War against the King, and for the form of Government which they establish in the kingdome a Superiour power that abolisheth the Royal, they have no Fundamental Law written: Is not this then marvellously to abuse the Justice of God, and the patience of reasonable creatures made after his Image, and indued with knowledge; to constrain them to prostitute their Consciences and Lives in a Quarrel for which they openly confess there is not any Law written, and for which there is not the least footing of Approbation, in all that hath been established, or left authentically written since *England* hath been a Nation? We have let you see before how they decline the Defences of Scripture against the resistance of Soveraigns; behold now they confess there is no funda-

mental

mental Law written for to justifie their Arms, and the superiority of the people above the King, which they would introduce with the sword; and thus they acknowledge they have no authority neither divine nor humane for what they do; as Cardinal *Perron* having maintained the power of the Pope over the Temporal of Kings, before the Estates of *France*, in conclusion affirmed, that it was an Article which was not decided, neither by the Scriptures nor the Ancient Church, so that the Pope and our Mutineers agree together to usurp an authority upon Kings, without any ground or warrant in the Word of God, and contradicted by all humane Constitutions, that is to say, that both God and man are contrary unto them.

In his Oration before the Three Estates, Jan. 15. 1605.

CHAP. VI.

What Examples in the Histories of England *the Covenanters make use of to authorize their Actions.*

But do we not much wrong them to say that there is nothing makes for them in all the ancient Writings and Histories of this Kingdom? Do they not alledg the two Parliaments that deposed *Edward* the second, and *Richard* the second, yea truly, and to their great shame, as the wisest of their party do acknowledg, affirming that those Acts of Parliament against *Richard* the second, were not properly the Acts of the two Houses, but of *Henry* the fourth, and his victorious Army, in which they say true, for the

Observations upon the Answers of his Majesty.

the Duke of *Lancaster*, who after caused himself to be called *Henry* the fourth, having prevailed with the people to rise against their lawful King, assembled a Parliament, which he made to do whatsoever he would, and having deposed and imprisoned this poor King, soon after caused him to be put to death; though this action were as just, as it is execrable, yet it would make nothing to the purpose, where the Question is, of that which the two Houses may do, separate from the King; for the deposing of King *Richard* was by another King sitting in Parliament; for until these last States, the two Houses never thought that they were able to conclude any thing without the Royal Consent; and since, the Parliaments held under the House of *York*, declared *Henry* the fourth Usurper of the Crown, and therefore condemned the Parliament which had confirmed his usurpation.

The other example is no better than this, the deposing of *Edward* the second, by the Conspiracy of his Wife, and the Favourites of this Queen, who served themselves of a Parliament to execute this wickedness, and having deposed the King, and crowned his Son, who was under age, caused the Father to be most cruelly put to death in prison, & yet the authority of the young K. must be made use of to make the resolution of the Parliament pass into an Act; for without the King the Parliament can no more act, than a Body without a Head: But when the young King came to age, he caused the Authors and Complices of his Fathers death to be executed, and caused all the Acts of this Parliament to be broken by another.

And less than these to the purpose is, which they alledg, concerning the accord the Barons extorted from King *John*, by which this unhappy and imprudent King being reduced to a straight, promised to put himself into the power of twenty five of his Barons, and submitted

ted himself to divers other dishonorable Conditions; and this accord was not made in Parliament, but in the field by force of Arms, there being no Parliament then sitting, and therefore was of no force, nor was ever kept.

These Articles of the Barons were much like those the two Houses sent the King to *Beverly*, *Oxford* and *New-Castle*; the Covenanters imitate these Barons in their affectation of Piety, for they called their General the Marshal of the Lords Army, and of his holy Church, and these perswaded their Chiefs that they led the Battels of the Lord of Hoasts, but these transferred not the Crown to another Prince, as the Barons did, but have taken away both his Crown and Life, having long before declared by writing to their King, that they dealt very favourably with him if they did not depose him, and that if they did, they should not exceed the Limits of Modesty, nor of their Duty. This Judgment was pronounced in the House of Commons without contradiction that, The King might fall from his Office, that the happiness of the Kingdom did not depend upon him, nor the Royal Branches of his House, and that he did not deserve to be King of *England*: The Authors of these Opinions are declared in a Declaration of his Majesties. *Dec. Aug. 12. 1642.* In one point the Barons and Covenanters are very different; for the Lords that remained with the Covenanters were without power, all places of Honour and Trust being taken out of their hands by their Inferiours, and at last their House abolished by the Commons, so that instead of producing this War of the Barons, the Covenanters should rather have alledged the Seditions and Commotions of *Watt Tyler* and *Jack Straw*, poor Artisans, and followed with people of the same rank; for these persons and the Cause of the Covenanters are far more alike.

Behold

Behold here with what authorities the Margins of their Books are stuffed! Behold the Examples which the politicians of the times present to the Gentlemen of the Parliament for to teach them what they ought to do; those infamous actions which were abhorred by the ages following them, are become the supporters of ours; and despair, which makes men snatch up any sorts of weapons, forceth our enemies to justifie their actions by the examples of Rebels and Paricides; 'tis not for nothing then that these Histories are so often alledged, though nothing to the purpose, and it's not without cause that they print them apart; for not being able to justifie their actions, they have declared their intentions, and made the King to see what he sholud trust to, if he fell into their hands: Certainly, if there had not been a design laid to come to that, both to prepare the people and intimidate the King, those incendiaries who by these horrible examples, and their Maximes of State grounded thereupon, teaching the deposing of Kings, should have been hanged long since with their Books about their necks: For so many men which are studied in the Laws of the Kingdom, and are at the helm of affairs, cannot be ignorant of that which King *James* of happy and glorious memory, marks in his Book of the Right of Kings, that in the time of *Edward* the Third, there was an Act of Parliament made, which declared all them Traytors, who imagined (it's the word of the Law) or conspired the death of the King; upon which Act the Judges grounding themselves, have alwaies judged them for Traytors who dared but to speak of deposing the King, because they believed that they could not take away the Crown from off the Kings Head without taking away his Life. It was heretofore a crime worthy of death to speak, yea to think evil against the King, and moreover the Word of God which is to be obeyed, forbids us to speak evil of the King, no not in

D our

our thought; but now it's the exercise of devout Souls to write Meditations upon the deposing of their King.

CHAP. VII.

Declaring wherein the Legislative Powers of Parliament consists.

Having no better Authorities in all the Examples of the Ages past, they establish a New one, which by the unlimited largeness, supplies what it wants of length of time; for when we require to be governed by the Laws, they answer us, that the Parliament is the Oracle of the Laws; that it is for that great Court to declare what is Law and what is not, to interpret the Laws, to dispense with them, or to make new ones.

That themselves are the Parliament, excluding all others; and that since they have declared that this War is according to Law, and that such Maximes as they give us, are fundamental Laws of the Kingdom, we must remit our selves to them, and receive for Law what they ordain.

But because strangers may read, who have no knowledge of the Government of *England*; for to examine this Imperious reason, we are obliged to declare here what we know touching the present affairs.

We have learned to acknowledg the Parliament of *England* for the Supream Court of the Kingdom, that can make and unmake Laws, and from whose Judgment there is no appeal: But of this Court the King is the principal part, and it's he that renders it soveraign; the two Houses in all their Legislative Acts acknowledg him their true and sole Soveraign, the House of Lords only can evert the Judgment of the Courts of Justice,

but

but not their own, without the consent of the King and the House of Commons; the House of Commons is not a Judicial Court, having not power to administer an Oath, inflict a Fine, or imprison any, but those of their own House; and these two neither apart nor together, cannot make a Law; but when they would enact any thing, they both together present a Writing to the King in form of a request; if the King approves of them; the Lord Keeper of the Great Seal answers for the King in these *French* words, *Le Roy le veult,* and then it is made an Act; but if the King refuseth it, he returns answer, *Le Roy S'avisera,* and the business passeth no further: Before the consent of the King, the proposition of the two Houses contained in the Writing, is like unto that which the *Romans* called *Rogatio*; but when the King grants it, they may then give it the name of *Lex*; and in effect, it is but a request before the pleasure of the King makes it pass into a Law; and was never other before this present Parliament.

Therefore the *English* Lawyers call the King the life of the Law, for though the King in Parliament cannot make any Law without the concurrence of the two Houses, yet nevertheless it's his Authority only that gives it the strength and Name of a Law; and they are so far from having any Legal Authority in their Commands, without the consent of the King, that the customary right gives them not so much as a Name, neither takes any Cognisance of them.

To say then that the Parliament hath declared this War lawful, and that the Orders of Parliament are Laws, is by an ambiguous term to abuse the ignorance of the people; for by the Parliament they understand sometimes one House, sometimes both; and sometimes the King and both Houses together; it's thus that men understand them, when they speak of the Supream Court of Parliament, and of Acts of Parliament; for

D 2

the

the King was ever accounted the first of the three Estate, without whom the two other had not power to conclude any thing lawfully, for all their Authority is derived from him, not only for a time, but by a continual Influence, which being interrupted, the power of necessity ceaseh.

These three together have power to interpret the Laws, to revoke them, and to make others, therein properly lies the Oracle of the Laws. A Judicious Writer of the Royal party, calls the union of the three Estates, the Sacred *Tripos*, from whence the Oracles of the Law are pronounced.

When any one of these three are separate from other, the other two stagger and are lame, nor cannot serve for a firm foundation for the safety of the State, and satisfaction of the Subjects Conscience.

But let us assume the business higher, you cannot more vex our Enemies than to tell them this Truth, that the Monarchy which is at this day, began by Conquest, this is that which by no means they will endure to hear of, but would perswade men that it began by an Election and Covenant, which indeed had never any being but in their own Fancies. If they would be believed for this, they should then produce some Records. For the bold conjecturers are less credible than all the Histories, which assures us of three Conquests in this Kingdom, since the *Romans* and *Picts*, Namely, that of the *Saxons, Danes* and *Normans*.

Moreover, those that would abolish this Office and Dignity, destroy that of their own Laws, for all the Lands of the Kingdom are held of the King by right of the Sword, as appears by the nature of Homages and Services that the Lords of Fiefes owe to the King, when *William* the Conqueror took possession of the Kingdome, strengthening the Right of his Conquest by the last Will and Testament of *Edward* the Confessor; he
declared

declared himself Master of all the Land, and disposed of it according to his pleasure.

His Son *Henry* the first eased the People somwhat of the severe and unlimited Government of his Father, and confirmed to the *English* their ancient priviledges, which since after long and bloudy wars, were anew confirmed, and the Quarrel determined by that wise King *Edward* the first, who having as much valour as wisdom, in condescending to the Rights of his Subjects, knew well how thereby to preserve his own, for after all, the Soveraignty of Kings remained inviolable, and those prerogatives were preserved which were only proper to him who is not subject but to God alone. Such also is the Court of Wards, by which a great many Orphans of the Kingdom are in Wardship to the King, and almost all the Lands appertaining to him until they be of Age. In this thing the Kings of *England* exceed all other Christian Princes. This being such an essential mark of absolute Soveraignty that there cannot be a greater. Certainly, if this Monarchy had begun either by Election or Covenant, the Subjects would never have given the King so vast a power over their Estates and Families.

Amongst the priviledges of the *English*, these three are the principal. That the King cannot make a Law without the consent of his Estates. That no Law made in Parliament, can be revoked but in Parliament; and that the King can levy no moneys of his Subjects besides his ordinary Revenues, without the concurrence of the Two Houses, in the intervals of Parliaments; the King according to his Supream Power may make Edicts seen burdensom to the Subjects, or to impair their Laws and Priviledges, they humbly present them in the next Parliament, & the K. when the complaint appears just unto him, easeth them; for to make their requests pass for Acts without the pleasure of the K. they cannot, neither can the K. make new Acts in Parl. without their consent.

D 3 In

In the mean while, the King makes not them partakers of his Authority, but assembling them in Parliament, he renders them capable to limit his Authority, in Cases that appertain to their cognisance; for there are many cases wherein they are not to meddle at all, in the point of the *Militia*, and for fear they should forget that, even this power they have to limit the King, comes from the Authority of the King, and he can take it away from them when he pleaseth; for when he breaks up the Parliament, he retires to himself the Authority that he gave them to limit his; and moreover if they stretch their priviledges beyond the pleasure of the King, he hath power to dissolve the Parliament, and after the word of the King is passed which dischargeth them, and sends them away, they have not power to sit or consult a minute.

Whence *Bodinus* (well versed in the nature of the States of Christendome) concludes the King of *England* to have Soveraign Authority; *The Estates of* England, saith he, *cannot be assembled nor dissolved, but by the Edict of the Prince, no more then in* France *and* Spain; which proves sufficiently that the Assemblies have no power of themselves to command or forbid a thing; and he laughs at the ignorance of *Bellaga*, who affirm the States of *Arragon* to be above their King, and yet nevertheless confesseth the States cannot assemble nor separate without him; *Illud Novum & plane absurdum*, That (saith he) is New, and altogether a most absurd Doctrine: And therefore it was that which occasioned them, who had a design to overthrow Church and State to labour to draw a promise from his Majesty, that the late long Parliament should not be dissolved without the consent of both Houses, well knowing, that without that granted, the King when he pleased might have overturned their designs; which they having obtained,

Bodin. de Repub. lib. 1. cap. 8.

shewed

shewed by their Actions that they thought themselves then priviledged to do what they would without his Authority, and thus it is with us at this day.

Yet so it is, that they themselves do confess that this grant did not alter the Nature of the two Houses, and the Gentlemen of the Parliament have often protested that they would not make use of this Act of Grace to the disadvantage of his Majesty: so then if there were no Soveraignty resident in the two Houses before this grant, there is no more after, and the pretended Fundamental Laws not written, that parts Soveraignty between the King and his Subjects, yea that transport it wholly to the people, are much to be suspected of falsity, since they never appear; but since the promise they obtained of the King (both to his and their great damage) to perpetuate this Parliament as long as they pleased, and since they have begun to exercise the Soveraignty by force of Arms. Thus the new Nobility after they had obtained the *Firs* by right or wrong, produce Coats of Arms and Titles which were heretofore unknown.

They maintain this their New Soveraignty by a Maxime of *Stephanus*, *Junius*, *Brutus*, *Rex est singulis Major & universis Minor*, That is to say (as they expound it) *That the King is the Soveraign of Particulars, but the Representative body of the State is greater then he, and have Soveraignty over him*; and all their Writers (and amongst others the Observator on the Kings Answers) attribute Majestie to the Commonalty, and not to the King or Supreme; if this be true, it's very strange how this Representative Body of the State, the Parliament, have left it so long time to the Kings, the Court of Wards, and many other Rights of Soveraignty, which they have enjoyed without Contradiction, until that present Parliament.

This vile Maxime then being destitute of all proofs

from the Laws and Customes of the State, ought to be despised; but moreover it is also void of all reason, for if the *English* be subject to their King in Retail, are they not in Gross; if in pieces, not in the whole? being born Subjects, have they power to give the Soveraignty to their Deputies or Parliament men, and make them Chief? that is to say, can they give them that which they have not? And seeing also that they cannot assemble in Parliament without the King or Supreme Magistrates Writ; this Writ of the Kings doth it render them forthwith Soveraigns above the King? The stile of the Writ calls them, *ad Consultandum de quibusdam arduis,* to consult with him, about some difficult affairs, and not to master him, and to dispose of his Authority.

And since they call this great Court, the *Body Representative of Subjects*, they must needs then be Subjects, otherwise they should not represent them who sent them, and that which the King accords to, should be granted to Soveraigns, but his Subjects should receive no benefit thereby: He who will well examine this Proposition; That the Soveraignty over the Soveraign rests in the Representative body of Subjects, shall find it full of contradictions, and to destroy it self.

Bodin. de Repub. lb. 1. cap. 8. *They cannot bring any probable reason* (saith *Bodin*.) *that the Subjects ought to command their Prince, and that the Assembly of Estates ought to have any power, unless when the Prince is under age,* or *distracted,* or *captive, then the Estates may depute him a Regent* or *Lieutenant. Otherwise, if Princes were subject to the Laws of the States, and Commands of the people, their Power were nothing, and the Title of a King would be a Name without the thing; moreover, under such a Prince the Common-wealth should not be governed by the people, but by some few persons equal in their Suffrages, who who would make Laws and Edicts, not by the Authority of the*

the Prince, but by their own; who for all that come and present him humbly with requests, every one apart by himself, and all in a body making shew of Faithfulness and Obedience, these things are as ridiculous as can be imagined: thus saith *Bodin*. Behold here the Form of State of our Covenanters in their beginning, so drawn to the life by this learned Person, that one would say, he took the very Copie from them: In effect, when (under a Monarchy) a Faction in an Assembly of States shall take upon them the Soveraignty, the State change not into an Aristocracy nor Democracy, but into a pure Obligarchy, which is the worst of all Forms of State, and but the corruption of others. The Royal Power being once usurped, 'tis not then the greatest, nor the best, nor the most, who govern the affairs; but some few unquiet and ambitious persons, who love contention, and know how to fish in troubled waters; and as these men deceive the King with a false Idea of Soveraignty, so they deceive their companions, perswading them that they have part in their Authority, because they have voices in the House, for in such Assemblies where the choice of persons, is more by hap then Judgment, the Suffrage is to all, but the Power is in a few. The same Author, numbring the Soveraign and absolute Monarchies of Christendom, places *England* and *Scotland* amongst them; and saith, *That without all Question, their Kings have all the rights of Majesty, and that it is not lawful for their Subjects neither apart nor in a Body, to attempt any thing against the Life, Reputation, or Goods of their Soveraign, be it either by ways of Force or Justice; although he were guilty of all the crimes a man could imagine in a Tyrant.* De Repub. lib. 2. cap. 5.

For the Subjection that the Parliament owe to their King, we can have no better witness then the Parliament it self; for that disloyal maxime, *that the body of the State is above the King*, is contradicted by the ordinary

dinary ſtile of their papers preſented to the King by this Body: *The Two Houſes moſt humbly beſeech their Soveraign Lord the King, and they qualifie themſelves, the moſt humble and loyal ſubjects of his Majeſty.* 'Tis the Preſentative Body of the Kingdome who ſpeaks, and nothing by way of Complement, but Duty. This Preface hath an excellent Grace in the beginning of a Declaration of the Two Houſes to their King, wherein they tell him, that they deal favourably with him, if they do not depoſe him, and that they may do it without exceeding the limits of their Duty and Modeſty. This diſcourſe is like the Locuſts of the bottomleſs pit, *Revelations 9.* which had the faces of men, but the tails of Scorpions; and therefore to avoid this diſproportion, in their Articles preſented to the King at *New-Caſtle*, they left out the Qualification of Subjects.

The ordinary Preface of Statutes do lively expreſs the Nature of the three Eſtates: *The King by the Advice and Conſent of the Prelates, Earls and Barons, and at the inſtance and requeſt of the Commonalty hath ordained, &c.* For it's the King alone properly that ordains; the Peers as Councellors adviſe and Conſent, the Commons as Suppliants require and ſolicite. The Parliament held in the twenty fourth year of *Henry* the Eight, ſpeaks thus: *By divers ancient and authentical Hiſtories, and Chronicles, it is manifeſtly declared that this Kingdome of* England *is an Empire, and for ſuch hath been known in the world, governed by one Soveraign Head, having the dignity and Royal greatneſs of the Emperial Crown, to which there is a Body Politick joyned, compoſed of all ſorts and degrees of people, as well Spiritual as Temporal, who are bound next to God, to render unto him Natural Obedience.* If the Body Politick be naturally ſubjected to him as to its Head, it's contrary to Nature, that it ſhould be ſubjected to the Body Politick;

and

and his maxime, *Rex est universis minor*, is condemned as false by the Parliament; they knew not in those daies what it was to make the Body of the State march with its head downward, and feet upward, but they were careful to maintain the Head in that eminent place where God had set it; and hither also tend the words following, *That the chief Soveraign is instituted and furnished by the goodness and permission of Almighty God, with full and entire Power, Preheminence, Authority, Prerogative and Jurisdiction, to execute Justice, and put a final determination in all Cases to all sorts of his Subjects within this Kingdome*; and that many Laws and Ordinances, had been made in preceding Parliaments for the full and sure conserving of the prerogative and preheminence of this Crown. These good Subjects, could not find words enough, nor consult of means sufficient according to their mind, to defend the Authority of their King, esteeming (and well they might) that the happiness and liberty of the Subjects lay in the inviolable power of their Soveraign, that the greatness of the State consisted in that of the Prince, and that there is no other way to crown the Body, but to place the Crown upon the Head.

This stile is very far from that of the nineteen Propositions presented to the King by the Two Houses in the beginning of the War; which required that all matters of State should be treated of only in Parliament, or if the King would treat of any Affairs in his Councel, this Councel should be limited to a certain number, and the old Councellors cashiered, unless such whom it pleased the Two Houses to retain, and that none hereafter should be admitted without their approbation; that the King should have no power in the Education and Marriage of his children without their advice; that all great Officers of the Crown, and the principal Judges, should alwayes be chosen by the

the approbation of the Two Houses, or by a Councel authorized by them; the same also in Governours of places, and in the Creation of Peers, which hath since been denied to the King in effect. And as for the *Militia*, they would have the King wholly put it into their hands, that is to say, he should take his Sword from his side and give it them, which he could not do without giving them the Crown; for the Crown and the Royal Sword are both of one piece; so also for the point of Religion, these propositions take from him all Authority and liberty of judgement, yea, even the liberty of Conscience; *for they require that his Majesty consent to such a Reformation as the Two Houses should conclude upon, without telling him what this Reformation is.* Let all the world here judge if these men speak like Subjects; they had reason to present these Articles with their swords in their hands, but the King had more reason to draw his to return them an answer.

All these propositions are founded upon one only proposition, which passeth amongst them for a Fundamental Law, *That the King is bound to grant to the People all their Demands:* but this is a Fundamental in the Ayr, and made void by the practise of all Ages since *Eng.* was a Monarchy, and by that Authentical Judgement of the States assembled under *Henry* the Fift; *That it belongs to the Supremacy of the King to grant or refuse, according to his pleasure, the Demands that are made to him in Parliament:* And in stead of the House of Commons, being as it is now the Soveraign Court, a thing never heard of until this present Age;

Ola. magna Charta Diar. Hen. 4.

2 Hen. 5.

The House supplicated Henry the Fourth, *not to employ himself in any Judgement in Parliament, but in such cases as in effect appertained to him, because it belonged to the King alone to judge, except in cases specified by the Statutes.*

The

The same House under *Edward* the
Third, acknowledged that it did not   3 *Edw.* 3.
belong to them to take Cognisance of such matters as
the keeping of the Seas, or the Marshes of the Kingdome; yea, even during the sitting of Parliaments,
the Kings have alwayes disposed of the *Militia*, and Ad-
miralty, of the Forts and Garrisons, the Two Houses
never interposing or pretending any right thereunto,
they declared ingeniously to *Edw.* the
First, *that to him belonged to make ex-*   7 *Edw.* 1.
press Command against all Force of Arms, and to that end
they were bound to assist him, as their Soveraign Lord.

They declared also to King *Henry* the Seventh, *that*
every Subject by the duty of his subjection, was bound to
serve and assist his Prince and Soveraign Lord upon all oc-
casions: by which they signified, that it was not for
them to meddle with the *Militia*; but that their duty
as Subjects bound them to be aiding and assisting to
him.

The Learned in the Laws tell us, *that to raise Troops*
of Horse or Foot without Commission of the King, or to
lend Aid, is esteemed and called by the Law of England, to
levy war against the King our Soveraign Lord, his Crown
and Dignity: In this point all that is done without him,
is done against him, and this is conformable to the general Right of all Nations; *As for the Royal Estate*
(saith *Bodin.*) *I believe there is no person that doubts that*
all the Power, both of making Peace and War, belongs to the
King, since none dare in the least manner do any thing in
this matter without the Command of the King, unless he
will forfeit and endanger his Head. If the Two Houses
were priviledged to the contrary by any Statute, we
should have heard them speak it, but for what they
have done, we see no other Authority then their practice.

Therefore none ought to wonder if this their new
practice

practice hath less Authority with persons of a sound judgement, then these practises of all ages past: and if we cannot perswade our selves that without the Authority of the King they cannot abolish those of Parliaments Authorized by the King, let them not then make such a loud noise with the Authority of Parliament; 'Tis in obedience to that Supreme Court of Parliament that we so earnestly strive to preserve the Princes Rights: those Acts of Parliament are in full force which have provided with great care to defend the Royal Prerogatives, judging aright, that the Soveraignty is the Pillar of the publick safety, and that it cannot be divided without being weakned, and without shaking the State that rests upon it; But we leave the reasons of the form of this Estate to them who formed it, contenting our selves to obey the Laws, until the same Authority that made them alters and changes them.

This Authority being that of the Prince sitting in Parliament, we hold not our selves bound by that which passeth in any House or Councel without him, and against him, accounting that where the Princes Authority shines not, their power is eclips'd; above all since the Houses at *Westminster* were reduced to the fourth part of their number, and the lesser part (the major part being frighted away) and filled their vacant places with persons of their own judgement, without the Kings Authority; if the Houses had ever any Power without him, it was like the light of the Moon without the Sun, *Exiguum & malignum Lumen*, as the *Astrologers* call it, it was a little light which did nought but hurt.

ut igitur in naturalibus Capite de truncato residuum non Corpus sed Truncum appellamus, sic in politicis sine Capite Communitus nulla tenus corporatur. Fortescue cap. 13.

Our great Lawyer *Fortescue* speaks well, that as a Natural Body when the Head is cut off, is not called a Body,

Body, but a Trunck; so in the Body Politick, the Commonalty without a Head, cannot any way incorporate or make a Body.

CHAP. VIII.

How the Covenanters will be Judges in their own Cause.

But was there ever any thing more unreasonable then this proceeding? They would that the judgement of the Lesser part of the Two Houses without the King, and against all former Parliaments, should be received, yea, in their own Quarrel; and that in the Controversie, whether the King hath Authority above this Assembly, or it above him, this Assembly will be judge; 'tis for them (they tell us) to declare what is Law, and to make the Law: Now that Assembly declares, that their Authority is above the King, that their Arms are just, and the Kings unjust; and that the Representative Body of the State cannot erre in Law, and that it's your duty to stand to their judgement.

These people would be ashamed to confess where they have learned thus to reason: Is it not of him who said, *Dic Ecclesiæ, hoc est tibi ipsi*; Tell it to the Church, that is to say, to thy self; and truly to confute them, we will do them the shame, to employ the same words we make use of against him, changing only the persons.

In the present Quarrel, one of the Controversies is, Whether the Two Houses at *Westminster*, without the King,

Judge of Controversie, cap. 5 p. 103.

King, are the Soveraign Judges in point of Law. In this Controversie should the Two Houses be Judges, they should then be Judges in their own Cause, and should be assured to gain their process. *Item*, if it be disputed whether they can erre in this Controversie also, they would judge they could not erre? Should they be Infallible Judges of their Infallibility? Who beholds not in this an evident contradiction? That it must be, that he that disputes whether the Two Houses can erre, must address himself to the Two Houses, as to Judges that cannot erre, to judge this Question; so likewise in the Question, whether the Authority of the Two Houses be above the King, it's certain that the Two Houses cannot be Judges, since by this same Question their Authority to Judge is called into doubt, the one pretends, that the difference hath been decided and judged by the Authority of a Soveraign and infallible Judge; it's certain that hereby he renders the wound incurable, the quarrel eternal, and beyond all terms of reconciliation.

It matters not to say, that between two parties that pretend to the Soveraignty, there can be no Judge, but that the strongest must carry it; for if the two parties desire peace, they may choose Arbiters. The King or Supreme being the Natural Soveraign of his Enemies, and he who gives vigor to the Laws, hath desired notwithstanding, that the difference should be determined by the Laws, he pretends not to infallibility: He hath also often chosen his Neighbours for Arbiters, and hath fully satisfied them by reasonable offers, and such as are worthy of him; witness the Report that the extraordinary Ambassadors of the States Generals made to their Lords, for which the Parliament of *London* declared their great discontent in writings: The King being to render account of his Actions to none but God alone, submitted himself notwithstanding

standing to Reason and Piety, remitting himself wholly to the Ancient Laws and Constitutions of his Kingdome.

He hath often protested, and oft-times published, and in this difference taken all *Christendome* for Arbiters; but what? in the Question whether his Subjects can make a Law against him, and whether they have right to make war on him, and would also that he should remit himself to their Ordinances; yea, even those which they have made without him, against his will, and against himself; and that he should acknowledge them for Supreme Judges in their own cause, without other Arbiters then their will: Now they have had their wills wholly, and have been Judges and parties both together, a priviledge that belongs to God alone, to whose Supreme Court we appeal.

CHAP. IX.

That the most Noble and best part of the Parliament retired to the King, being driven away by the worser.

THat which doth strongly perswade us to believe, that the Priviledges of Parliament, which they would extend even *in infinitum*, have an ill foundation, is because we have seen them opposed by the better part of the Parliament; both in Quality and Dignity: For besides the King, an hundred seventy five of the House of Commons, and the best qualified, withdrew themselves from amongst them, and of the Lords eighty three, so that scarcely the third part remained at *Westm:*

E Almost

Almost all the Gentry wholly followed the King; and when we consider the persons, the Condition and Revenues of those that withdrew themselves, we cannot see that they had any need to fish in troubled waters, or to warm themselves at the Great Fire that began to flame, as those had that remained. Without doubt that great Body of Lords and Gentlemen of the Kingdome loved their Liberty, and would never have assisted the King to have obtained an unlimited power, break their Priviledges, and impose a perpetual yoak of slavery upon them and their posterity.

When need was, these Members of Parliament assembled themselves, and the King deferred to their Councels as much as their Priviledges required: Whereupon those of the Parliament of *London* were extraordinarily vexed, maintaining that the Name and Power of Parliament, was from that time fastened to the place where they sate, which is a point that we will not dispute, how strange soever it be; but we would have them remember, that they have had their sitting in other places, and have not for all that thought they had left their Authority at *Westminster*; and we dare answer for them, that if the Lords and Commons which held with the King, had driven them away, and taken their place, they would soon have changed their Opinion.

Besides this strong consideration of numbers and persons, all those who know that the King is the Fountain of Authority, and that without him there is no more lawful Power, then day without the sun, would never make question which were the true Parliament, that which acted with him, or that which rose up and fought against him. But alas since, force and necessity hath constrained many poor Lords to return & bow to their unjust power.

It would be too long to relate all the reasons that moved in the beginning, so many persons of Honour to withdraw themselves from *London*, in the general they
loved

loved their Religion, their King and Country, and could not consent to the general disorder of Church and State, nor hinder it in gainsaying.

For a Sample of their proceedings, which they used to drive them away, we will only commend to the Judicious Reader the Petition of the baser sort of people of *London*, presented to the House of Commons, and by that House, to the House of Lords; *Anno* 1641. *To exhort the Lords to sit no longer apart from the House of Commons, but to make one whole and entire body together, and to joyn with them, and that they would agree to an equality in the State, to procure an equality in the Church, and for a while to forsake their power of Lords to subdue the pride of the King*; adding withal, That if they gave not a speedy remedy to the obstructions which retarded the happy progress of the great pains they took, they should be forced to have recourse to the Remedy they had in their hands, and to destroy the Disturbers of their peace; requiring the House that they would *publickly declare to them who they were.*

Judge ye in what Common-wealth these people lived, who durst present such a Petition, and if there appeared not a sworn hatred against all Greatness and Superiority, and a design formed to change this Noble and Ancient Monarchy into a Common-wealth; like that of *Munster*. Oh what impudence! to dare to solicite the House of Lords at one blow to lose both their Rights and Honours, to consent to an equality in the State, which was to debase them, and even to put them in their shirts, and oblige them to depose the King, and to render him like to the meanest of the people: For observe, they would have an equality in the State, like unto that of the Church, where all Ministers are Companions. The Royal Dignity they call pride, and would seduce the Nobility, which is the Kings right hand, to ruine the head from whence their honour takes life and mo.ion; and this urged with Menaces to destroy them, and Bravado's that the lives of the great ones were in their hands. Behold here that of the Prophet *Isaiah* fulfilled, *Isa.*3.5. *The base shall behave himself proudly against the Honourable.*

These Petitioners in the Title of their Petition qualified themselves, *The poorest of the people,* and such indeed they were; so little in their condition, that a great person offended would have scorned to have taken notice of them, and yet so strong in their number, that there was neither greatness nor power that could resist them; in this double regard they were chosen, to speak aloud the intentions that their Leaders would, but durst not otherwise make known, and that they might bear the blame without danger, as proceeding from the insolence and ignorance of a brutish and ill bred people.

Notwithstanding the charity of the House of Commons discharged this poor people of the blame, and took it upon themselves. For these Gentlemen, did they not in a body themselves present this so unworthy a Petition to the House of Lords, witnessing thereby that the Petition, and the seditious souls of those people which clamoured at their doors, was a work of their own. Oh how will they palliate over this vile action? All the water in the Sea cannot wash away their shame, to favour so villanous a Petition, in stead of making the bearers feel the effects of their just indignation. This base multitude might have been frighted and dispersed by an angry look or word of this great and Noble House of Lords, but this rascality had friends in the Parliament, who emboldened them to rise, thereby to make use of their assistance: For the same day (the seditious Rabble remaining there to serve them who sent for them) the

This Story is related in the Kings declaration of August 12, Anno 1642.

Ordinance

Ordinance to take the Militia from the King, which had twice been cast out of the Lords House, was again presented to them the third time by the House of Commons, with threatnings, giving them openly to understand, that if the House of Lords did not joyn with the Commons in point of the Militia, those amongst them that were of the Commons opinion, should do wisely to make them publickly known, that so they might distinguish their Friends from their Foes. This being seconded by the great cries of the mutinous people about the House of Parliament, the most part of the Lords arose and left their places, and amongst the Lords who remained, those who were for the Militia, for fear or otherwise, carried it by some voices.

Soon after many of both Houses withdrew themselves without ever returning; it was time to part company, when thy could not Vote without hazzarding their lives or Consciences: For the Names of the Lords and Commons which pleased not the Zealous party, were posted up to make them flee, or to be torn a pieces by the enraged multitude.

And thus the small party of the two Houses drave away the greater, as a few Hornets which dispeoples the whole Hive; being assisted herein by the insolent, hypocritical and meaner sort of people, which were at their beck, through the Industry of some seditious Preachers of the populous Parishes of *London*, where the Brownists and Anabaptists abounded.

By the same Instruments the Lords had been before constrained to pass the Ordinance for taking away the Bishops Votes in Parliament.

By the same Instruments also the King was driven from his House and chief City, when the Factious affrighted a peaceable and disarmed King, arming the people, and manning out Vessels of War on the Thames, besieging the Royal Palace, under colour of being a Guard to the six Members, whom the King had accused of high Treason, to conduct them to *Westminster*, in spight of him; but the King some hours before retired himself to save his life, and returned not after.

In requital of the many good services of the people, their Masters at *Westminster* permitted them all kind of liberty, and indeed they taught the people that lewd licentiousness, who before were kept in obedience by an excellent Government, and could hardly be brought to become so vile and insolent; but there is nothing but in time one may learn, by exhortations and examples; and it appeared by their actions, how well they had profited in this Art, for when the House of Lords would have reproved them, the House of Commons were offended with the Lords, and made this open profession to them, *That they should not discourage their friends, and that they had need of their service.* And thus these Masters and the Factious people, granted one another mutual liberty, and they forgave the people their passed Insolencies, on condition they would commit new ones.

But when the honest and most understanding of the City came in a good number to petition the two Houses to hearken to peace, and satisfie the King, they were severely rebuked, as seditious; and these Gentlemen let them know that they loved no noise but of their own making. Behold here the waies whereby the Parliament of *London* obtained their absolute power! Behold the Foundations they laid for a most holy Reformation!

Posterity will be ashamed of the Actions of their Fathers; all Forreign Nations will abhor these proceedings; remorse and sorrow may in the end enter into the hearts of the *Londoners*, when they shall behold themselves the sole object of publick Execrations and curses. Those of *Gaunt* and *Paris* have only reason to pardon them, when they shall remember their Baracado's, and the estate of the Nobles during the holy League.

Chap.

CHAP. X.

A Parallel of the Covenant with the holy League of France, under Henry the 3d.

WHo so shall compare the holy League of *France* with the *English* Covenant, shall find that they are sisters, daughters of the same Father, and that the younger is to the life after the Image of the Elder; in both you shall find an Oath of mutual assistance to extirpate Heresie, without the Authority of the King, and which at last is turned against the King himself: A Jealousie without ground of the Religion of their Soveraign, and a War of Religion against a King of the same Religion, which they would make the world believe was a Heretick. A League with strangers, and Armies raised in the Kingdom against their natural Prince, who gave them no other occasion of the War but his too much Gentleness. A King submitting himself to reason, offering himself to remedy all the grievances of his Subjects, and a people refusing to admit him to bring a remedy, and resolved to give order without him, the King driven from his chief City, which he had honoured by his ordinary presence. The fire of civil war blown about by seditious preachers. The superstitious people tributary to the ambition of some particulars, weak Conscience instructed to cut the throat of their King, for the love of God, and to gain Paradise; fastings frequent, Devotions doubled, Prophetical Inspirations, Examples of Angelical Holiness, and all this to perswade the superstitious people, that God favoured their Seditions as his cause, and that their Leaders took Counsel of none but the Holy Ghost, and
had

had no other aim but the setting up of the Kingdom of Jesus Christ: Writers under pay to write scandalous libels against their King, the people fed with lies to drain money out of their purses, one while amazing them with fears where there was none, another while flattering them with false hopes and with forged news; A Parliament in the principal City, but in it a small number, who wanting the Royal assistance, support themselves by granting liberty to an inveagled people, and by power of rich and foolish Citizens. Nobility scorned; Artificers and Banquerouts bearing the sway, all Order Divine and Humane overturned, the ancient Laws and Customes broken, and new fundamental Laws never heard of before, in their places. In brief, it appears at this day, that the Devil marches abroad, and walks in the same paths he did about fifty years since.

CHAP. XI.

The Doctrine of the English Covenanters parallel'd with the Doctrine of the Jesuits.

Since the League of *France* and the *English* Covenant were both made upon pretence of Religion, it's not unworthy our paines to consider the conformity of the Doctrines they employed to maintain both the one and the other, and how the Jesuits Maximes were the chief support of the Covenant.

Both in the League and Covenant, the people were encouraged to take up Arms against their King, by this opinion of Car. *Bellar.* who teacheth, *that in the Kingdoms of men the power of the*

Bel. de Con. l. 2. c. 19

the K. comes from the people, because it's the people that makes the King, and that the people do never so transfer their power over to the King, but they retain it in habitu, and so that in certain cases they may in effect re-assume it again, which was also the judgment of *Navarrus*, whom the Cardinal highly extols.

And thus also the Author of the Observations upon the Kings Declarations, who is the *Master of the Sentences* with the Covenanters, teacheth us, *That originally the power is in the people, who are the fountain and efficient cause, and that the Authority is not in the Prince, but secondarily, and derivatively*: All these State Philosophers are full of School terms, but little reason; and he adds, *That this Authority founded by the people, cannot be dissolved but by that power which gave it constitution.* Which is as much as to say, That the people may take away the Kings power and authority when they please.

Another of the Sect, but more antient tells us; *That Princes and Governours have their authority from the people, who when they find it convenient, may resume and take it from them again, as every man may revoke when he please his own procuration, or warrant*, but this reason shall by and by be examined and refuted.

Gilby lib. de obedientia, p. 25. & 105.

The Cardinal explains himself more clearly in that which before he had written in covert Terms, saying, *That a King, such as he there describes, may, yea ought, by the consent of all, to be deprived of his Authority*: and Goodman is of his opinion, *That evil Princes ought to be deposed, and that this alone belongs to the inferiour Magistrates to put in execution.*

Bellarm. l. 3. De Pontif. cap. 7. Goodman p. 144. and 149.

We learn from Doctor *Charron* that the *French Leaguers*

Leaguers eluded the ſtrength of S. *Pauls*-Texts, which forbids the oppoſing of Soveraigns in ſaying, That the commands had regard and reſpect only to the State of the Chriſtians of

Charron in his Chriſtian Diſcourſe about the end of his Book of Wiſdom.

thoſe times, becauſe they were not then ſtrong enough to make reſiſtance. I have before ſhewed how *Bellarmine*, *Buchanan*, and the Champions of Covenant, make uſe of the ſame reaſon and expoſition.

But to clear the way, and make it ſmooth to come to depoſing of Soveraign Princes: Theſe two parties are wont to abſolve their Subjects from their Oaths of Allegiance, *Emanuel Sa* the Jeſuite ſaith, *That the people may depoſe their Prince, even after they have ſworn perpetual obedience to him*. And Mr. *Knox* ſaith, That if Princes prove Tyrants againſt God and his Truth, their Subjects are free from their Oaths of Allegiance, &c.

Emanuel Sa in voce Tyrannus.
Knox to Engl. and Scotl. 78.

To the excommunication and depoſing of the Prince ordinarily, there follows execution according to the Authentick Bull: *That its not Homicide to kill an excommunicated perſon*. The French League produced two examples in the perſons of their Kings; and this accords with the Doctrine of *Buchanan*, *That Miniſters may excommunicate Princes, and that a King after he is caſt into Hell by Excommunication, is unworthy to live, or to enjoy life upon earth*: But obſerve in paſſing, the Reformed Churches do not teach that the *Excommunicatio Major* do caſt any perſon into Hell, but onely excludes them from the outward communion of the viſible Church, and in this, as in other things, *Buchanan* hath ſhewed himſelf to be leſs skilled in Divinity, then in Poetry.

Papa Urban. cauſa 23. Qu. 5. Can. Excommunicatorum.
Buchanan de jure Regni p. 70.

The

The best excuse which can be alledged in his Defence is that which Mr. *Du Moulin* lends him, which may also serve for Mr. *Knox*, That if he hath written any thing which passeth moderation, we must not attribute *Hyparaspishes,* l. 3. cap. 10. it to his Religion but nature; for its most certain both these were hot headed men, and had a great Antipathy against Monarchy.

As for the doctrine of King-killing, which is a familiar doctrine amongst the Jesuits, and is oft their shame and reproach; they to render us as odious as themselves, and by way of exchange, alledge and quote in their writings the passages of *Buchanan, Knox* and *Goodman,* who together with them teach the same Doctrine. That cunning Jesuite *Petra Sancta* is very curious in searching into their writings, whom that excellent person Mr *Rivet* answers, and tels him, that none amongst us approve or allow those wicked Maximes, and imputes the cause to their supposed persecution, *Jesuita vapulans,* cap. 13. which had exasperated their spirits, and to the hot heads of the Nations of this Iland.

After this so wise and charitable a reprehension, coming from a person of such eminency; men of learning amongst them, ought at least to have learned modesty, since they refused to learn obedience of their Parliaments, which condemned these Doctrines of *Knox,* and *Buchanan* by their publike Acts, or by the determinations of their principal Divines who have learnedly refuted them; and also by considering what great pains Mr. *Bloudil,* Mr. *Valade,* and other judicious and learned men of Forraign Churches, have taken to wash off the filth of their doctrines and behaviours, which have exceedingly scandalized the Evangelical profession; after so many Iterated saving advertisements, one would have thought they should have preserved themselves from falling into the same offences, and from giving new occasions

casions of rejoycing to their enemies, and of shame to their brethren; but behold of late worse then ever, their hot heads have produced such new effects of violence, as gives a challenge of defiance to the very Jesuits themselves.

Sions Plea, page 240.

The Author of *Sions Plea*, animates the people to war and to pull down the Bishops, speaking thus, *Smite neither small, nor great, but the troublers of Israel,* wound that *Hazael* in the fifth Rib: *Yea if your father and mother stand in your way to prevent you, dispatch them suddenly, pull down the ensign of the Dragon, set up the standard of Jesus Christ.* What? If the father of the State stand in your way, now when ye are busie in this holy cause, must he be dispatched? no doubt but they would tread upon him to make way, and would serve the Son, as they had done the Father; 'tis a point resolved on by the same Author, *They must strike the Basilike vein, none but that can heal the Pluresie of State,* which is as much as to say in good *English*, that they must cut the throat of the King for the publike good. This Author were a good Scholler of the two Jesuites, *Guignard* and *Scribanius*, had he not too grosly borrowed their Terms,

Anticorum. Amphitheatrnm Honoris.

for (say they) *France was sick, and they must cut the Basilike vein to heal her;* and Scribanius, *that they committed a great error on* S. Bartholomews *even that they cut not that vein.* That is, that those of the *Guisian* Faction spared the lives of the King of *Navar*, and the Prince of *Condie*.

Oh rare Flowers of Diabolical Rhetorick! Oh the shame of Christian Religion! Is this the simplicity and meekness of the Gospel? Is this the way to guide Conscience into the way of peace, and to set up the Kingdom of Jesus Christ, or Christ on his Throne? If S. *Paul* were alive, doubtless these men would even maintain to his face, that he understood not the nature

of

of the spiritual Kingdome, when he said, *Rom.* 14. 7. *That the Kingdome of God is righteousness, peace and joy in the Holy Ghost:* And when he read this lesson to the Christians, *Let the peace of God rule in your hearts, to which peace ye are called in one body.*

They would have taught him that the Kingdome of Jesus Christ ought to be set up by the murthering of Kings, the destruction of the people, and the overthrow of States, and would have sent him to their Catechise to be instructed, *That the Parliament Souldiers at the present ought not to consider us as their Fellow-Citizens, or their Parents, or their companions in Religion, but as Enemies of God, upholders of Anti-Christ, and therefore their eye should not pity us, nor their sword spare us.*

These are the words of that abominable Catechism published by Authority, for the use of the Covenanters Army: Oh behold the principles of Faith, wherewith these dull souls are instructed: Behold the Bread of Life wherewith their Divines feed the consciences of the poor people, *Jer.* 23. 4. *I have seen in the Prophets of Hierusalem an horrible thing, they commit adultery, and walk in lies, they strengthen also the hands of evil doers;* Israel, *the daies of thy visitation are come, thy Prophets are fools, and thy men of Revelations are mad.*

The Souldiers Catechism composed for the Parliaments Army by Robert Ram, Minister, published by Authority, page 14, 15. *of the seventh Edition.*

To these prodigious Doctrines we will joyn that Aphorism in the book entituled, *Altare Damascenum, That all Kings have a natural hatred against Christ:* If ye would believe this man, every one that loves Christ, must bear an irreconcileable hatred to all Kings; was there ever a more seditious and execrable Maxime: after such a Doctrine pronounced by an Author of such account, should we ask who hath put weapons into the hands of this superstitious people against their Soveraign,

raign, for these poor miserable people, hate the King for the love of God, yea, many account him an Enemy of Jesus Christ, even because he is a King.

That we may the better discover by what spirit this man is led, observe how he deals with his natural Prince, he calls King *James* of most happy and glorious memory, *Infestissimus Ecclesiæ Hostes*, the most mortal enemy of the Church, without doubt those who read this, will question what Religion this man is of, who so qualifies the incomparable Defender of the Faith, who hath so vigorously and sincerely maintained the truth, that if there were a Christian in the world, who knew not that great Prince, neither by his admirable writings, nor by the Renown of his Piety and Wisdome, and should hear him call'd the most spiteful and mortal Enemy of the Church, he might well imagine that King *James* had turned *Turk*, and changed the Churches of his Kingdome into *Mosques*, and sold his Christian Subjects for slaves to the *Moors*.

It were to do wrong to the testimony that himself hath given by the Immortal Monuments of his Religious Wisdome, and by his truly Christian and Fatherly Government, to undertake here to defend him against so unequal an Adversary, wherein the injuries spoken of this excellent King, turns to the ruine and perdition of him that spake them, like unto the bitings of the weasel, who consumes his teeth by gnawing of steel.

Certainly when the Divines of *France*, defend in their writings, the Confession of Faith of his Majesty, against the Doctors of the contrary Religion, they account not that King, *a most mortal enemy of the Church*. That most holy Confession confirmed by the practice of that great Prince, will serve as a bright shining light in the Church in after Ages, and cover the memory of them who injured and reproached him with perpetual shame. But

But for the present, these rare Adages which curse the best of Kings, and Royalty in general, are gather'd as choice and golden sentences. Witnesse this other, which comes from the Authority of his Companion, as great a liar as himself, who hath this passage: *He erres not much who saith, that there is in all Kings a mortal hatred against the Gospel, they will not suffer willingly the King of Kings to govern in their Kingdomes, yet God hath some amongst the Kings who pertain to him, but very few, it may be one in an hundred.* Vindiciæ Philadel. But since he is upon the number, instead of counting a hundred Kings one after another, let him account only a hundred years without going out of *England*, and we intreat this good man to consider what Kings have raigned over this Kingdome within this hundred years, and let him in good earnest tell us, which of them he would leave to God, and which he would give to the Devil; let them consider the piety of him, whom God hath made a Saint, and they a Martyr, let them find if they can in all his Kingdome, a man more just and meek, more temperate and religious, and let envy and rebellion, who finding nothing to bite at, in the life of this *Monarch*, burst asunder at his feet, and hide themselves in their own confusion.

Let us say the same to the Observator upon his Majesties Declarations, who speaking of all Kings now raigning, but with a particular application to his Soveraign saith, *That to be the delight of mankind* (as Titus Vespasian) *is now a sordid thing amongst Princes, but to be tormentors and executioners of the Publique, to plot and contrive the ruine of their subjects, which they ought naturally to protect, is now accounted a work worthy of* Cæsar. If reviling and speaking reproachful words against the King were Blasphemy, according to the stile of the civil Laws of *Israel*, 1 *King.* 21. 10. then this impious person is a

Blasphe-

Blaspheme in the highest degree against the sacred Majesty of Kings, and moreover exceeding ridiculous as well as wicked, to appropriate this description to his King, whose known piety, justice and clemency deserved rather the title of the delights of mankind, then that Emperour upon whom the love of the people conferred it: The like I may speak of the Kings of *France* within these fifty years, all the Lists of the French Kings furnisheth not such excellent Princes, wherefore Aphorismes of Rebellion, could never have been pronounced in an age more proper to give the Authors the lye.

The Lord rebuke these black souls, who curse God in the person of his Anointed, their sentence is written, and their qualities painted out to the life by St. *Peter*, 2 Pet. 2. 10, 11, 12. *who despise Dominions, presumptuous self-willed, they are not afraid to speak evil of dignities, whereas Angels which are greater in power, bring not raling accusations against them before the Lord; but these are natural bruit beasts, made to be taken and destroy'd, speak evil of things which they understand not; and shall utterly perish in their own corruption.*

I might heap up many more passages of our enemies, which teach murther, rebellion, and hatred of Kings, in which they seem to dispute with the very Jesuites themselves, this description of their devotion, *A seditious piety, a factious Religion which would be Judge of the consciences of Princes, who abhor their Religion, because they hate their Government, who make good subjects, and good Christians to be things incompatible.*

usurpations des Papes c. 5. pag. 81.

Whosoever would weary his patience, and behold how ingenious the Covenanters have been even to exercise the patience of God, and insult over the persons and authority of Kings, let them read their Sermons which were daily printed by authority, after they had preached them before the House of Commons, wherein the

the filthy Torrent of seditious Eloquence, and the fantasticalness of a Bastard Devotion were imploy'd to tear apieces the King, to disfigure him in odious colours, and stir up the people to all cruel and bloody courses against him, out of which books we might collect thousands of Modern Authorities in favour of the wickedness of these times, which passed from them as Doctrines of Religion; but we esteem our selves worthy of a better imployment, then to be poring on Carrion, and stirring in sinks and puddles: That which we have cited out of known Authors shall suffice to let the world see with whom we have to do, and that we are call'd to the condition of S. *Paul*, to fight with beasts.

CHAP. XII.

How the Covenanters wrong the Reformed Churches, in inviting them to joyn with them; with an answer for the Churches of France.

AS 'tis the vice of those who are strucken with the Leprosie, to endeavour to infect others, so the Covenanters, like to them, labour by all means possible to spread abroad the poyson of their impiety: Those who have preached and published their most infamous Doctrines, which renders Christianity hateful both to Turks and Pagans, were so bold as to address their publike Declarations to the Reformed Churches of *France*, the *Low Countryes*, and *Switzerland*, as if they made profession of the same Doctrines; they had the impudence to invite these so pure Churches, to have society with them, and to pray them to esteem the Cause of the Covenant, that

F   of

of all the Churches. In this the Assembly of Divines at *London* were imployed by their Masters.

The Epistle of the venerable Assembly of English Divines, and the Deputies of Scotland, to the Reformed Churches of France, the Low-Countries, and Switzerland, &c.

That which makes this Temptation less dangerous, is, That the Letter they wrote upon this subject to their Neighbours, could very hardly be understood: This Venerable Company of Divines of Consummate Knowledge, and the Flower of Eloquence of that Party, writ a Latine Letter to the *French*, *Flemens*, and *Switzers*; wherein there wants nothing in the Outward but Language and Common sense, a most worthy Cover for the Inward; for so evil a drogue there needed not a Better Box. This Epistle, amongst a ridiculous affectation of Criticismes, Greek and Poetical phrases, and many Rhetorical Figures, is here and there fill'd with Solecismes, Barbarismes, and the like Grammar Elegancies, like a foundred horse that goes up and down; and it's pity to behold how their Eloquence stumbles in Capriolinge.

This piece of Latine was much admired, and many praises heaped upon the Authors, and publick thanks, by special command, given to them by the House of Commons, so much is knowledge valued in this Reformed party. It's likely many hands contributed to the composing of it, for it's a patched discourse, made up of divers pieces altogether unlike one another, and goes by leaps and skips, as an empty Cart in a craggy and stony way, I will not burthen my discourse, with the faults of Children. I will only give you a taste in the Margin.

For the Margin.

In the Title *Litteræ a Conventus Theologorum in Anglia*, a barbarous phrase.

The

The same, *Prout Ordinaverat Honoratissima Domus Communium*; *Ordinare*, doth not signifie *to Command*; but *to put in Order*. *Honoratissima* is wholly barbarous.

In the first Page, *Diu est ex quo credidimus calicem hunc quem epotandum vindex Dei manus exhibuit vestris auribus insonuisse.* Rare Tavern Eloquence, to make the Cups and Goblets to sound.

In the second Page, *Reformationis impedimenta*, They would have said, *Hinderances of Reformation*; These Masters knew not that the Plural *Impedimenta* signifies *Baggage*.

In the same, *Eo usque profecit sceleratissima factio*; Surely they should have said, *progressa est*, for *proficere* signifies to advance in that which is good.

In the same period there is a Solecisme, *Eousque profecit, ut oportet*, they should have said *oporteat*.

There is a Solecisme of the same nature in the third Page, *Hosce cum gens illa rejecerat*, they should have said *rejecisset*; I wish these grave Divines would learn that the Prepositions *ut* & *cum* govern the Conjunctive in the signification they give it.

In the second Page, *Cœnobia Angliæ tolerata*, this is another Solecisme, for according to their sense, they should have said, *in Anglia*; in these words there are yet more incongruities in the Truth, than in the Grammar, for both God and men know that it is false, that there hath been any Convent or Monastery tolerated in *England* for above these eighty years.

In the third Page, *Missi hinc trans Alpes, mandatari & ab ipsa Roma recepti nuntii*, there can be nothing spoken more barbarous nor more false.

In the same Page, *Dicam dicere*, they have heard speak of *Dicam scribere*, which signifies to appeal in Justice.

In the same Page, *Injurias in apricum proferre*, Excellent

lent Elegance, to put the injuries in the Sunne.

In the fourth Page, *Natio altera triumphaſſet in alterius ſanguine*; they ſhould have ſaid, *de ſanguine*.

In the ſame Page, *Deus qui rodentem ſenſim tineam prius egerat rugientem Leonem induit*, that is to ſay, that God had plaied the perſon of a gnawing moth, which is a very ſtrange conception. Let theſe Divines correct either their ſenſe or their Latine.

In the ſame Page, where they would ſay, the Principals of *Ireland*, they call'd them *Principulares*, which is a word of Campagne, and doth not ſignifie that they would ſay, and yet the true word is *Principulos*.

In the fifth Page, *Delitendum*, they would have ſaid, *delitescendum*: They ſhould do well to read over their Conjugations again.

In the ſame Page, *undique* in ſtead of *ubique*.

In the ſame Page, *Cluet* in ſtead of *Cluit*, and yet the word is nothing worth in proſe.

In Page the ſixth, *Sacratiſſimam*, the word is barbarous.

In the ſame Page, *Gladius Anglicam ſaginatus carne*, that is to ſay, the ſword fatted with the fleſh of the *Engliſh*, the word *ſaginare* is not proper, but for a creature or beaſt that a man feeds; its a very extravagant fancy to fat a ſword as a hog.

In the ſame Page, That which the *Iriſh* had invaded by Arms, they call *quod nacti ſunt*, as if they had met with it by chance or hazard.

In the ſeventh Page, *Modo evenire poſſit, ut Eccleſia redimeretur*: Its a Soleciſm, they ſhould have ſaid, *redimatur*: This people are wholly out of Tenſe and Mood.

In the ſame, *Veritatis pediſſequi ſumus & amaſii puritatis*; *amaſius* is a diſhoneſt word, and *pediſſequi* ridiculous, and both the one and the other very improper: Behold the ſenſe in Engliſh, We are Lacqueys of the
Truth,

Truth, and Paramours of the Court of purity; these are lofty imaginations, fit to entertain the brave wits with.

A little after they enrich the Latine tongue with a new word, *Remonstrantias*, peradventure in their next Edition they will consider whether they should write *Remonstrantias* or *Remonstrationes*.

There is also a Solecism; they make use of the Adverb *utroque*, which is an Adverb of Motion, as if it were an Adverb of Rest.

In the eighth Page, *Potestati sumanus*, its a barbarous word, and is found in no good Author: But I think not my self bound to write out all their faults, the most part whereof hath this commodity, that the intricateness and obscurity of their stile hinders our sight.

The next time they write to strangers in this stile, I counsel them to send an Interpreter with their Letter; for this Latine Monsieur *Salmasius* the Prince of Learning of this age, could not understand: And in the mean while, these Gray Beards should do well to employ some time, when their State-affairs will give them leave, to learn their Grammar, that strangers may not laugh at their childish Eloquence.

And for the present they are obliged in Charity (for this their Epistle being printed and sent to seventeen States and Churches beyond sea) to some stranger, who out of compassion lent it good Latine, but it was a year and half after: 'Tis pity he spoil'd their work, for he should have left the form and the matter, the one being sutable to the other.

Now should we impute their Latine to their want of knowledge, did they not in this their Epistle tell us, *That they were a most venerable Company of excellent persons in Wisdom, Learning and Piety.* The same also sufficiently proved by the Testimony of some of their company,

Mulus Mulum fricat.

which were Members of the same Assembly, in which the other are not behind them in requital, and in magnifying their persons and actions to the Skies.

It's the old custom of this Faction to commend one another, and when they print any Book, they borrow of one or two of their Friends Epistles and Prefaces in commendation of the Work, wherein ordinarily they give the Author excessive praises: Never did the Bishops assume half the Titles that they give one another. As the Dunghil Cocks have the greatest Combs, so the meanest spirits are most arrogant and proud, taking on them many high Titles. A great man in *France* compared such kind of persons to the old Writings, full of abbreviations, saying, that where there are many Titles, there is little Learning.

But we will labour to decypher their Latine so far as may serve our present purpose, for which the last Interpreter will much help us. They pray

Liceat interim apud Fratres quos salutat hæc Epistola, dilectissimos innocentiæ nostræ testimonium & in sacris eorum cœtibus quandocunq; opus fuerit Apologiam obtinere.

the Forraign Churches, but almost in a commanding way, that they would recommend their cause to God in their publick prayers, and require it *sine conditione*, without any condition, and will not be refused, and they would have them make Apologies for the innocency of the Covenanters in their Assemblies. Must the Churches then of *France* for to content them, without considering the salvation of their souls, the safety of their persons, make publick prayers in their Assemblies for the Covenanters? Preach to the people that their War is lawful and holy? and that after being questioned by the Magistrates of a contrary Religion, constantly maintain that it is the cause of God, whatsoever may happen to their Goods, Lives and the profession of the Gospel?

But

But behold here that which is worse, in the conclusion of the Oath of the Covenant, which they sent with their Epistle to all the Neighbour Churches, they invite them earnestly to take *this Oath or the like:* And above all, they invite those Churches who live under the power of a contrary Religion: The Invitation is in form of a Prayer, *That it would please God to encline by their examples, the other Churches that groan under the yoke of Antichrist's Tyranny, to associate themselves with this Covenant or the like.* For to take then their Summons in their own sense, that is to say, That the Churches of *France* to please them, would make a Covenant against their Soveraign; expecting, as a thing which they need not doubt, that the English Covenanters would overcome their enemies in an instant, and would be ready at the day appointed, to succour their Confederates beyond the Seas, with their victorious Armies, before their King justly provoked, should ruine them. The Covenanters Declarations, especially in the year 1642. flatter these poor Churches with this hope, and through all their discourse clearly resolv'd to go forth and pull down Antichrist in all Countries, and make a general conquest for Jesus Christ. These are very like the Messages that *John* of *Leyden* sent to *Munster*, to make all the Commons in *Germany* to rise, and all the world if it were possible.

Not that the Leaders of the Covenant considering their strength and interest, thought themselves capable of so vast a design, but according to my opinion, they had two ends in making this so open a profession: The one, to draw to their party the weak and passionate, who in enterprises, have regard to the lustre and promise of the design, and not to the possibility of the execution. Of such spirits the great Herd of the world is composed, who in the great and publick Motions, suffer their fancies to be bewitched with Poetical hopes, incompatible with the nature of the affairs.   F 4   Such

Such was the promise of another Declaration, which lul'd the imaginations of the adherents, *That this War would bring them deliverance from all their sufferings and fears, and be the beginning of a new world of joy and peace, which God would create for their consolation.* For this new world of peace and joy which was but three skips and a stride off, as they thought, they found such besotted spirits who cast themselves headlong into a Gulph of evils, without bottom or bounds.

The Scots Declaration in the year 1644.

The Scots now feel it.

The other apparent end was to gain credit to their party by the applause of Forreign Churches, to fortifie themselves by the powerful association of the *Low-Countries*, and to try whether the *French* of the Reformed Religion were so ill affectionate as to take up Arms against their King, without ever caring what should come after, when they were once engaged in a war wherein formerly they had ill success. And these people were so void of charity and humanity, that they were content to buy an unprofitable reputation to their party, by the certain ruine of those they invite to alliance with them: As he that cared not to cut down his Neighbours Oak, were it but to make himself a pick-tooth.

For suppose that the *French* Churches should have suffered themselves to be gained by their perswasions: In what condition were they in to succour them? Could they have furnished Money, Armes, Men and Shipping? Had they the means to put out the Fire, when they had once kindled it? All the Succours that these Gentlemen could give them, would be to declare the Votes of the two Houses, That the Armes of the Churches of *France* were Defensive and Just, and those of their King, Offensive and Unlawful: Or have Declared

clared his Majesty fallen from his Dignity and Crown of *France*, as they declared those two Illustrious Princes, Prince *Rupert* and Prince *Maurice*, Sons of the late King of *Bohemia*, excluded from Succession in the *Palatinate*; which Vote shall take place, when the Masters of the Covenant shall have Conquered the *Palatinate* by their Armes, in spight of the Forces of *France*, the Emperour, and *Spains*, and they become sole Arbiters of the Empire. Before the Covenanters come to the end of this design, a little too far off, these brave Princes will have leasure to make their peace, and many things may intervene, which will induce their Judges to abate of their so great severity.

For to perswade these poor Churches to cast themselves headlong into ruine, the Assembly at *London*, in their Epistle labour to exasperate them, by the remembrance of all that they had suffered, and perswaded them that all Churches on this side, as well as on the other side of the Seas, were concluded to be ruined by the same Agents; that after the Churches of *England* and *Scotland* should be devoured, they would then fall upon their Neighbours; and that it was not against the men, but against the profession of the true Religion, and against Godliness, that their Enemies made War: Whereby they would make the Neighbour Churches believe, that King *Charles* confederated with the Pope to ruine the Reformed Religion, and that after he had dispatched his own subjects, he would do the like to his Neighbours of the same Religion.

There needs no great measure of the Gift of discerning Spirits, to judge by what spirit these Grave Divines were led, who take such pains to send their Brethren to the slaughter, within and out of their Kingdome, and to make the Doctrine of the Gospel a Trumpet of Sedition, to arm subjects against their Princes, and put all Christendome into a flame of bloody and unnatural wars. And

And therefore they had reason to confess themselves thus to Forraign Churches, they beseech them *to excuse them that they had not writ sooner, alledging* (according to the second Interpretation of their Friend) *That since they were assembled, they found themselves so amazed with the Wine of Astonishment, that God had given them to drink, that they had wholly forgot their duty:* But in the Addition which they disperse amongst all the Churches, *they do not acknowledge themselves only* Attonitos, *amazed, but* Ebrios, *drunken*; and both in the one and the other they had great reason. Oh the force of Truth! Oh the wonderful Providence and Justice of God, to draw from these subtil and crafty souls, their own condemnation! How is it possible that so many choice and picked Divines, whereof this Assembly was composed, should be so blinded, as to let pass from them so shameful a Confession in the name of all their Body, and of all their Party, to be divulged through all the Churches of *Europe*? And yet we are herein to praise God, that in this their astonishment, he hath given them a little interval, that they came to their senses to make this acknowlegement.

They needed not to specifie to us *in what they were forgetful of their Duty*; their comportments justifie their words, *that they had wholly forgotten it*. It appears also that they had forgot their duty to God, their King, their Countrey, and to the Church from which they received their Ministry, and to which they had sworn Obedience, and towards them also to whom they write: For if they had born any Brotherly affection, they would not have been so forgetful as to write to them, and in such a stile, and by a publick Declaration. They would have taken heed to render them odious and suspected without cause, and to draw upon them persecution, from which there could proceed no other fruit, unlesse to make them Companions in their miseries.

miseries; for to render us Companions in their crimes, we hope they shall never obtain. But these Divines, and their Masters who employ them, shall find themselves deceived in their design, to induce the Reformed Churches of *France* to shake off the yoke of their King, under colour of shaking off the yoke of Antichrist.

The fidelity and peaceable conversation of these Churches, doth take away even the shadow of such things from their Superiours, whose justice is such, that they will not condemn the Subjects of their King for the offences of strangers, but will be more careful to protect the innocent, then their ill neighbours are active to render them blame-worthy and unhappy. The King and his Councel need not fear the *French* of the Reformed Religion will take the Oath of the Covenant, to which they are invited with so much earnestness and craft: For to speak of them in the terms of one of their beloved Pastors, *They take no Oaths to others, but to their Soveraign Princes, they cast not their eyes on a stranger, they hold that it is not for a Subject to find occasion of disobedience in the Religion of his Prince, making Religion a Match to give fire to Rebellion, they are ready to expose their lives for the preservation of their King against whomsoever it be, were it one of their own Religion; whosoever should do otherwise, should not defend Religion, but serve his ambition, and should draw a great scandal upon the truth of the Gospel.* This is the Doctrine wherein they are instructed; this is the Profession in which all good *Frenchmen* of the Reformed Religion will live and die.

Usurpation des papes.

But if strangers, whose heads run round with the wine of astonishment, will force the Churches of *France* to drink of their Cup, they will use the *French* freedome, refuse to pledge them, and behold their zeal to press them to do as they do, with despite and compassi-

compassion: Let them not think it strange that they run not with them into the same excess of riot, they do not offend them, for whilst they have this strong wine in their heads, they keep their sobriety, and are filled; beseeching God to shew mercy upon those who would seduce them. Now as it is the custome of drunken persons, who would draw others into the same excess with themselves, and to drink according to their pleasure, to make them believe that they have seen them themselves in that condition; so the *English* Covenanters to defend their actions, and augment their Party, alledge very often to the *French* Churches their wars for Religion, the remembrance whereof is very sad; and to use this Argument to seduce them, is no other thing then to counsel them to be miserable because they have been so, and to go with their eyes shut, and run the remains of their broken vessel against the rock where they were shipwrackt.

Moreover, its very unjust in them to impute to the whole body the actions of a party; for in the late wars all the Churches on this side the River *Loyre*, continued in their obedience, and very neer the half of the other Churches. The people were carefully preserved in their duties by their faithful Pastors. This holy Doctrine which condemns the resisting of higher powers, and commands to wait patiently deliverance from God, and to suffer for righteousness sake, was most pressed and urged in their Churches; and whilst some of the Religion were in Arms during the minority of the King, they preached at *Paris*, *Their strength was to sit still.* Isai. 30. 7.

There fell lately into my hands an Epistle well penn'd, which was sent to the State-Assembly of *Rochel*, in the beginning of their sitting, to encline them to peace, and the obedience of his Majesty. Behold here a passage of it.

I think it very profitable for you to be informed the truth, what the opinions and dispositions of our Churches are, by persons that have a particular knowledge of them: You are now debating (Gentlemen) of the separation of your Assembly for to obey his Majesty, or of its subsistence, and to give order to your affairs; I am bound to tell you, that the general desire of our Churches is, that it would please God to continue peace unto us under the obedience of his Majesty, and that seeing the King is resolved to employ his Armies to make you obey, they promise themselves so much of you, that you will do what possibly you can to avoid this tempest, and yield rather to necessity, then enter into a war, wherein the ruine of a great part of our Churches are certain, and into a trouble wherein we may behold the entrance, but cannot see the issue, and that ye will take away the pretext from them who drive on the King to fall upon us. Those that fear God desire that if we must be persecuted, it should be in bearing the Cross of Christ, and for the profession of the Gospel. In brief, I assure you that the greatest and best part of our people desire you to decline this unjust enterprise.

Here is not the Authority of a Single Person, 'tis the testimony of *the greatest and best part* of the Churches of *France*, 'tis a general Declaration of the Churches, and of those *amongst them who feared God*, that the duty of Christians persecuted is, *to bear the Crosse*, not Arms. It's then very falsly and injuriously done, that the example of the *French* Churches should be so often and importunately alledged by the Covenanters to justifie the Subjects resisting their Sovereign, since that ever in the time of war, the greatest and best part were against it.

A *French* Divine, who loved both his Religion and King, found himself so prick'd by this reproach made to the generality of his Party, that he prayed us to insert here this expression of his judgement, and of the soundest part of the Churches of *France*. The war for
Reli-

Religion in this Kingdome is a wound yet fresh, and ye can hardly touch it, but ye will hurt it, and make it smart; and its very sore against my will that I must touch it: But I am constrained to it, by the frequent Declarations of the Covenanters, who have nothing so strong nor so frequent for to move the people to take up Arms against their King, as to propose to them the example of the *French* Churches, as a pattern which they ought and are bound to follow. Would to God that in leaving us there, they would have given us liberty to hold our peace; but since they will not give over publishing abroad, and making all places ring with our calamities, the remembrance whereof we rather desire should be for ever buried, since they impute the actions of some few to the generality of our Churches, and even to Religion it self; and since that they alledge our errors, for to exhort us to return to them again, and since they change the subject of our repentance and sorrow, into rules for their imitation, and into precepts of the Gospel. Is it not now high time to speak, and prefer the Interest of Gods Glory, and of the Truth of his Word, above the credit of men whatsoever they be, yea, and of our own too. *Let God be true and every man a Liar*, Rom. 3. 4. *Confess thy fault, and give glory to the Lord God of Israel*, Jo. 7. 19. Mr. Rivet *was not ashamed to call these our stirrings*, *culpam nostrorum*, the fault of his Countrymen; and this was spoken as a Champion of the truth, to confess it so freely, that it was both to our sin and dammage, wherein (as he himself declares) he agrees with *Monsieur du Moulin*, who in his second Epistle to *Monsieur Balzak*, makes the same confession in equivalent terms. Such was the Piety and ingenuity of these godly and learned persons, that all their care and pains was to defend the Truth only, and not their persons.

Jesuita vapulans, Cap. 26. Art.2.

It

It would be a great honor for the Churches of *France* with one consent publikely to declare that they judge all wars of Subjects against their Soveraign, unlawful, and to exhort their Brethren of *England* to Obedience and fidelity to their Prince, then for to preserve the credit of some of their party, and suffer their actions to serve as snares to the weak consciences of their Neighbours, and of pretext to those who labour to corrupt the Doctrine of the Gospel.

My self being a member of the Reformed Church of *France*, doubt not but I shall be owned and approved to give an Answer for them to the Summons of a strange Covenant.

An Answer for the Churches of *France*.

" Its a very great affliction to us to
" behold the famous Churches of
" Great *Britain* to destroy themselves,
" for controversies without necessity;
" and which might have been easily composed. And that
" which toucheth us most, is, the danger of the Truth,
" which is much weakned by these divisions; for its to
" be feared, that in your contending and striving one
" with another, you over-turn not the Candlestick of
" the Gospel, and that God being provoked, takes not
" away his saving Light, which was not given to lighten
" you one to fight against another.

" We will not enter into the causes of your quarrels,
" and could wish that you had left out the remembrance
" of ours, and had not imployed the unfortunate actions
" of your poor Neighbours, which anguish and terrour
" produced, to serve as example to your people to take
" up Arms against their King. They were but the lesser
" part of our Churches, that were involved in that party.
" The signal testimonies of our fidelity to the Crown,
" ever since the reducing of *Rochel*, and other places
" which were in our hands, do efface the memory of the
" troubles moved in their behalf; and the cause of these
" moti-

"motions being equitably confidered by fober and mo-
"derate fpirits, would beget pity rather then ha-
"tred: For if juft fear could juftifie Arms againft their
"lawful Soveraign, thofe of our Religion who bare
"Arms in this occafion, could reprefent to you, that
"when the King demanded back again the places that
"he had granted them for their fecurity, they had great
"occafion to fear, that with thefe places, they fhould
"lofe the fecurity of their confciences and lives, in which
"they were happily deceived: For the late King who

<small>A rare pattern for a Conquerour.</small> "was as gentle in making ufe of a vi-
"ctory, as valiant in gaining one, e-
"ver laboured more to comfort, than
"to punifh, and compaffion ftifling his anger, made
"them know that the ftrongeft place for the fecurity
"of Subjects, is the Clemency and Juftice of their
"Soveraign. Oh thefe Royal Vertues were eminent-
"ly manifeft in him, whom God had given you for
"your King! Who being the Defender of the Reform-
"ed Chriftian Faith, and publifhing his moft holy Pro-
"feffion, with fuch proteftations which gave us full fa-
"tisfaction, we cannot fee, how you can alledge the ex-
"ample of our taking up of Arms, fhould they be the
"moft juft of the world, having not the fame fubjects
"of fear. The fecurity of your confciences and lives
"were without queftion. But you are not the firft whom
"eafe and long profperity hath carried to the fame im-
"patience, to which others have been driven by af-
"fliction.

"And fince then ye addrefs your felves to us to give
"you advice: We befeech you confider, that to take
"counfel of your Friends, it muft not be when their
"fwords are in their hands, and their enemies before
"them; but when they are quiet and at peace: 'Tis
"not from our Souldiers, but our Divines, that you
"fhould enquire whether you fhould draw your
"fwords

"swords against your Prince, if you refer your selves
"to them, they will all conclude for the Negative.
"For whilst our Wars continued, whereof you have
"too good a memory, not one of all our Divines
"maintained those dangerous Maximes which is now
"defended by your Sermons and Writings: *They that*
"*say most for their Party, excuse it, and lay it upon neces-*
"*sity.*

"'Tis not from any of our Books that ye have drawn
"these vile Maximes, That the Authority of the Sove-
"reign Magistrate is of Humane Right. That the peo-
"ple is above their King, That the people gave the
"power to the Prince, and may take it away when they
"please, That Kings are not the anointed of the Lord,
"That if the King fail in performing the Oath at his Co-
"ronation, the Subjects are absolved from their Oaths
"of Allegiance, That if the Prince falls from the Grace
"of God, the people are loosed from their subjection,
"That for to establish a Discipline, which they ac-
"count to be the only Kingdom of Jesus Christ, Sub-
"jects may take up Arms against their Prince, That
"Kings are to be judged before their Subjects, That
"the Civil Government ought to be formed according
"to the pattern of the Ecclesiastical, which is not Mo-
"narchical. This Maxime tends to the abolition of
"Royalty in all States.

"In all the Writings of our Divines, ye find no such
"matters, but such as teach Subjects Loyalty, Humi-
"lity, Obedience and Patience. All agree together,
"with the ancient Christians, and say that prayers and
"tears are the weapons of the Church. Buckler of Faith,
"*We never spake of deposing our Kings,* Sect. 182.
"*and do not believe that any man living*
"*can depose the King, or dispense with their Subjects Oath*
"*of Allegiance.* If any of ours speak otherwise, we
"are ready to disavow it.

"Very

"Very often those that teach well are seduced to do
"ill, being overcome by temptation, and yet very few
"ever go so far, as to teach ill to justifie their Actions;
"God hath kept us hitherto from that: And although
"it may happen unto us, as unto others, to *break the*
"*Commandments of God*, Mat. 5.19. but we hope never
"so to be forsaken of him, *to teach others to do so*; Then
"is the evil desperate when vices become manners;
"and yet more evil, when the evil manners become
"Doctrines, that poor souls are instructed to sin for
"Conscience sake. Oh observe! that there is not a more
"certain sign of a people forsaken of God, than this.

"Therefore with the same liberty you invite us to
"maintain your Opinions by a publike Association, we
"earnestly beseech you to correct your own, and con-
"demn all your Maximes, contrary to sound Doctrine,
"Enemies to the peace of States, Majesty, and the safe-
"ty of Kings, taking heed of drawing reproach and
"persecution upon the profession of the Gospel, and
"to render your neighbours suspected for the faults of
"others. Also that you re-establish the use of the
"Lords Supper, intermitted in divers places these ma-
"ny years, that ye give order for children to be bapti-
"zed, and that there be no more aged persons rebapti-

Vindication of the Royal Commission of Jesus Christ.

"zed. That they print not any more
"that all Churches which baptize In-
"fants, are a faction of Antichristians,
"that none teach any more that the
"Sacraments are not necessary, and that for a quarrel of
"State, they dispossess not faithful Orthodox Pastors of
"their Benefices, to put Hereticks in their places.

"As for the quarrel ye have against Antichrist, we
"should be very glad to joyn with you, provided that ye
"observe these two conditions; the one not to call An-
"tichrist that which is not, for we gather by your E-
"pistles and Declarations, that you give the Title of
"upholders

"upholders of Antichrist to many of our Brethren,
"whose confession agrees with ours, and with whom you
"ought to bear, and with Charity amend their faults on
"condition that they may deal the like with you.

"The other condition is, That ye fight against Ant-
"christ by lawful ways prescribed in the Word of
"God; *namely, by the Spirit of his mouth,* that is, by
"the power of the Gospel; for as they were not the war-
"like Engines of *Joshua,* but the Trumpets of the San-
"ctuary that made the walls of *Jericho* to fall down, so
"it is not the Cannon, but the Trumpet of the Gospel
"which is required to pull down the walls of *Babylon.*
"These are the weapons of our warfare, *which are mighty*
"*through God to the pulling down of strong holds,* 2 Cor. 10.
"4. they are not carnal: And besides Divine Authority,
"experience should have have taught you, that God bles-
"seth not these designs of pulling down Antichrist by the
"Sword: It was the Epidemical Phrensie of *Germa-*
"*ny* now sixscore years since, which turn'd into smoak
"and confusion.

"Indeed if our King should Covenant in a just quar-
"rel against Antichrist, and *Lewis* the 14th assume for the
"devisoe of his Mony, that which *Lewis* the 12th stamp-
"ed upon his Crowns at *Pisa, Perdam Nomen Babilonis,*
"we would with a great deal of cheerfulness follow him
"in this War, but we cannot approve of a Covenant or
"League against Antichrist, made and agreed upon
"in spight of the Supreme Powers, who chuse Chiefs
"other then their Soveraigns. For such Leagues or
"Covenants are the open Rebellion of Subjects again't
"their Prince. Upon which, the Observation attri-
"buted to *Bullinger* is very remarkable, and which
"should extreamly move you, That the Anabaptists
"began with the destruction of Bishops, accounting as
"you, the Office and dignity of Bishops was an appur-
"tenance of Antichrist, but they ended with the destru-
"ction of Magistrates. "Our

"Our Churches look upon the predictions of the fall of Antichrist, and the establishment of the Kingdom of Jesus Christ, as objects of their Hope, and not as Rules of their Duty. They govern not themselves by Prophesies, but by Commands, and make Conscience of transgressing the Laws of God, out of zeal to advance his Kingdom; so leaving to God the execution of his counsels, we keep our selves in a peaceable obedience to our Sovereign; and in doing that we yield obedience to God, who commands, *to submit to every Ordinance of man for the Lords sake,* 1 Pet. 2. 13. and *to pray for Kings, and for all that are in Authority, that we may lead a quiet and peaceable life in all godliness and honesty, for this is good and acceptable in the sight of God, and our Saviour,* 1 Tim. 2. 2.

"If we embrace your Covenant, or make one like it, we cannot obey these commands of the Gospel; for to Covenant without permission of our Sovereign, would be to Covenant against him; to take up Arms in the Kingdom, without him, or against him, comes all to the same thing. What? Cannot our sufferings which you remember so often to us, perswade you from following so dangerous a Councel? for we retain and per- *Buckler of Faith,* "severe in the Instruction given us, Sect. 182. "that we must not remedy an evil by sin, nor defend Piety by Disloyalty; God hath no need of our sins to defend his cause; the preservation of the true Religion is the Cause of God, and his work, which he will never forsake, and even then when all humane means seems to fail, he watcheth for the preservation of his Church, which if he is pleased to afflict, its our duty to humble our selves; and when he is pleased also to raise her up, we need not carry to his help Sedition and Rebellion.

"In fine, We love the King that God hath given us by duty and inclination, trembling at the mention of your

"Covenant;

" Covenant; and the younger his Majesty is, the more we
" account our selves bound to endeavour to preserve
" peace in his State, hoping that when he comes of
" years he will acknowledge the services we have done
" him in his Minority, and that he will consider with
" what Fidelity and Integrity his Subjects of the Re-
" formed Religion have cast off the instant solicitations
" of Strangers, conceiving they can never be good
" Christians, without being good Subjects; and that
" to obey their King, and to offer up their Goods and
" Lives to his service, is a great part of the service they
" owe to God.

" The English Covenanters may receive this Answer
" as the Answer of the Churches of *France*, until they
" have disavowed it by a publick Declaration.

CHAP. XIII.

The preceding Answer confirmed by Divines of the Reformed Religion, with an Answer to some Objections of the Covenanters upon this Subject.

TO the end it may better appear, that the preceding Answer for the Reformed Churches of *France*, is drawn from the Model of their Doctrine, behold here some few passages.

Calvin speaks thus, *If we be persecuted for piety by a wicked and sacrilegious Prince, before all things let us remember* (Institut. l. 4 c. 20. Art. 29.) *our sins, not doubting but God sends us these scourges for our sins; by this, our impatience will be bridled by Humility: Moreover lets remember that it is not for us to remedy these evils; and that all that we have to do, is to beg help of God, in whose hands the hearts of Kings, and motions in King-*

Art. 25.   *Kingdoms are.* He said a little before, *That the Word of God bound us not only to be subject to Princes that are worthy of our duty, but to all Princes whatsoever and howsoever they came to the Soveraignty, and although they do nothing less then perform the duties of good Soveraigns.*

Com. upon Dan. c. 4. v. 19.   In his Commentary upon *Daniel,* *Let us learn,* saith he, *by the example of the Prophet, to beseech God for Tirants, if it shall please him to subject us to their inordinate pleasure; for what though they be unworthy of all Offices of Humanity, yet neverthelesse becanse it is by the will of God that he commands, its our duty to bear the yoke patiently, not only because of wrath, as Saint* Paul *admonisheth, but also for Conscience sake, otherwise we are not only Rebels against them, but against God.*

Instit. l. 4. c. 20. Sect. ult.   This Lesson is of the same Authors, *Let this be ever in our memory, that the same Divine Authority that gives Authority to Kings, establisheth also the most wicked Kings: Oh let never these seditious thoughts enter into our spirits, that we should deal with the King as he deserves, and that it is not reasonable to yield the duty of Subjects to him who will not perform the duty of King to us.* Which is notwithstanding the arguing of the Covenanters.

Pet. Martyr. Claf. 4. loc. 20.   *Peter Martyr* an *Italian,* but a Minister in those Churches our enemies invite to associate with them, is not less contrary to them. Expounding that place of the Proverbs, *By me Kings reign,* saith, *That under the name of Kings, the Text understands also Tyrants:* Whence he collects this consequence, *Therefore learning hence that thy K. is established by God, beware thou never conspirest any seditious thing in the State, all that thou must do when thou art oppressed, is to appeal to the Tribunal of God, there being no other superiour power to whom a Tyrant ought to obey.*

He

He saith also very pertinently, & worthy our best observation, *That then when God would chastise the Kings of Judah for their sins, he did not do it by the Jews, but by the Babylonians, Assyrians, and Egyptians, shewing by the conduct of his justice and providence, that it is not for subjects to take knowledge of the faults of their soveraigns, but that they ought to leave them wholly to God, who hath other means in his hand to punish them, and reduce them to their duty.*

Surely if *Calvin* and *Martyr* had lived in these days, and were beneficed in *England*, they would eject them out of their benefices for this troublesom doctrine, which hinders the progress of the holy Covenant, and fils their consciences full of scruples, whom they instruct to rebel against their Soveraign for the Lords sake.

And above all Monsieur *Deodati* would be very ill dealt with by them, for being Author of that excellent Epistle sent from the Church of *Genevah*, to the Ecclesiastical Assembly at *London*; in which your good King is highly prais'd for the justice and clemency of his proceedings in this present quarrel; the popular tumults condemned, which forced him to retire from his Parliament, and these Gentlemen earnestly entreated to dispossess their spirits of all factious inclinations, and to wash off this foul spot by which they have and do defame the pure profession of the Gospel, giving occasion for the world to believe, that the reformed Religion hath a secret hatred and antipathy against the Majesty of Kings and soveraign authority; against this Epistle, our enemies vomited out many outragious words in their books, maintaining that it was supposititious and invented by some prophane Atheist. Behold here the thanks that this great and learned person, and the reverend Ministers his brethren, received for their charitable and truly Christian counsel.

And this is further to be observed, that the Assembly at *London* having sent their Epistle and Oath of their

Covenant to seventeen forraign Churches, whereof the Churches of *France* made but one, they make no noise of the Answers they received, which doth evidently testifie they did not satisfie them, and that they durst not produce them, for fear of making it appear that the generality of the reformed Churches were ashamed of their actions, and condemned the insurrections of Subjects against their Severaign under pretence of reformation.

En fundum & fundamentum totius paracidialis doctrinæ. Potestas à populo Regi data est fiduciaria.

This Divinity of Rebellion being founded upon one only Maxime, that the power of Kings is of humane and not divine right, and that their right to the Kingdom is but a paction between them and the people. Its much to purpose to produce here what the Churches of *France* hold hereupon, and how they refuse the reasons of the Jesuits which are the same with the Covenanters: Behold the last Chapter of the Buckler of Faith, which is a garment so fit for the size of both parties, that after the one hath made use of it, the other may put it on, they need change nothing but the persons.

Section 183.

Tho. 2 2. qu. 10. Art. 10.

Dominiū & prælatio introducta sunt ex jure humano, & Qu. 12. Art 2. Dominium introductū est de jure gentium quod est jus humanum. Casabon in epist. ad frontenem ductum Jesuitam.

Thomas the Prince of the School Divines, saith, that the power of Princes and Lords, is but of humane institution, and comes not from God; to whom we may joyn Cardinal *Bellarmine* in his Book against *Barkley* and Monsieur *Arnoux*, who upon the second Article of our confession, cals the power of the Magistrate a humane law, conformable to the Apothegme of reverend Father *Binet* the Jesuit, who told Mr. *Casaubon*, that it were better all Kings were killed, than a confession should be revealed,

vealed, because the power of Kings is but an humane right, but confession is of Divine right.

The Reasons they bring for this opinion, are,

"1. That the first King that was raised in the world, namely *Nimrod*, was raised by violence, and not by the ordinance of God.

"2. That the most part of the Empires and Kingdoms that ever have been, came by conquest, one Nation overcoming the other; or by some Prince, whose ambition moved him to pick an unjust quarrel with his Neighbour.

"3. That Emperors and Kings are established by humane ways, whether they come to the Crown by hereditary succession, or by election, since there is no extraordinary revelation, nor no rule in the Word of God, that a Nation are bound to follow rather Succession which is hereditary, than that which is by Election.

"4. That there is no express command of God, to obey *Henry* rather than *Lewis*, or to acknowledge this man rather than that for King.

"5. That for these considerations, the Apostle S^t. *Peter* calls our obedience to Kings, an Ordinance of man; saying, *Submit your selves to every Ordinance of man for the Lords sake, whether it be to the King as supream, or unto Governours*, &c. 1 Pet. 2. 15.

These are the ordinary reasons of the Covenanters, if they should disavow them, their Books would witness against them, for they are full of them. But I would they could get them out of the Schools of the Jesuits, and come and learn the Doctrine of the Reformed Churches, which speak thus:

"Wee on the contrary maintain, that Obedience to Kings and Magistrates is of Divine right, and founded upon an Ordinance of God, for which purpose those passages serve, which commands obedience to Kings, and the higher Powers, as to Persons whom

" whom God hath set up, and whom we cannot resist,
" without resisting God. *There is no power but of God,
" the powers that be, are ordained of God, whosoever there-
" fore resisteth the power, resisteth the Ordinance of God,*
" Rom. 13.1,2.

" Item, *We must be subject, not only for wrath, but
" also for Conscience sake*, V.5,7. And Saint *Peter*, in
" that place they object against us, wills *that we yield
" our selves Subjects to Kings for the Lords sake.* So that
" although *Nebuchadnezzar* was a wicked King, and a
" Rod in the hand of God, to destroy the Na-
" tions, notwithstanding God speaks thus to him by
" his Prophet *Daniel, Thou O King, art a King of Kings,
" for the God of Heaven hath given thee a Kingdom, pow-
" er, strength and glory,* Dan.2.37. *Moses* the first Prince
" & Lawgiver of *Israel*, was established by an Ordinance
" of God, and *Joshua* after him, *Num*.27.18. *Saul*,
" the first King of *Israel*, and *David* his Successor, were
" anointed by *Samuel*, and consecrated to be Kings, ac-
" cording to the Ordinance of God, 2 *Kings* 9. God
" sent to *Jehu*, a Prophet, for to anoint him King of *Is-
" rael*. *Its God that girdeth the loins of Kings with a gir-
" dle,* Job 12.18. God is he that governs, or as our
" Translation read it, *God is the Judge, he putteth down
" one, and setteth up another,* Psal.75.7. *The Lord rais-
" eth the poor out of the dust, and lifteth the needy out of the
" dunghil, that he may set him with Princes,* Psal.113.7,8.
" Certainly, if the providence of God extends it self e-
" ven to the feeding of Fowls, and giving food to the
" young Ravens, when they cry unto him, *Psal.*147. Yea,
" as to number the very hairs on your head, so that not
" one of them falls without his Providence, who be-
" lieves, that when God will establish or set up a man
" on the top of mankind, and make him Head of Milli-
" ons of people, the counsel of God doth not intervene,
" and that he leaves not all things to go at adventure
" and by chance. " The

"The reasons they alledge against so evident and
"apparent a truth, are lame and interfere.

"1. They say, that *Nimrod*, the
"first King in the World was raised
"by violence: But that is false, that
"before *Nimrod* there was no Sove-
"raign Prince in the World. Before
"*Nimrod*, the Fathers and Heads of
"Families, were Kings and Priests,
"and Soveraign Princes of their Fa-
"milies; For after the Flood men
"lived five or six hundred years; So
"that it was easie for one man to be-
"hold five hundred, yea, a thousand
"persons of his Posterity, over whom

Hunc ordinem, Regendi inturbavit Nimrodus, qui novo Titulo principatum acquisivit scil. Jure Bello. Nimrod arripuit insuetam primus in populo Tyrannidem, Regnavitq; in Babylone. Hier. in Trad. Hebraic. ad Gen. 10. v. 10.

"he exercised a paternal power, and by consequence a
"Soveraignty, for there was no other form of Royalty in
"the earth; whose children & servants being joyned to-
"gether, one Family could make a great Commonweal:
"And even in the time of *Abraham*, then when the life
"of man was shorter, we read how *Abraham* was called
"by the Children of *Heath*, a Prince of God, *Gen.* 23. 6.
"that is to say, a mighty Prince; and of his own Fa-
"mily he drew out three hundred and eighteen Souldi-
"ers, to whom if we joyn the Maid-servants, and those
"servants who were not fit to bear arms in war; ye
"cannot but confess, that although he had no children,
"yet his own Family were capable to fill a good Town.

2. "They object to us also, that the most part of the
"Empires and Kingdomes, have had their beginning
"by Conquest and violence, and therefore not by the
"Ordinance of God: And that if the Conqueror had
"invaded the Country of another, by the Ordinance of
"God, the Inhabitants of the Country had offended
"God in opposing and resisting him. Upon which, I
"say, that those Inhabitants in a Country whom a
"strange

"strange Prince will invade, do well to oppose and re-
"sist him, and if in this defensive war, the Usurper is
"slain, he is justly punished. But if he become Master
"of them, and if all the ancient Possessors of the
"Kingdome are extinguished, and the States of the
"Country assembled contrive a new form of State, and
"all the Officers throughout the Kingdome give to the
"new King an Oath of Fidelity, then we must believe,
"that God hath established such a Prince in the King-
"dome; then, I say, the people ought to submit to
"the Will of God, who for the sins of Kings and Peo-
"ple, transfers Kingdomes, and disposeth of the events
"of Battels according to his good pleasure.

"3. It matters not to say, that Princes, who enter
"Kingdomes by Hereditary Succession, or by Election,
"come in by wayes introduced by Custome, and not
"by the Ordinance of God: For the Question is not
"by what wayes or means a Prince comes to the King-
"dome, but whether, if being once established by the
"Ordinance of God, we are bound to obey him? Our
"Adversaries indeed would have the Power of Parlia-
"ment, of Divine Right, although the Members of
"Parliament enter by Election, and oft-times by close
"and under-hand dealing, and by some crafty Ca-
"balle.

"Let them hold that the Parliament is by Divine
"Right; it appears by their authentique Catechisme,
"that they teach us this Doctrine: Page 5. *It's a gross
error to say, that the King is the Supreme Power, but that
power appertains to the Soveraign Court of Parliament, which
not to obey, is to resist the Ordinance of God:* But let us
hearken to a better Author.

"4. That if there be no Command in the Word of
"God to obey *Henry* rather then *Lewis, &c.* It's suffici-
"ent that there is a command for to obey the King, and
"a command to keep our Oath and Fidelity we have
"sworn,

"sworn, and by consequence to be faithful to the King
"to whom we have taken the Oath of Allegiance.
"There is no more command of God found to injoyn
"us particularly to obey the Parliament that began *No-*
"*vember* the third, 1640. to which neverthelefs, our
"adverfaries, accounted themfelves to be fubject by
"Divine Right. So that if this confideration fhould
"take place, it would follow, that none of them that
"are now in the world, are obliged by Divine Right,
"to fear God, or to believe in Jefus Chrift, becaufe
"the Scripture hath not particularly appointed *Thibalt*,
"*Antony* or *William*, that they fhould fear God, and be-
"lieve in Jefus Chrift; It fufficeth that the Word of
"God contains Rules, which bind particulars without
"naming them.

"S. *Peter* truly in the place before cited calls the obe-
"dience we owe to Kings, a humane Ordinance, and
"that either becaufe Kings command many things,
"which in their nature are not of Divine Right, as
"their commands which forbid wearing of gold or fil-
"ver, or the like things on their apparrel, or becaufe
"they attain this power by certain humane means in-
"troduced by cuftome, which notwithstanding hinders
"not but their power may be founded in the Word of
"God, when they are once eftablifhed; for as we faid
"before, the Queftion is not of the means by which a
"Prince comes to the Kingdome, but what Obedience
"is due to him, after he is once inftaled. And there-
"fore Saint *Peter* after he had called this Ordinance
"an humane Ordinance, commands us to fubject our
"felves for the Lords fake, and to obey his command.

"Whofoever makes the Authority of Kings de-
"pend upon the infticution of men, and not upon the
"Ordinance of God, leffens their Majefty more then
"three quarters, and takes from them that which fe-
"cures their lives and Crowns, more then their Guards,
"or

"or mighty Armies, which plants in the Subjects
"hearts, Fear instead of Love and Reverence. Then
"the fidelity and obedience of Subjects will be firm
"and lasting, when it shall be incorporated with piety,
"and accounted a part of Religion, and of the service
"we owe to God.

This foundation being over-turned, that the Authority of Kings is but an humane Ordinance, that which they build upon it, must necessarily fall; for to reason thus, that the people may take away their Authority from the King, because they gave it him, is to prove one absurdity by another; as if one should prove the Moon might be burnt, because its made of wood. For to say the people gave the power to the King, is to imagine that which never was, no not in Kingdomes which are Elective. The People give not the King his Authority, for they cannot give that they have not, but he defers his obedience to *Henry* or *Charles*. But this Prince being elected, receives his Authority from God, as the beginning and source from whence all power flowes. *By me Kings Raign, Pro. 8. 15. And there is no Power but of God, Rom.* 13. 1. None ought therefore to take this Power which God hath given him.

Thus the Wife choseth her Husband, and gives him a promise of obedience in marriage, but it is not she that gives him his Authority, that comes from above: And there is as great an absurdity to say, that the People may depose the King, because they chuse him, as to affirm, that the Woman may put away her Husband, or subject him to her, when she shall judge expedient, because that she made choice of him: For the woman loseth the liberty of her choice by the bond of marriage, and the People likewise lose the liberty to revoke their choice when the Prince Elected is declared King. 'Tis a strange consequence to say that the people may take away the Kings Authority, because they have sworn

obedience

obedience to him, the Election is no other thing. And it's a reason that overthrows it self, to say that the people may take from the King his Authority, because they gave it him: For put the case that it were true that the people gave Authority to the King whom they Elect; since then the people have given away their Authority, 'tis no more in them. This maxime being once admitted, that it is lawful for every one to take back again what he hath given, it would break the Laws of Society, and fill the world with injustice and confusion: But let our enemies know, that although the Authority of the King had not begun, before the Oath of Allegiance, which this Parliament took in a Body at the beginning of their sitting, yet the Body of the State made thereby an irrevocable gift of their obedience to the King, and from this Oath we draw a better consequence then theirs; namely, that they cannot dispose of their obedience since they have given it to the King: So that were their reasons good, they would be of no force, but in Kingdomes which were Elective, and make nothing against King *Charles*; for neither he, nor any of the Kings his Ancestors in all ages past, ever came to the Crown by Election.

It's not to purpose to alledge the Oath the King took at his Coronation, as an agreement and paction made with his people, equivalent to an Election; for the King receives not his Kingdome at his Coronation, he is King before his Crown is put on, and therefore *Watson* and *Clark*, who conspired against King *James* of glorious memory, were justly condemned as guilty of High Treason, although they alledged that the King was not then Crowned, and it was judged by the Court, that the Crowning was but a ceremony, for to make the King known to his people.

It's the like also in *France, I judge* (saith *Bodin*) *that no man doubts but the King enjoyes before his Anointing,*

the

the possession and propriety of his Kingdome. Before this ceremony, the King enjoyes as fully all his Rights as after, and according to the Laws of *France* and *England*, the King never dies, whilst there remains any of the Royal Blood, for in the same hour that the King expires, the lawful Heir is totally invested of the Kingdome. Wherefore the Eldest Sonne of *Edward* the Fourth, who was murthered by his Uncle *Richard*, is by general consent numbered amongst the Kings, and named *Edward* the Fifth, although he never wore the Crown, nor took any Oath, nor exercised any Authority. *Henry* the Sixth was not Crowned but in the ninth year of his Reign, and yet before his Coronation, many were attainted of High Treason; which could not have been done, if he had not been acknowledged King.

In the Oaths of the Kings of *France* and *England*, at their Coronation, there is no image of stipulation, covenant or agreement betwixt them and their subjects. They receive not their Crowns upon any condition, and their people owe their obedience, whether they perform or violate their promises. This Oath is a laudible custome, profitable to bear up the Authority of the Prince, by the love of his Subjects, and to give to the people this satisfaction, that the King whom God hath given them, hath an intention to govern them with Justice and Clemency, and to preserve their Rights and Liberties.

If the King by his Oath should bind himself to fall from the Right to his Kingdome, when he should violate his Promises, he would then be lesser after his Oath then before; and surely if the Kings did believe they should diminish their propriety by their Oath, they would never take it; and to shew that their Authority depends not of their Oath, but their Oath of their Authority, the Kings of *England* form it at their pleasure.

Very

Very hardly shall you find three that have taken the same Oath without changing some things. That which was presented to *Henry* the Eighth, which is to be seen in the Rolls, was corrected by his own hand, and interlined.

And moreover, the Oath is made to God, and not to the People, and binds the Conscience of the Prince, but doth not limit his Soveraignty; if the intention of this solemnity were to make a stipulation or agreement with the people, the people at the same time should also take a reciprocal Oath, and in a paction of such importance, there should also pass some publick contract, things which are not practised; so that hereby it evidently appears, that this imagination of the enemies of Monarchy, have not any foundation neither in Law nor Custome.

Some persons think they speak very finely, in saying that the Authority of the King is an Usurpation of the Sword, confirmed by Custome, & that if they could gain their liberty by the sword, and confirm it by custome, their Right would be as good as his; and upon this they Phylosophy upon the Resolutions of States, which are in the hand of God, and teach us to follow the course of his Providence.

But by speaking thus they commit a double errour, against conscience, and against prudence.

As for conscience, the antient constitution of the State confirmed by so many ages, Statutes, Oaths of Allegiance, do suffice to learn all Christians that live under this Monarchy, that it was God that established it, and that by the command of God, they are bound to defend the State under which they are born, and whom the Body of the Kingdome hath sworn to maintain. These discourses of following the Providence of God in matters of Revolutions of States, are then only seasonable, when the Royal Blood is extinguished, or when

when Usurpation hath gained prescription through length of years, but not when they are neer to overthrow the Estate, and ruine the King; these considerations are good when the evil is done, and out of remedy, but not when they are acting ill, and when the obedience and loyalty of the subjects may remedy all. The providence of God will never serve for excuse of the wickedness of men; let us do that which we ought to do, and leave God to do what he pleaseth; and above all, these moralities of revolution of States are worst in their mouths, who labour to make this revolution in the State, for it's their duty to prevent this revolution with all their power; posterity may excuse themselves by the providence of God in following a new form of State, whilst those that introduced it, shall be condemned by his Justice.

Besides all this, there is a great want of prudence in this reasoning, for in quarrelling the Rights of the King as usurpations of violence and custome, they teach the King to quarrel at their liberties and priviledges for the same reason; yea, and by one much greater, for the Priviledges of Parliament are much newer then the Royal Authority, and the King may say they were obtained by force after many long and bloody wars: he might cast off all prescription gained upon the unlimited power of the first *Norman* Kings, and put himself into all the rights of their Conquests by another. Wise

Neque unquam libertas gratior extat quam sub Reg. Pio.
subjects who would keep their priviledges, ought by all means to preserve peace, for there is nothing renders Kings more absolute then war.

Under a Royal Estate the principal means to preserve the peoples liberty, is to maintain the only authority of the King; dividing it amongst many, they do but multiply their Masters: For its better to have one evil Master, then many good ones.

CHAP.

CHAP. XIV.

How the Covenanters have no reason to invite the Reformed Churches, to their Allyance, since they differ from them in many things of great importance.

WE wonder exceedingly how our Enemies dare solicite the Reformed Churches to Covenant with them: From whence comes this great familiarity? Is it because of their great resemblance one with another? Its that we cannot find. As for obedience due to the King, which is the principal point of the Covenanters, we have made it already appear, that the Divines of the Reformed Religion are as contrary to the Covenanters, as they are to the Jesuites, their Brethren and Companions in blood and war.

This point being denied them, they care not much for the society of any Church in other points of Doctrine. This is the first and great Commandment of the Covenant, to obey the people against their King, maintain but this their fundamental maxime, and they will give you leave to chuse your Religion, but in many other things this faction differ from the Reformed Churches.

Concerning the Doctrine of the Lords Day, they have a great quarrel against *Calvin*, who is so far from constraining the Church to a *Jewish* observation of the Sabbath, that he accounts that the Church is not subjected to the keeping of the seventh day, a passage which

Calvin. Institut. l. 2. c. 8. River Explicatione Decalogi precep. 4.

Learned *Rivet* alledgeth and approves; and to both these, doth Doctor *Prideaux*, since Bishop of *Worcester* joyn; who in a discourse of the Sabbath, complains that the *English* Sabbatarians lean towards *Judaisme*, and go against the common received Doctrine of Divines; never considering into what captivity they cast themselves, in establishing the observation of the seventh day under Christianity, by the authority of a Mosaical Precept. Master *Primrose*, Minister of *Rohan*, hath writ a very Learned Book full of profound knowledge, upon this Subject; where amongst other things, he proves at large how all the Reformed Churches are contrary to this opinion.

Although God hath no need of the errour of men to establish his service, we so much love the reverence due to that holy day, that we would not lightly quarrel at any thing thereupon. Let every one enjoy his Opinion, so that God may be served, and the day which is dedicated to him, be not violated, neither by prophaneness nor superstition. But since the Covenanters in this point are so contrary to the Reformed Churches, and have so often condemned it by their writings, the Assembly at *London* did very ill to plead conformity with these Churches in this Article, and complain to them of the Liberty the King gave to poor servants to sport on Sunday after Divine Service.

So also for the Festivals, although Mr. *Rivet* declares his desire, that those daies which carry the Names of Saints, should be abolished in *England*, because of the abuses of these Festivals in the Church of *Rome*; nevertheless he acknowledgeth and commends the Protestation of the *English* Church hereupon, that they observe them not for the Service of Saints, but for to glorifie God, in imitation of the

Rivet about the end of his Exposition of the 4 Command.

the Primitive Church, by the memory of those whom God was pleased to serve himself by, to build up his Church, and exceedingly blames those who accuse them of Idolatry for this observation.

King *James* of happy and glorious memory, speaks thus in his Confession of Faith; *As for the Saints departed, I reverence their memory, in honour of whom, our Church hath established so many daies of Solemnity as there are Saints enrolled by the Authority of the Scripture.* The Festivals of Saints scarce exceed the number of the Apostles and Evangelists: Monsieur *du Moulin* his Champion defends this Confession of his Majesty. *Indeed* (saith he) *we condemn not this celebration of the memory of Martyrs and Saints; we find the custome good of the* English *Church, who have daies set apart for the commemoration of the Apostles*: And a little after he gives the reason why the *French* Churches do not follow their example, *Because living in a Country where Superstition abounds, the people would be easily drawn to abuse them, and be tainted with the common contagion.* The Prudent and Religious acknowledge with him, *That in this the Churches have liberty to govern themselves, according to the exigencies of time and place*; and that if in the *English* Calender there be some festivals which might well be passed by, and whereof there might be some fear of the consequence; these things ought to have been fairly represented, with the humility of subjects, and the charity of Christians, and not defame the reputation of the *English* Church, as idolatrous, and a member of Antichrist, nor reform the Church and the King by the Sword, since the Reformed Churches in this point acquits them, and the example of the Primitive justifies them.

But although they make a great shew of their agreement with other Churches, they make but use of them in some points where they like and approve of, and spare not to accuse them of idolatry as well as others when

when they pleaſe. 'Tis that which they do without naming them, then when they reject, as groſs idolatry, the obſervation of the memory of the daies dedicated to the Nativity, Paſſion, Reſurrection, and Aſcenſion of Chriſt, and the ſending of the Holy Ghoſt into the Church. Behold here the Opinion and Practiſe of the Reformed Churches, declared by that Godly and Learned *Feſtus Hominius, Its a thing of very great profit to the edification of the Church, to commemorate and preſs ſolemnly to the people at certain ordinary times the principal manifeſtations of God, and his moſt ſignal Benefits to his Church, ſince that the Primitive Church, even in the times of the Apoſtles, dedicated certain daies to the Anniverſary Celebration of the Nativity, Death, Reſurrection, and Aſcenſion of Chriſt, and ſending of the Holy Spirit. Its very well done to retain the practiſe of the ancient Church in a thing which is not ſimply indifferent, but ſingularly profitable to edification, provided that none attribute ſuperſtitiouſly any Sanctity to be in the daies; and impoſe not upon the conſciences of Chriſtians a yoke of abſolute neceſſity, contrary to the Liberty of the Goſpel.*

Diſput.1. Theſ. 3.

Our new Reformers cannot affirm in ſincerity that the Clergy of *England* attributed any Inherent Sanctity to be in the daies, or made uſe of them to impoſe a yoke of abſolute neceſſity upon their conſciences, there was no need then to aboliſh them with ſuch rigour, nor to ſcandalize ſo many pious ſouls, nor reſiſt a vain fear of ſuperſtition by inſolence and prophaneneſs, which is a remedy worſe then the evil. The day of the Nativity in the year 1644. was changed by an expreſs publick Order into a Faſt, which was the firſt time ſince the Apoſtles that there was any Faſt kept that day in the Chriſtian Church, and becauſe many would not Faſt, they ſent Souldiers into their houſes a little before dinner, to viſit their Kitchins and Ovens, who carried a-

way

way the meat, and eat it, though it was a fasting day, who were exempted from fasting, provided they made others fast; such insolencies were ordinary, if we may call them insolent actions which were done by Authority. *Senatus-Consultus scelera patrantur.*

And as for Easter day, on which and the daies following the people are enjoyned by Act of Parliament to receive the Blessed Sacrament; the devotion of the people in many places have been opposed by violence. We have heard of a Parish, where by main force the Bread and Wine was taken away from the people, who were assembled at Church for this holy action. Behold their wayes to change the times, and to reform abuses, which is to resist a supposed superstition, with a true and manifest one, and to make Sacriledge fight for Religion.

Lets pass to other differences: The Reformed Churches do not believe as they, that all significant ceremonies excepting in the Sacraments, are unlawful; for then, it would follow that to keep off the Hat, and kneel at Prayer, should be unlawful, for these are ceremonies which signifie reverence; whence many of the Covenanters for this reason refuse to put off their Hats, or kneel at prayer, without being taken notice of, and reproved by authority.

Also the Reformed Churches do not believe as they, that to be tyed to written prayers, or forms of prayers in the Administration of the Sacraments, is to binde the Spirit of God, many of the Covenanters are come so far as to call the usage of forms of prayer idolatry; yea, even the use of the Lords Prayer, which the most part of this faction refuse to say; although by a special priviledge its permitted the Minister by their Directory to make use of it if he please; for its not commanded him.

According to this Directory (as they call it) that is to say, an instruction how the Minister should govern himself in the Church. The Minister must not say the Apostles Creed, nor repeat the ten Commandments of God, whereby the people shall be without any form of what they are to believe, or what they are to do; therefore in the families of most part of this faction, they teach not their children neither the Creed, the Lords Prayer, nor the ten Commandments; and as for the children which have learned these holy forms, they teach them to forget them: Above all things, they take a special care that the Minister tyes not himself to any form of words, as a thing of dangerous consequence, and which hath a taint of Antichrist. Henceforward then there will be no uniformity in the Divine Service, nor no more help for the infirmity of aged Ministers, nor for the understanding and memory of simple and dull Auditors, who cannot comprehend at the first aboard what the Minister saith, but had need to be well accustomed to him.

Also there will be no more bounds to devout phantastical spirits, which is the principal vice of this Nation: Every Church will have a particular Order, or rather will have none at all; for the Pastor hath liberty to alter it every time he pleases, nothing being forbidden but to make use of the long established forms, by the Authentical Acts of many Parliaments, sanctified by the publick devotion of so many years; and composed by the first Reformers, persons excellent in piety and wisdome, whose books these are not worthy to carry after them.

If these Directors had had any fear of scandalizing the Churches, whom they invited to associate with them, they would never have abolished the custome received in all the Reformed Churches, and generally in all the Christian Churches of the World, who have

certain

certain forms for the publick Service of God. If they had born any respect to Antiquity, and to the universal consent of the Christian Church in all ages, and in all places, they would not have begun in this age a custome so prodigiously singular, as to banish out of the Church all forms and orders of prayers, the Apostles Creed, and the ten Commandments.

There rests yet some Liturgies of the ancient Churches, and Hymns used in the Publick Service, as the eighteenth Canon of the Councel of *Laodicea*, That the form or Liturgy of prayers Morning and Evening ought alwayes to be the same. There hath not, nor ever was there a Church, who had not some forms of prayers, but above all for the higher Powers, but that being abolished in *England* by the Directors, we need not wonder if many Ministers of the new Edition have long since forgot to make mention of the King in their prayers, and those that pray for him, do it in odious terms, thrust on by a perverse and malignant zeal, telling God a long story of the sins they impute unto their King, as if they would poure all their choler into the Bosome of God. If any amongst them should thus pray for his Father in the Pulpit, Lord grant Repentance to my Father of all his extortions, perjuries, thefts, murthers and adulteries, they would account him a fool, or exceedingly wicked, but against their King all things were permitted. Behold the fruits of abolishing the Divine Service, and the liberty of the Prophetique Spirits of the times, fomented by publick order.

CHAP.

CHAP. XV.

Of Abolishing the Liturgy, in doing whereof, the Covenanters oppose the Reformed Churches.

Amongst their reasons for the Abolishing such good prayers in this time of Rebellion, this none of the least, because in the Liturgy there are divers clauses which teach the people the Soveraignty of their Prince, and the obedience they owe unto him. There the King is called *our most Gracious Soveraign*: This would give the Minister the Lie, if after that he should call him a most cruel Tirant, as it was their custom: There they pray, *that it would please God to strengthen the King, that he might overcome all his enemies*, which were to pray to God for the ruine of their holy Covenant: there God is called *the only Governour of Princes*, which would contradict the Doctrine and Practise of the times, which gives other Governours to Princes besides God, and subject the King to his Subjects.

There they pray to God that the Subjects of the King may *duly consider whose Authority he hath*, namely Gods. If his Subjects duly come to consider this, they would lay down their Arms which they had taken up against him, for fear of fighting against God, and would reject the instruction taught them, that the King holds his Authority of men.

There they pray that the Subjects of the King *may faithfully serve, honour, and humbly obey him,* a prayer of a most dangerous consequence, and would utterly spoil the affairs of the Covenanters, if the Lord should hear them. There they also pray, the Lord would so bless the King, *that under him we may be godly and quietly governed,* but it is not *under him* but *without him,* that
they

they would govern us, there being not according to their saying, any means to live godly and quietly under his obedience.

In the same manner they pray for *all those who are established in authority under him*; but according to the form of the State turned the bottom upward, as the Presbyterians would have it, they must now pray for all those established in *authority over him*. 'Tis also a most dangerous clause in that same Prayer, which prays *to God to punish all wickednesse and vice, and to preserve true Religion and Piety*. For if this Prayer were once heard, the Zealots of the State who draw their swords against the King, and the Preachers of Rebellion, would be constrained to make their Speeches to the people on the Gallowes, and their hypocrisie would be unmasqued, and they rendered the publick object of contempt and scorn, and the Brownist and Anabaptist sent into the Islands of *America*.

Also the Prayer *that God would give peace in our daies*, would be very unsuitable to the Intentions of the Covenanters, who preach no other thing in substance, then that Text ill applied, *Cursed is he that withholds his sword from shedding blood*.

They have therefore voted it a point of prudence to lay aside the Liturgy out of their way, which is so contrary to their politick intentions; as for Conscience and the Government of the Church, which is dislocated and dismembred by this Abolition of the Divine Service, they will then consider of, after these Gentlemen have served themselves of the general disorder, to build themselves an Empire in the confusion.

Its most certain that in this change God is far worse served, there are indeed some certain Ministers capable without the Divine Service, to make prayers full of Edification, and truly every Minister of the Gospel ought thus to be prepared, but how many are there amongst them

them who for lack of being tied to certain prayers in publick, abuse the patience of God and holiness of prayer: If the Judicious Auditory at *Charenton*, should but hear what tales and news these people tell God, the insolent familiarity whereby they discourse and reason with him, their Maledictions against their King, their humorous, mad and phantastical tricks, which pass for sallies of zeal, they would mark out lodgings for them in the *petites Maisons* (with us here called Bedlam) which might exempt them from the *Chatelet* (but with us from New-gate.)

Charenton the name of the Protestant Church at Paris.

    Certainly as Liberty ought not to be a Cloak of maliciousness, so it ought not to be a door open for folly. The Libertine and capricious humour of the Climate in matter of the Service of God, should have taught these Directors to have restrained this licentiousness rather than to have let loose the rains, and the importunity of those that demanded this liberty, should have the more induced them to refuse it. But what? those who accorded this most pernicious liberty, were the same persons who only demanded it.

    The prophane contempt wherewith they used this so holy Liturgy, ought not to be imputed to the Insolency of the Souldiers, but unto the Instructions which were given them. The Parliaments Souldiers Catechisme published and recommended by special Authority, teacheth them to tear it a peeces wheresoever they find it, *Pag.* 22. Calling it a most Abominable Idol, and a Nurse of Ignorance and blindness, which foments an Idle, Lazy and dissolute Ministry, and that therefore they should reduce it to Ashes, as *Hezekiah* did the Brasen Serpent, as the occasion of much evil and an object of Idolatry.

    But seeing in so great a change they oppose the general consent of their Church, and that for one whom
they

they please hereby, they offend more than a hundred.

They labour to turn the eyes of the ignorant people towards the Churches beyond the Seas, hoping as well they might, that looking so far off, they could not know what they did. The Authors of the Directory affirm, *That by a long and sad experience they find that the English Liturgy is offensive to the Forreign Reformed Churches.* [In the Preface to the Directory.] And they add a little after, *That it is to answer the expectation of those Churches, that they reject the ordinary Liturgy.* Oh our good God! these persons do they meddle to preach the Truth? Because that *France* and *England* are separated by Sea and Language, do they think their people shall never be informed the truth of the opinion of their neighbours touching the *English* Liturgy, nor the manner of their practise in matter of their publick Service? I hope they will leave to others the practise of this Maxime, *Lie boldly, although you be refuted after, there will remain some impression upon the spirits of the hearers;* And therefore we will believe charitably, that the most part of these Divines knew not what they said, but referred themselves to the Faith of others, and hoping that after they are better informed, they will change their opinion, we will say to them, as St. *Paul* to the *Galatians*, *I have confidence in you through the Lord, that ye will be none otherwise minded, but he that troubleth you shall bear his judgment, whosoever he be,* Gal. 5. 10. Since then they speak of their long experience, let us take it from the beginning, soon after the Liturgy was compiled, it was sent to good *Calvin* who thus writ to the Protector of *England, as for the form of prayers, and Ecclesiastical ceremonies, I much approve that they should be established as a certain form from which it may not be lawful for the Pastors to go in the execution of their charge.* [Epistola ad Protectorem Angliæ.] Behold two points very contrary to the

Cove-

Covenanters, the one that he very well approves of the Book of Common prayer, and the Ecclesiastical Ceremonies; the other, that there ought to be a certain form of Divine Service, from which it should not be lawful for the Pastors to digress: Will they not say in reading these words of *Calvin, Durus sermo,* this is *a hard saying, who can hear it?* What cruelty is this, to undertake to bind the Spirit of Zeal? And to dare to speak of a Rule to them, *who will stand fast in the liberty Christ hath made them free, and will not again be entangled in the yoke of bondage,* for they make use of this Text for that subject; we will leave them this Text of *Calvin* to ruminate, and pray them not to begin the date of their long experience, till after his Decease.

Bucer Scripta Anglicana, p. 455.

Martin Bucer will yet shorten it some years, he speaks thus to the Churches of *England* of the form of their Divine "Service, I give thanks to God who hath given you grace "to reform these Ceremonies in such a purity, for I "have found nothing in it, which is not taken out of "the Word of God, or at least is not contrary to it, be-"ing rightly interpreted.

That which the Directors and their party find most to be reprehended in this Book, is of so small consideration with *Beza*, that he wrote thus to those who were so enraged against it, " The Surplice (saith he) "is not a thing of such importance,

Beza ad quosdam Anglicarum Ecclesiarum fratres.

"that Ministers should be so scrupu-"lous, as to leave their Function ra-"ther than wear it, or that the peo-"ple should forbear to feed of the bread of life, rather "than hear their Pastors preach who wear them. And as for receiving the blessed Sacrament of the Lords Supper kneeling, Musick in Churches, and things of the like nature, he saith to them, "That
"these

"these are such small and indifferent things which
"should not much trouble them. Behold here
their long experience much shortned, for its little
above fourty years since *Beza* died.

Gualter and *Bullinger* likewise commending the *English*
Liturgy, condemned the affected tenderness of some
who made use of it for a cloak of their Sedition and Rebellion, speaking thus in an Epistle which they both
joyntly wrote to their discontented Brethren in *England* upon this Subject, "That if any of the people
"perswade themselves that these things smell of Pope-
"ry, let them learn to know the contrary, and let
"them be perfectly instructed, and that if the clamours
"of any of them raise up troubles amongst the multi-
"tude, let them beware lest in doing so, they draw
"upon your necks a more heavy yoke, and provoke not
"his Majesty, and bring not many Ministers into such
"dangers out of which they shall find no means to
"escape. This advertisement might well be turned
into a Prophesie, and these persons who falsly alledge
the Reformed Churches are offended with the Liturgy of *England*, repent too soon that they had not
followed their exhortations, and submitted themselves.

Now the King hath offered to exempt tender Consciences from the observation of certain things which
offend them; yea to submit the whole Reformation to a
lawful Synod: But in stead of receiving this Gracious
offer of his Majesty, they persecute him and his Clergy
with all violence; manifesting thereby that it is not
our Reformation, but our destruction which is capable
to content them, and these tender Consciences which
tremble at the sight of a Surplice, or the sound of an
Organ, are strong and lusty enough to commit murder
and Sacriledge; like the Pharisees, who strained at a
Gnat, and swallowed a Camel.

His Majesty made a Declaration to all the reformed
Churches

Churches, of the sincerity of his Profession and intention to live and die in the holy Religion which he had maintained, and because the Factious of his Kingdom had used all their endeavours to alienate Forreign Churches from the Church of *England* upon the outward of Religion, his Majesty remembers them there how at the Synod of *Dort* both the Discipline and Liturgy of *England* was approved by word and writing by the most eminent Divines of *Germany*, *France*, *Denmark*, *Sweden* and *Switzerland*, as appears in the Acts of that Synod, and yet nevertheless the Covenanters at this day, are so impudently bold as to publish *that by long and sad experience they have found that the* English *Lyturgy was offensive to the Forreign Reformed Churches.* Where is their honesty? Where is their sincerity? Do they hope by these wicked waies to draw down a blessing of God upon their cause? The Truth which they pretend to advance, must it be established and set up by lying?

By all this then it appears that their long experience comes to nothing, but if they are wanting in the old experience, let them produce the new. Where are the Forreign Churches that require of them the abolition of the publike Service? Would they could cause them to speak for themselves: By Forreign Churches they cannot understand the *Scotch* Church; for since the beginning of this war, the Covenanters would not acknowledge them for strangers, for fear of being reproached for inviting and bringing in Forreign Forces, and keeping them under pay in the Kingdom. And as for other Churches, we account the experience of the Authors of the Directory do not much exceed ours: Now we have not known any Protestant stranger ever made it any difficulty to joyn in the publick prayers of the Church of *England*, except some walking Anabaptists, as in *London* they have lately made to appear; and neither

in

in *France* nor the *Low Countries*, we never knew or understood the least trace of dissention hereupon, and if the fashion of some Particulars amongst us displease other Churches, they do not less displease ours.

The Reformed Churches are better instructed than lightly to quarrel at the exteriour circumstance of Divine Service, where the substance is whole and sound; they have learned to speak after *Calvin*, in the Confession presented in the Name of the Churches of *France* to the Emperour and Princes of *Germany*, *We acknowledg that all and every Church have this right to make Laws and Statutes, and for to establish a common Policy amongst them, provided that all things be done in the House of God decently and in order, and they owe obedience to these Statutes, so that they do not inthrall the Conscience, nor impose Superstition, and those that refuse this are accounted by us seditious and wilful.*

<small>*Confessio Ecclesiarum Gallicarum inter opuscula Calvin.*</small>

Beza goes yet a little further, and maintains that in the outward of Religion, *Many things may, yea ought to be born, notwithstanding they are not justly commanded.*

<small>In his Epistle before alledged.</small>

St. *Augustin* hath an Epistle upon this Subject, which is a Golden Epistle, wherein he instructs *Januarius* of the indifferency of Ecclesiastical Observations, as of the times of Fasting, and the divers customs of receiving the Blessed Sacrament of the Lords Supper. *All things of this kind* (saith he) *have their Observations free, and for this there is no better of Discipline for a grave and prudent Christian, then to do as he seeth them do in all the Churches whither he goes, for that which is neither against faith and good manners ought to be held indifferent, and ought to be observed according to the company with whom we live and converse*; and hereupon he reports how his Mother being come to *Millan* found her self

<small>Tom. 2. Epist. ad Januarium.</small>

I in

in great perplexity, becaufe they did not faft on the Saturday, as they did in the Church from whence fhe came, and he to refolve her, went to ask counfel of St. *Ambrofe* Archbifhop of *Millan*, who anfwered him; *When I* (faith he) *go to* Rome, *I faft on the Saturday, when I am here I faft not on that day, do ye the fame: Into whatfoever Church ye go, obferve their cuftomes; if you your felf will not give offence to perfons, and will that no perfon fhould give you offence.* All Proteftants of *Europe* except the Faction of the Covenant, govern themfelves thus, in whatfoever place they are, they joyn with the Reformed Church, whatfoever their form of Difcipline be, which as fome fay is divers in all Nations.

To this grave counfel of S. *Ambr.* S. *Auftin* adds a Character to the life, of the imperious and fcrupulous humour of our melancholy zealots, whom one would think had an intention to paint them out: *I have oft perceived* (faith he) *with much grief and forrow, that many weak and infirm perfons have been much troubled through their Contentions, wilfulnefs and fuperftitious fearfulnefs at fome of their Brethren, for doing fome things which could not be certainly defined by the Authority of the Holy Scriptures, nor by the tradition of the univerfal Church, nor by the utility that might thereby come for the bettering and amendment of our lives; only becaufe there is fome matter for their conceptions to reafon and difcourfe upon, or becaufe they think the farther they go, or are able to feparate themfelves from the Cuftoms received, is the moft exquifite and neareft to perfection, moving fuch litigious and idle Queftions, that they make appear to all, that they will never allow of any thing well done unlefs they do it themfelves.*

The Reformed Churches take and give this Liberty, that every one form an outward Order of Divine Service according to their prudence, and its more to be wifhed than expected, that there fhould be one and the fame same order throughout all Churches. But I know not any Church that reject and cast off all certain Forms as the Covenanters. The Declaration following made some few years since, by persons of account in the Churches of *France*, is notable.

As for the Ceremonies and Customs of Ecclesiastical Service and Discipline, we judge convenient to leave to every Church his own, without altering or changing any thing. One day when it shall please God to perfect and confirm amity amongst these Churches, we may be able by an universal councel and confe, *to form a certain Liturgy which may be as a Symbole and Bond of Concord.* Sententia Quorundam Ecclesiæ in Gallia pastorum eximiorum edita à D. Johanne Duræo Londini, An. 1638.

The Churches of the Covenanters ought to be exempted out of this Number, for the Liturgy is become to them an Apple of Discord, which hath made them quarrel with all Churches of the world; being in this point like unto *Esau*, whose hands were against every one, and every ones hands against him. Therefore the Directors refute themselves by a manifest contradiction, then when by their publike Declaration they tell the people, that it is to conform themselves to the Reformed Churches, that they prescribe not an ordinary form of publike Prayers and Administration of the Sacraments. Seeing that it is a thing most notoriously known, that all the Reformed Churches have certain Forms of Prayers: But they do as if they should apparrel themselves with Green and Yellow, because the Ministers of *France* apparel themselves with black: 'Tis the Doctrine of the Brownists, which now predominate in *England*, that for to have a Liturgie or Form of Prayers, is to have another Gospel: Now after all this, Do Barrow Refut. 224 they not well, think you, to court the Churches of *France*, and to make a great noise of their conformity with them, having so openly condemned them? and their

their phanatical Phrenſie in this point is proceeded ſo far, that neither the Lords Prayer, nor the Ten Commandements, nor the Apoſtles Creed, are repeated in their Churches, nor are taught their Children in their Houſes; much leſs any Form of Catechiſm: Behold here a Faction who reject the Books of Chriſtian Religion: An horrible and unheard of thing in all ages, and in all Churches ſince Chriſtianity entred the world. And dare theſe people ſpeak of Reformation and Conformity with the Reformed Churches?

CHAP. XVI.

Of the great prudence and wiſdome of the firſt Engliſh Reformers, and of the fool-hardineſs of theſe at preſent.

IF theſe directors who boaſt themſelves of a new Light, had had at leaſt the light of Prudence, they would have conſidered that they had to deal with popular Spirits, who were accuſtomed to a good and holy Liturgie, but ſince on a ſudden interdicted the uſe, they could not but think they were ſuddenly tranſported into another Goſpel, for the people are dull, and faſtned upon the exterior, and that if they be once faſtened to a form of devotion which is good, although below perfection, there is occaſion to praiſe God that the people have any taſt of devotion, even in any Form, and it ſhould be cheriſhed and encouraged. And if there be any thing in this Form to be amended, it ſhould be done ſo mildly and dexterouſly, that the people be not exaſperated, and the change made in the outward skin of Religion, make not the ſubſtance diſtaſted; for the moſt part mens ſpirits

rits penetrates not much further than the superficies, as indeed no further did theirs who came to reform us with the sword. Its a very dangerous thing to overthrow an Order wherein the Devotion of the people hath taken root. For besides the disorder that follows commonly in the Church and State, they shall find that in transplanting Devotion into a new soil, they cause it to die; some being prophane, others desperate and atheistical.

For an exemplary conduct of Christian prudence in this great point of publick Reformation, all after ages will admire the *English* Reformers under the Reign of *Edward* the Sixth, who intrapt the people, as Saint *Paul* beguiled the *Corinthians*, who confessed that being subtile, *he caught them by guile*, for to establish the Doctrine, so as it is contained in the Confession of Faith in *English* Church, and agrees with that of other reformed Churches, they kept themselves from going openly and suddenly against the inclination of the people, above all in the exteriour, which although it is of less importance, hath notwithstanding a very strong influence upon the common people. After the Reformation was concluded upon by the Prelates and Nobles, Mattins were said in the Cathedral Churches at their accustomed hours, with the same Garments they were wont to wear, and the same ordinary singing, but the Hymns and Psalms they read in *English*, and their Scriptures were not read in pieces, but by whole Chapters, and Prayers were put to God only in the Name of Jesus Christ, and in a known tongue; a thing which did much content the people, and much edifie them, and being accustomed to these things, they passed by the Mass. Sermons became more frequent, simply instructing the people in the Truth and Holiness without any bitterness or contest; whereby they gained the spirits of the people by charity, which is the only method for to decide controversies, and in a short time, that which Superstition had drawn over the Service of God, was insensibly abolished, and there was a general conversion of the Kingdom wrought without any noise.

This prudent way wrought better effects than all the combats of Religion, whether fought by Armies or Letters, which have been since above these hundred years: Their enemies of the Church of *Rome* would much rather the Reformers had disputed concerning the Doctrine and Discipline, and that they had set upon them with their utmost strength.

Our melancholy and peevish Zelots would have done no great good upon them by the waies they now take, if this task had fallen into their hands; for such a great work there was need of better notions of piety and prudence than the fundamental Maximes of the reformation at present, *That the purest Religion is that which hath least conformity with the Church of Rome.* That for to do well, they must do quite contrary to that which the Church of *Rome* doth, and hereby they make all that remains of the Institution of the Apostles to become Antichristian, because the Papist hath practised them. Maximes which are only proper for poor seditious Spirits, whose nature is like the Crab-fishes, who know not how to go but backward. Religion consists not in negation, the saving Truths are affirmative, and it would be a dangerous rule to believe altogether contrary to that which the Devil believes, which would oblige us to deny the Divinity.

The Book called Chirist upon his Throne, p. 23.

For so high an enterprise, which is equally as necessary as dangerous, there is required clear, seeing judgments, firm & stable, ready & charitable; who are able to penetrate and dive into the inside of Religion, and discern

cern the meat from the shell; who without bending the Truth to the times, know how to accomodate their work to the nature of men and affairs; and who have the discretion recommended by Saint *Paul*, *Prove all things, hold fast that which is good*, wisely distinguishing betwixt the Apostolical Institution, and the rust that is grown on it through length of time.

These excellent persons manifest to the world that they well understood this secret, that the matter of Religion is a thing rather adored than known by the people; but the Form and Ceremony is that their eyes are fixed upon, and which fills their spirits, and he that pleaseth them in the exteriour, shall easily prevail with them for the inward of Doctrine.

Now it appears that Superstition is alwayes of the same Nature, although she changeth her object; for the Fanaticall zeal of the people of the Covenant being fleshed and egged on to destroy the exteriour Order, perceived not in the mean while that they undermined the foundations of Faith; For we find amongst our enemies, many different Sects; Some denying the Trinity, the Incarnation of the Son of God, and his Divinity, who neverthelesse agree altogether to hate & abolish our Lyturgie with the sword, without contending amongst themselves for these essential differences; neither are they moved for these monstrous errors, which directly oppose the glory of God and salvation of men; so much are men for the most part children, yea brutish in matters of Piety, fastening themselves upon appearances, and not upon things, considering more the garment then the body of Religion.

The vulgar being every where of this disposition, God shewed great favour to the ignorant people in times of our Fathers, to put them into so good hands, who knew how to lead them mildly to the Truth, without exasperating them for the Discipline. For to provoke and irritate them, was not the means to instruct them.

Let all the world judge if the Reformers at present follow this example, and whether they search to instruct or to provoke the people; for after we have made the best and soundest party amongst them to confess that the Doctrine of the Church of *England* was good and holy, and they be demanded hereupon, why they persecute the King and his people with such rage? They pay us with this miserable reason, that the people are affectionate to certain things as necessary, which are not necessary, and they would wean them from this opinion: And must they for this drown three famous Kingdoms in bloud, and snatch the Crown from off the Head, and the Sword out of the hand of a good King?

We may well tell them that they undertake an impossible thing; for there is no Religion, no Nation, nor almost person, who is not lodged there; but they themselves, are they not more superstitious in this point, than those whom they would correct? For what greater superstition, for to make a necessity to contradict and oppose things, where there is no necessity, yea to account the abolishing of things not necessary, so necessary, that for it they will massacre the King, and bathe themselves in the blood of the Church and State. Can there be in the world a more pernicious superstition? No verily, if they consider that this superstition kils the soul as well as the body. For those from whom they take the use of their holy prayers, have great cause to fear they will also take from them their Religion, whereupon some have fallen into a desperate Melancholy; if they deal thus with us, because they have a greater measure of light then we, it is much to be desired that they had a little more; that they fall not into the offence condemned by S. *Paul*, and *through thy knowledge shall thy weak brother perish for whom Christ died, but when*

when ye sin against the Brethren, and wound their weak conscience, ye sin against Christ, 1 Cor. 8.11,12.

Heretofore this faction would be spar'd in their disobedience to the Ecclesiastical Laws, pretending tenderness and weakness of Conscience; but now that they are become Masters of the Laws, they regard not our weakness, but force us to follow their fantasies, without considering our doubts and scruples. The King by the Articles of *Uxbridge,* offered them liberty of Conscience, but they will not give neither the King nor his subjects the like liberty: Either take the Covenant or leave your Benefice, was the choice they gave many Ministers.

Alledge to them the great and deep affliction of the people, because they had taken from them their Common Prayers, their Forms for the celebration of the Sacraments, and of Marriage, their customs of receiving the Sacrament at Christmas, Easter, and Pentecost, and the decent manner of burying their dead, with some Prayers and Texts of Scripture, which put the living in mind of their mortality, and raised up in them an assurance of their resurrection. They will answer you, that these observations are not necessary, and mock at the affliction of the ignorant people: But we hold that it is necessary to obey God, who *hath commanded us to do nothing whereby thy weak brother stumbleth, is offended, or made weak, but be such as give none offence, neither to the Jew, nor to the Gentiles, nor to the Church of God,* Rom. 14.21. Also the imaginary danger which they fear of things that may come to passe, is a thousand times less then the present scandal and offence done to pious souls, to behold all Ecclesiastical order overthrown, and Liberty given to prophane and fanatique spirits, to whom any thing is permitted, unless to obey the King, and the orders established by Lawfull Authority.

But let us pass to other offences: There are many more besides the violation of Orders, the very substance

of

of Religion is endamaged. What care do many people take to Baptize their children? How do they reprove them that Baptize no more in the Name of the Father, the Son, and the holy Ghost? Is it not permitted to every one to Baptize or not Baptize their children? and Baptism is it not refused to many Infants, which are presented to be Baptized?

These new Reformers find so many difficulties in the capacity of their Parents, that they are constrained many times to carry their children far from their dwellings to be received into the Christian Church; for 'tis one of the Errors of the Times, that if the Father hath not Faith (that is to say a Faith after their mode) the Infant must not be Baptized; In stead whereof the Reformed Churches in Baptizing Infants, consider not the Faith of the Parents, but of the Church in which they are born; and the Doctrine, not according as it is believed, but according as it is taught, *Fidem non subjectivam sed objectivam.* For if they must be certain whether the Father hath Faith, they should also be certain that he is the Father of the Infant, which the Charity of the Church questioneth not.

Also it is an ordinary custom amongst them to rebaptize aged persons, and to plunge women naked into the Water untill they say they feel faith.

The abuse of the blessed Sacrament of the Lords Supper is yet worse, because it is more universal, and maintained by the body of their Divines. We beseech all lovers of the Christian Religion to enquire themselves of these Ministers, how long time they have forborn to receive or administer this holy Sacrament? when was it that the heads of the Covenanters received it? when is it that their Souldiers were partakers of it, those zealous murtherers, whose assassinations and plunderings are steeped in piety? Is it because they dare not receive the body and blood of our Lord, with hands defiled with
rapine

rapine and innocent blood? But this reason cannot serve for the Churches where the Ministers are laid hold on, and forbidden to administer the Sacrament where they are Ministers. How many Churches are there where there hath been no speaking of a Sacrament these fifteen or sixteen years? And is it not for them to mock God to make a Directory of the manner of receiving the Lords Supper, and not to make use of it, yea by force to hinder execution and performance of it?

Our Lord Jesus hath commanded us, *To do this in remembrance of him*, 1 *Cor.* 11.26. But behold here persons, who impose a necessity not to do, because they know not those who are worthy, and therefore they hinder others to obey Jesus Christ, taking by force the Bread and Wine from the people, who were assembled to communicate, and carried away the Minister out of the Church, for fear he should administer the Sacrament. These actions cry to heaven, and will one day draw down a just vengeance. These proceedings make us fear, least they rank the Lords Supper amongst the superannuated ceremonies which must be abolished; for in many Churches where the Covenanters are it's not used, which is a horrible thing to hear; the Church of God, since Chrifts time, never before brought forth such examples.

Certainly since Jesus Christ would, *that we should do this in remembrance of him, until his coming again*; if he should come now, he would find it very strange, that they had left before his coming this celebration of the memory of his death, which he had so expresly commanded, and it is to be presumed that he will receive no reason against his Command: for the coming of Jesus Christ is the only reason which ought to make this holy Ordinance cease.

By this scruple, that they dare not administer the
holy

holy Supper, but to those alone whom they know to be worthy (which is the general pretext of their party for their total abstinence) they condemn not only the Reformed Churches, who exclude none from the holy Communion, unless they be ignorant and scandalous persons, but also Jesus Christ, who administred to the Disciple that betrayed him; even then when he was plotting his treason in his heart.

By this also they even bind themselves not to celebrate the Supper of the Lord until they be inspectors and lookers into Conscience, that is to say, Gods: For otherwise they cannot be fully satisfied of the worthiness of persons, and all those who have a holy desire to partake of the Lords Table, shall not be admitted, until these principal Clerks of the Councel-Chamber of God have formed a Church, which consists purely of Elect.

Its great pity when men will be too wise, and introduce Laws of Severity into the Church which God hath not required at our hands: These men should meditate on the Text of *Solomon*, Eccles. 7. 16. *Be not righteous over-much, neither make thy self over-wise, why shouldest thou destroy thy self?* Or otherwise, *Why shouldest thou draw desolation on thy self?* Thus the Pharisees by an impertinent wisdome and affected Authority, and a sublime Divinity of *Chymeras*, were confounded in the vanity of their understandings, and drew desolation upon themselves, and their Church.

But yet there is a mystery of Iniquity under this scruple, which doth deeply stain the Divines of the Covenant; for their Masters foment them for to advance their affairs, and it is easie to see, that if they once become the strongest, they will exclude from the Sacrament of the Lords Supper all those who cannot banish from their heart the love of their King, and the Church wherein they were born and brought up: In a Sermon preached

preached before the House of Commons, and printed by command, we learn that their Party will no more communicate with the Antichristian Faction; the Preacher explains himself, and tells us he means all those that adhere to the King in this quarrel: They have many times preached that none should receive the Lords Supper, but those who had taken the Covenant; yea, they have spoke aloud, that the Oath of the Covenant, and the Lords Supper should be administred together, so that the Communicants must swear upon the Body & Blood of our Lord, and upon the hope of their Salvation, that they would be Rebels to their King as long as they live; and the Blood of Jesus Christ must be imployed for the same use, the cup of mans blood which the confederates with *Cataline* drunk round one to another, in taking the Oath of Conjuration to murder their Superiours, and ruine their country. But this design is not yet ripe for execution, they defer it for a time: In the mean time, these Gentlemen and the Spiritual Fathers deny themselves the Seal of their Union with Jesus Christ, and hereafter they will dispose of this Sacrament according as the necessity of the Covenanters do require. They forgot to put down this Article of their reservation in the Epistle they sent to forreign Churches, but in inviting them in general to conform themselves unto them, they exhort them to this amongst the rest. What? Must the Reformed Churches then abstain from the Lords Supper, and chuse to interdict the Ordinance of Jesus Christ, rather then put themselves in danger of administring to the unworthy? Must the Universal Christian Church be gulled by their scruples, composed of the folly of some, and the malice of others? Must all believers in the World hold their Faith in suspence, and deprive themselves of the Sacrament of their Union with Jesus

By Mr. Francis Cheynall.

sus Christ, until the Covenanters of *England* have found a proper time to make use of the Body and Blood of Christ, to bind together a wicked faction, and have made the mysteries of Salvation their footstool for ambition.

Rather then suffer by a criminal complacency, that Religion should be so destroyed, and that these horrible things should pass for Doctrines of the Reformed Churches, let all those who bear this title, defend the honour of the Gospel, and thereby a publick detestation of so great a corruption. Let all those who love God testifie by a just anger they hate the evil. It matters not what fraternity these Innovators pretend with other Churches, if they corrupt the Christian Religion, and invite them to do the like, *Familiaris accipere haud familiariter*, let them manifest, they have no fraternity with heresie, and impiety, repulse boldly the temptation of those who invite so basely to do ill, that they may have no more courage to return.

But there is one consideration which should mitigate your indignation against them. That amongst this most impious extravaganfie, there is a malady and disease of the spirit, for many of this party have their brains dislocated and displaced. Some whereof have taken their children, and gone and sacrificed them, pretending a particular command, like that God gave to *Abraham*; others have shut themselves up with a Bible, and resolved to eat nothing, because it is written, *That man shall not live by bread alone, but by every word which proceedeth out of the mouth of God.* Some have killed their cat, because she had taken a mouse on Sunday, but defer'd the execution until Munday. And there are women and tradesmen amongst them, who preach by the spirit without call, knowledge, or premeditation;

A woman at Dover cut off her childs head and alledged this Scripture.
The Quaker that fasted and died at Colchester.

ditation, others who account the receiving of the Sacrament on their knees, is to communicate at Mass, and that the Surplice is the Smock of the Whore of *Babylon*, the Publick Prayers Mass refined, the sound of the Organs, the Hoboyes of Antichrist; ye need not wonder the Covenanters have so great a party, since fools and Ideots are on their side.

The like weakness is seen in the Epistle of the Assembly to the Reformed Churches, they highly aggravate the persecutions prepared for all those who would not bear the mark of the beast, meaning by this mark, their obedience to the order of Episcopacy, and the use of the Publick Service, for the King required no other thing of them; but as beasts which being cast into the river, ordinarily swim against the stream, so many of these brutish spirits, think they can never be saved, but in going against the ancient received customes, how good soever they be, and make all their piety and honesty to consist in a sullen and dogged devotion, fantastical and turbulent, which will give no rest to themselves, nor others.

This scrupulous humour hath produced strange effects, witness he that killed his mother and brother in cold blood, having no other quarrel against them, but that they loved the Liturgy. *Enoch ap Evan neer to Shrewsbury.* This was a preamble of the devil, who the year after began this war for the same subject, in which he made use of the melancholy humour of the people to cut the throats of their brethren for devotion, according to the instructions before alledged out of Sions Plea, and the Souldiers Catechisme.

In effect their spirit of contradiction, and their bloody inclination, which hath formed this maxime of the times, that the Reformation must be made by blood, are the productions of a sharp choler, predominant

minant in the Hipocondres or bowels, whose vapours besiege the animal spirits, which carries them into a savage rage, which hath something of the nature of the Licanthropy.

There is alwayes in the worst parties excellent natures, which are carried away with the stream, and we know amongst the party of the Covenant, some very brave men; but the churlish zealots, whose fierceness and number govern even the Governours themselves, are of weak and malignant spirits, whose temper is like that of *Tiberius*, that is of dung kneaded and wrought together with blood, these are men of sad, sordid, and reserved natures, which a wild melancholy renders fearful, superstitious, suspitious and cruel; and when all these ingredients meet together, ignorance, superstition, presumption and wilfulness, and a flitting and imperious humour, all steeped in a black and hot melancholy, they make the most malignant composition of the world, pernicious to Church and State, to families and all societies, causing every where ruine and combustion, like a Granado fired, that makes all fly a pieces that is near it.

<small>πηλ☉ ἅιματι πε-
Συεγμενος, Suet.
Tiber.</small>

CHAP.

CHAP. XVII.

How the Covenanters labour in vain to sow dissention between the Churches of England *and* France, *upon the point of discipline; Of the Christian prudence of the* French *Reformers, and of the nature of discipline in general.*

Hitherto we have found no such conformity as might induce the Covenanters of *England* to invite the Reformed Churches to espouse their quarrel, for they every where carefully administer the Lords Supper, they take order that Infants be baptized, they suffer none to be re-baptized, they suppress heresies, scandals, the liberty of fanatique spirits, they repeat to the people the ten Commandments of God, the Articles of the Christian Faith, they make use of certain forms of prayer in administring the Sacraments, and other parts of the Divine Service. They teach the people to submit to every Ordinance of man for the Lords sake, and not to resist Supreme Powers, but to suffer for righteousness sake; they are free from a capricious weakness in matters of indifferency which are peculiar to our enemies; also these Churches approve of the English Liturgy, and without scruple joyn with it in prayer when occasion serves; what is there then which should oblige them to associate together. The Reformed Churches, say they, have no Bishops; but we demand of them, whether all those Churches which have Bishops are not Reformed? They incline doubtless to this opinion, for in the title of their Epistle to the Reformed Churches, they name but

K those

those of *France*, the Low Countries, and *Switzerland*, they let the other pass under an &c. If that be their opinion, they have much forgot themselves in their Copies which they sent to particular States, for they writ to the Churches of *Hesse*, and those of *Anhalt*, which are governed by Superintendents, that is to say in our Language, Bishops.

In all those Countries subject to the Crowns of *Denmark* and *Sweden*, The Episcopal degree is kept; so almost through all *Germany*, this degree is preserved under the name of Superintendent, and in some places (as in *Brene*) the name of Bishops remain; although part of these Churches be *Lutherans*, we will not refuse them the name of Reformed, there wanting but a little charity in them, to make both them and us to accord. So likewise in the large Territories of *Bohemia, Polonia*, and *Transylvania*, the Evangelical Churches are governed by Seniors, (as they call them) who have Episcopal power.

They should not then boast of the consent of the Reformed Churches, nor complain to them, that the King would not admit a Reformation, which pretends to abolish the Episcopal degree as an appurtenance of Antichrist, which is in effect to condemn all Churches where there is any preheminence amongst the Clergy. I forbear to speak of the Churches of *Russia, Grecia* and *India*, and of the rest of the world, whose Doctrine is less known to us, then the point of their Discipline, which are all governed by Bishops.

But the Covenanters Magisterially prescribe their Discipline to all the World, although they themselves have none, vaunting themselves of a piety without pair, and yet will not leave to other Churches any liberty.

Therefore their Declarations give all to understand, that after they have planted it in *England*, they will go and do as much beyond the Seas. The *Donatists*
shut

shut up the Church within the confines of *Africa*, which then was a small thing, unfitly applying that Text of the *Canticles*, *Tell us where thou feedest, where thou makest thy flocks to rest at noon*, Cant. 1.7. but the French translation readeth, *to rest towards the south*. At present the Kingdom of Jesus Christ is in danger to be confined within *England*, whither other Nations must come and search it, saying, *Tell us where thou feedest, where thou makest thy flocks to rest towards the North*.

It's easie to make the consent of the Churches named in the title of the Epistle to sound high, because they have no Bishops, but to prove their agreement with the Covenanters in this point, they should do well to make these two things to appear; the one, that these Churches condemn the Episcopal Order as unlawful and Antichristian; the other, that these Churches do conform to the discipline of the Covenanters, things which they will find false.

As for the first, we see not that the other Churches quarrel at the Church of *England* hereupon, but pray God to bless them in the order; against this it matters not to alledge the thirtieth Article of the Churches of *France* confession of Faith. *We believe that all true Pastors in what place soever they be, have the same authority and equal power under one head Jesus Christ, and that for this cause no Church ought to pretend any dominion or Lordship over the other.*

He that speaks for the General, expounds this Article, *Ye must know* (saith he) *that the equality of Pastors in that which is of Authority to declare the Gospel, and administer the Sacraments, and for the use of the keyes is held necessary amongst all; for Baptism, the Lords Supper, and the declaring of the remission of sins is of equal dignity in the mouth of Pastors, whether they be of great or little Authority. But as* Buckler of Faith, Sect. 124.

for

for Ecclesiastical policy, we do not hold the equality of Pastors absolutely necessary, we do not account this Order a point of faith, nor a Doctrine of salvation, we live (God be thanked) in brotherly concord with our neighbour-Churches, which follow another form, and where the Bishops have superiority.

In his disputations of Divinity in the University of *Sedam*, this is one of his Theses, *We maintain that the Bishops of* England *after their conversion to the faith, and their abjuration of Papistry were faithful servants of God, and ought not to forsake, neither the name nor title of Bishops.*

Calvin himself spake as much before in his Epistle to Cardinal *Sadolet*, speaking of the Church of *Rome*; *Let them* (faith he) *establish such an Hierarchy, where the Bishops having the dignity, refuse not to submit themselves to Christ, and depend of him as their onely Head, and refer themselves to him, and let them maintain amongst them such a brotherly society, which is not entertained but by the bond of truth. Then if there be found any persons who refuse to respect such an Hierarchy with reverence and Soveraign obedience, I acknowledge and confess him worthy of all sorts of Anathema's*

This passage serves for the Episcopal degree in general: This other of *Jacobus Lectius* Professor at *Geneva* hath a singular regard to the Bishops of *England*, He saith, *That those Bishops only were true and lawful Bishops, and such as* S. Paul *writes of in his Epistles to* Timothy *and* Titus; *and we deny not* (faith he) *but there hath been formerly such Bishops, and that there are some now, and that they elect such now in the Kingdom of* England.

Jacobus Lectius præscriptionum Theologicarum, lib. 2.

Beza writes thus to Archbishop *Whitgift*, Archbishop of *Canterbury, In my writings touching the Ecclesiastical Government, I have ever*

March 1591.

ever opposed the Roman Hierarchy, but it was never in my intention to oppose the Ecclesiastical policy of your English Church, nor to require of you to form your Church according to the pattern of our Presbyterian Discipline, for whilst the substance of your Doctrine is uniform with the Church of Christ, it is lawful for us to differ in other matters, according as the circumstances of times, places and persons require, and is avowed by the prescription of antiquity; and for this effect, I desire and hope that the sacred and holy society of your Bishops will continue, and maintain for ever their right and title in the government of the Church, with all Christian equity and moderation. Moreover the Churches, yea the English Bishops render to their Brethren beyond the Seas the like charity: Thus speaks Famous and Reverend Bishop *Hall*, *I most cordially respect, and with me our Church their dear sister, those excellent forreign* In his Treatise of Episcopacy. *Churches, who have chosen and followed an outward form of government, which in every respect, is most expedient, and sutable for their condition.*

With the like charity, an excellent Bishop whose Title of his Book being without name, binds us not to name him: Having proved that according to the antient Institution of the Christian Church, the Bishops always gave the imposition, or laying on of hands. *I write not here* (saith he) *to prejudice our neighbour Churches, I dare not limit the extraordinary working and operation of the Holy Ghost, there where the ordinary means is wanting, without the fault of the persons; God gave his people Manna so long as they were in the Wilderness, necessity is a strong pleader, many Reformed Churches live under Kings and Bishops of another Communion; Others have particular Reasons, why they could not continue nor introduce Bishops, but it is not so amongst us,* speaking of the Church of his own Country.

The Serpent Salve, 111.

K 3

A few lines after he adds, *As for my self, I am very much inclined to believe, that the Lord looks upon his people with pity in all their prejudices, and that there is a great Latitude left to particular Churches in the constitution of their Ecclesiastical government, according to the exigence of place and persons, provided that the Divine Order and Institution be observed.*

Now after these charitable judgements, the Reformed Churches do not believe, that which the Epistle of the Assembly of Divines would perswade them; that the Bishops hate forraign Churches, and teach that without Bishops they could have no Church nor lawful call of Ministers, so that if any of ours have offended of late the Reformed Church in the point of Discipline, they are disavowed in it by their Bishops.

Here is, thanks be to God, a Christian Harmony, the Churches which have no Bishops say, Let them that would and can injoy the Order of Episcopacy, let them injoy it, far be it from us that we should either proudly or rashly reprove them for it. The Bishops respect cordially the Forraign Churches, which have not the same Order, and account the Government established amongst them in all respects, the most expedient for them. Let both the one and the other hold themselves there, and let them grant one another the Liberty to govern in the outward, according to prudence and exigencies; and let them joyn brotherly together to maintain the substance of Religion constant and uncorrupted.

It is the councel of the Reverend Bishop before alledged, *There are some Plants* (saith he) *which thrive best in the shadow, if then this form of government without Bishops, agree best to the constitution of some Common-wealths, we pray to God to give them joy in it; and pray them to say as much for us. Petimus damusque vicissim.* This is spoken Christianly and wisely; if our enemies had the charity

Serpent salve, p. 219.

rity to have said so much, there would have been no Covenant, neither would they have pulled down Monarchy, for to pull down Bishops, under colour of pulling down the Kingdom of Antichrist: But if they would that in this quarrel the Reformed Churches should joyn with them, they should first have drawn from them a Declaration, that they held the Episcopal degree unlawful, and a mark of Antichrist, and incompatible with the Gospel; and that rather then suffer it, they should overthrow the State, and dispossess your Kings; for lesse then this persivasion could not induce the Reformed Churches to espouse the quarrel of the Covenant.

We will proceed no further in this controversie, only because the Covenanters build their rules of Reformation upon the example of the *French* Churches, which the *French* Reformers never thought of, we beseech all equal persons to consider the Christian prudence of those that put their hand to this great work in *France*, having the Court and Clergy contrary to them.

The best that they were able to do in the matter of Discipline, was to provide Pastors who should teach purely, and leave them in a simple equality, there being no question of governing in times of persecution, but to instruct and suffer; and it being a thing subject to danger and envy, to erect new degrees, which could not be done without quarrelling at them which were established. Necessity contributes to prudence, for the Reformation in *France* having begun by the common people, and some few of the inferiour Clergy, who were opposed by the Civil and Ecclesiastical Power, we cannot wonder, if the Government which they established according to the time, was popular; if the Reformation had begun by Bishops, the Government had been Episcopal; the Priests that were converted had not power to convert their Bishops; as the English who began the

Reformation, helped by their Authority, the conversion of their Clergy and people. For the inferiour Orbs, having a contrary motion to the superiour, have not the power to make them follow their course: But the superiour Orbs carry along with them the inferiour. It was a great matter that the Reformed people could gain any retrogation against the rapidity and swiftness of the greater Sphears.

The discipline of the *French* Churches is most commodious to their present estate, and hardly could there be found a more proper for a Church that lives under Magistrates of a contrary Religion, in expectation of the reformation of them who possess the Ecclesiastical degrees. The *French* Ministers in this humble and equal order keep themselves in a state of obedience proper to submit themselves to their Diocesans when it shall please God to convert them, and we believe that their Fathers did chose this equality, not as an opposition to the degrees of the Clergy, but as a way to dispose them, and as a plank ready to invite the Bishops to pass over to their Reformation.

But if the Churches of *France* should come to maintain this Doctrine of the Covenanters, that the Order of Episcopacy, is an appurtenance of Antichrist, and that there is no Kingdome of Jesus Christ, but there where the Ministers are equal and poor; This would put the conversion of the *French* Churches out of all hope. But for as much as we desire the advancement of the Gospel, we keep our selves from re-inforcing the considerations of flesh and blood, or from augmenting the reproach of the Gospel; we are not offended at the degrees, nor revenues of the Clergy, we render not the entrance into the Church more thorny then it is: For to preach Reformation to a Clergy of a divers Religion, and bind them to degrade and strip themselves for to reform them; what other thing is this, but at
-once

once to call them, and to shut the door against them? It's true, that notwithstanding all earthly considerations, God may do miracles for to convert them, but that hinders not but that we should carry our selves prudently to invite them, and we ought not of deliberate purpose to make new Barracadoes between them and us, because God can, if he please, break them.

But to the end that the difference of disciplines move no quarrel amongst the Reformed Churches, this truth ought wisely to be considered, that there is no entire rule of discipline laid down in Scripture; and that not to have an outward order in the Church, all the parts whereof not being expresly set down in the Word of God, is to involve themselves in great difficulties, and shut themselves up into straight bounds, it's to search that in the Word of God, which is not there to be found. *Let all things be done decently, and in order*, 1 Cor. 15. Its a Scripture that may be stretched very far, and which remits to the Christian prudence of the Ministers of the Word of God, to advise of such an order which is most expedient for the times and places wherein they live, provided that nothing be done against Divine Institution.

It's then necessary that to the Divine Institution the humane should be joyned, and it was never otherwise in Church: Now that which is humane in the discipline, can never be so well united and fitted with the Divine, that there may be made of these two, a form entirely regular, and a perfect composition: It's like the iron and clay in the feet of the Statue of *Nebuchadnezzar*, which could never well joyn themselves one with another, for the Ecclesiastical Ordinances are the feet of Religion, bearing on them a head of gold, and a brest of silver, that is striving to uphold a Doctrine of great price? but they themselves touch the earth, and are mingled, and there is not such a prudence

dence and sanctity of Reformation, which can form a discipline purely celestial, nor joyn that which it hath of humane and Divine in it with such a justness, as to compose a perfect order, with materials of so different a nature.

This here is the cause of so many faults which may be found in all Ecclesiastical Order. For notwithstanding the confusion of Schismes and Heresies, the sharpness of persecutions, the infinite revolutions of States, during sixteen ages, a pure and divine Doctrine remains in the World, as gold which is found alwayes at the bottom of the Furnace: The same cannot be said of the discipline, for that is defective in all Churches, and varieth; yea, ought to vary according to the times and places, and it hath so much of man in it, that what it hath of Divine, is alwayes more or less Sophisticated by humane inventions; and will be alwayes so, until Jesus Christ hath withdrawn his Church from the earth, and raised it to that great Ecclesiastical Government, which is the Rule of Heaven.

Surely though there be certain rules of discipline Divine and certain, there yet remains ever something for Prudence to form, which ought to accommodate it self to necessity; So bending according as occasions serve, the rules that God hath left, to the wisdome of men, as the Divine be not damnified, and that the Government of the Church thwarts not that of the State, which is our misery at this day.

Whosoever shall consider the Kingdomes and Commonwealths of Christendome, shall find that every where the Religion of the State hath a discipline suitable to the civil Government, the Church taking hold of the State, as the Ivy that groweth about a tree: But the Covenanters pretend the quite contrary, labouring to form the State to their new pattern of Ecclesiastical Discipline. Hither tended the Petition of the rabble of
London,

London, to the House of Commons; which was after by the same House in a Body, presented to the House of Lords; wherein they required an equality in the State, that thereby there might be one in the Church. An action which will leave for ever to posterity, an infamous and true character of the intentions of the Covenanters: But in this they have but followed the Doctrine of their Sect. *Cartwright* had taught them before, as the Tapestries or Hangings are fitted to the House, so the Commonwealth ought to be fitted and accommodated to the Church, and the Government of the State to the Ecclesiastical Government. This design is wholly void of all prudence and possibility, and being ruinous to the State, must of necessity be the ruine of it self. Reply to *whitgift*, page 181.

It's certain that the Doctrine of Religion must not be accommodated to the State, but that which is humane in the discipline, ought to be subject to humane Laws, and the authority of the Magistrate, since God demands it of us, *Submit your selves to every Ordinance of man for the Lords sake*: But these men make no difference between the Doctrine and the Discipline, and would perswade us, that they have a whole Body of Discipline altogether Divine, and which is even the substance of the Gospel, without which there is no true Religion, but it is that we cannot find in the Gospel, but in stead of that, they prove it by the Sword. *Cartwright*, 247.

CHAP.

CHAP. XVIII.

How the Discipline of the Covenanters is far from the practice of other Churches.

THere is another point which the Covenanters ought to prove, before they associate themselves with the Churches of *France* in matter of Discipline.

They must prove that they have an Ecclesiastical discipline like unto theirs; For all Churches which had no Bishops, have not for all that the same discipline. As for the discipline of the Covenanters, they need make none by theirs, nor receive any from them, for they have none at all, and they take the way never to have any. If the menaces of the *Scotch* Army, cause them to make an Ordinance in favour of the Presbytery, they make presently an honourable reparation to the Independents; And much of their prudence lies in this, to accord all to the different Parties, but give them nothing; in making use of the service of the divers Sects of Religion, they take no care of their Order, but of their Liberty to convert all; which will one day turn to their ruine, and confusion, when they shall have no enemy to unite them. But in the mean while Religion is destroyed, and all the world behold with astonishment that the *English* Reformers have left the Church without any discipline, now these many years; they have done much worse then he who began to build, but was not able to finish, for these have overthrown the antient order, without ever considering what they would build in the place; and yet they are not agreed thereupon, they made a great noise of the building they would erect; but this noise proceeded from their contestation, and their building advanced like that

that of *Babel*, that which the one builded, the other pull'd down, and in the end the division of tongues will make them forsake their work.

It's an easie thing to ruine, 'tis a work of ignorance and insolence; 'tis the pastime of the devil, and the occupation of his children: *Destruction and unhappiness is in their wayes, and the way of peace they have not known*, Rom. 3. 16. And ordinarily those that burn down the house, know not what it is to build it up, and those who build up a Church or State, proceed by wayes and rules quite contrary to those that ruine them, the sharp and rigorous proceeding of our enemies wholly to raze the established order, witness they want knowledge to build an order in the Church; for to this purpose there is not only required to conceive an Idea of Reformation, but to consider the matter they have in hand, and how to frame it; For as he is not the best Engenier who knows best how to make a Regular platform upon paper, but he that can best accommodate his rules to the nature of the place which he fortifies; and it would be a strange method to pull down and lay level the place for to build it again regularly. But its that wherein our new Reformers have laboured; Certainly they neither understand the Theory, nor the Practick of the work they undertake, and their knowledge goes no further then destruction: It's true, many of the Assembly desired the *Scotch* Discipline, and to establish it, courted the *Scotch* Armies.

We also respect these Armies, hoping that God will one day touch their hearts to defend the rights and person of their Soveraign, and we pray God for their prosperity: But let them give us leave to tell them mildly our advice of their Discipline, the wisest amongst us commend the subordination, and concatenation of their Synods, and do confess that that was
want-

wanting in the *English* Order, judging that the Synodal Power is not incompatible with the Episcopal; but in an order well made, both the one, and the other is requisite, and it is impossible that the *English* Bishops, excellent in knowledge and piety, who have lived within these ninety yeares, should not know this very well, above all those who were imploid in the Reformation.

But behold that which hath hindred the ordinary use of Synods amongst us, incontinent after the Reformation, it had been to ill purpose to have given all the Clergy liberty to assemble in a Synod, Papistry being not then well rooted out of the Priests and Curates, and before the *English* Church was well healed of this old malady she fell into a new one, and was infected with a fanatick and malignant Sect, who made piety consist in overthrowing all order and superiority in the Church, and to controle that of the Magistrate, whereupon our Soveraigns and their Prelates beholding the body of the Church swollen with evil humours, and mutinous superstition, continually ready to break forth, feared least the frequent use of Synods, should not be made use of by the discontented, to gather and associate a faction; and therefore accounted the surest way to maintain peace and truth, was to keep these violent spirits in their duty by the Episcopal rod, assisted with the Royal Scepter, and certainly this way would have had better success, if they had not let the bridle too loose for such hard mouths.

The Synod is proper to make Ordinances, and the Bishop is proper to cause them to be observed: The Synod to hinder tyranny, the Bishop to prevent confusion; the Synod to determine in point of Doctrine, the Bishop to maintain order and discipline; the Synod to remedy inveterate evils, the Bishop to suppress immergent evils; and in the mean while, both the one

and

and the other serve to all these uses, and ought not to be separated in a Church where there is freedom, and where the estate upholds the Religion.

But in a Church which lives under a state of a contrary Religion, order must bend to necessity; and as it is not possible to have all the parts of Ecclesiastical Government, also there is less need, for common adversity unite affections, and take away many occasions of scandal and disorder. *Bodin. Method. Histor. de Repub. Geneva.*

Such are the Reformed Churches of *France*, where the order is sutable to their condition; and the native piety and simplicity of their Discipline is commended even by those of a diverse Profession.

Now having had leisure to examine their Discipline, we find not that it doth much resemble the *Scotch* discipline; for the Consistories and Synods of *France* have not Ruling Elders, whose voices alwaies carry it, as they do in *Scotland*. Their Elders pass not any sentence in matter of Doctrine, neither have they the power of the Keys to determine Censures: All that *Calvin* granted them, was but *præesse moribus*, to have an eye to the manners and behaviour of the flock in which they served as Assistants to the Pastors, and this was a commendable use. But in *Scotland* the Elders command, for the Lord of the Parish is ordinarily the ruling Elder of the Consistory, and in some manner is a Lay Bishop, and although the Minister is alwaies Moderator, its but for form, for the Elders have the principal power, and being Deputies to the Assemblies, they keep there the same credit, above all in the General Assembly, where Dukes, Marquesses, Earles and Barons have their voices, and decide the points of controversies and the censures of the Church.

We greatly respect the power of Synods, but we require that it be purely Ecclesiastical, and that it be managed

naged by none, but by those who are appointed of God; lay persons have not to do, but to assist them, except the King, who ought to have the exterior power (which the *Sco.ch* deny him) to convocate and dissolve their Assemblies, to suppress disorders, without medling himself with the interiour or spiritual, for it seems to us a thing unreasonable and contradictory to it self, that the other Laiques should be admitted to the full capacity of the spiritual power equal or above the Ministers, and that the King only should be excluded, and hath not so much as the exercise of his temporal and purely Royal power in the Assembly.

We could wish also that the power of their Consistories and Synods were a little more limited, for these Assemblies being Courts of Conscience, which takes cognisance of all the offences of the Church, they may enclose in their Jurisdiction, all criminal and civil causes of the Kingdom, there being no cause which hath not in it a point of Conscience: And so hereby it may come, that the sentences of Judges may be controuled in the Consistory, and the Officers of the Crown questioned about their managing of publick affairs, and so the Government of the State become purely arbitrary.

And the power of the Ecclesiastical Councel being such, the most unquiet and ambitious will be ever pressing to be of it, whereupon sidings and factions will abound, revenge and particular interest will turn the ballance; There they will form factions in the State, and parties against the King, for what is there that they dare not enterprise who have so vast a power, which have no other limits than the extent of the flitting and moveable conscience of particulars, which give account to none, who pretend to have their authority only of Divine right, and therefore are not subject to be controuled? These are not conjectures nor suppositions,

but

but observations of long experience; certainly that personal citation which was sent by the National Synod of *Scotland* to their King, when he was in the midst of his Armies in *England*, *Feb.* 1645. filled Forreign Churches with amazement and scandal: And no less is the Authority they exercise even over their Parliaments, which having demanded advice of the Synod, concerning what they were to do with their King, the Ministers concluded that they should not bring the King into *Scotland*, and that the Kingdom of *Scotland* ought not to espouse his quarrel, for to maintain his Rites in *England*, and their advice passed for an Ordinance; after this they cannot reprove the Bishops for being Councellours of State.

Monarchy which can endure neither Master, nor Companion, can hardly comply with this Court of Conscience, which gives Laws, but receives none, unless themselves make them, and limit the King, but refuse to be limited by him; but the Magistrates of an Aristocratick, or popular Common-wealth will shift better with them, for this Court pretending an Ecclesiastical Jurisdiction, purely Soveraign and Divine, yet nevertheless admit lay men to the participation of this power; The Lords never fail to be Members of this consistory, and to govern there. And thus the question touching the Ecclesiastical authority is Eluded.

Now although above all we desire to enjoy an Apostolical and Episcopal Discipline, where the Bishop, assisted with the Councel of his Clergy governs the Church, and admits other Pastors according to their degree and quality, to the participation of the power of the Keies, yet nevertheless if the revolution of the State brings in another Discipline, our Ministers submit themselves to it, not to be Actors there, remembring themselves of their duties and promise made at their reception

reception of Orders, but to suffer themselves to be governed, remembring that they are call'd to preach the Gospel, and whether there be a good or an evil Order in the Church, or even none at all, the vocation binds them to feed the Flock and to maintain the holy Doctrine.

But indeed its great pity to be reduced to expect a Discipline of those that have none, and yet make the Kingdom of Christ to consist in it, for which they made such clamours, in their licentiousness, and overthrow of all Order and lawful Vocation in the Church.

The Reformed Churches of *France* who employ all their Zeal and Industry to maintain the purity of the Gospel, without contending with any about the outward Discipline, look upon with contempt and compassion the impetuous weakness of our enemies, who overthrow the holy Doctrine, and ruine Church and State for points of Discipline, which is to lose the end for the accessaries, yea although these accessaries are not good in this regard, there being but two things to reprove in the Covenanters, their end, and the means which they employ to attain that end.

CHAP.

CHAP. XIX.

That the Covenanters ruine the Ministers of the Gospel under colour of Reformation.

ONE of the points of Reformation for which they laboured so much with Cannon shot, was to abase and pull down the Clergy, which is a work already done without proceeding further.

As for their greatness, the only thing wherein it consisted was taken from them in the year 1645. Which was the Bishops sitting and having power to vote in the Lords House, the rest is a smal thing.

As for their Revenues, they are confiscated and sequestred, and even the Revenues of the Bishops were such as might cause rather pitty then envy, except four or five Bishopricks; the rest were so poor, that for to help them to uphold their Degree, and pay their dues to the King, Tenths and first Fruits, his Majesty ever out of compassion, gave them some other Benefices, otherwise very few would have hazzarded the taking of them, the Bishopricks of *England* being like the ruined Monasteries in some Countries, which have nothing remaining but the wals, with nothing in them.

The children of those parents who had formerly fitted themselves by the Bishopricks, have now swallowed the rest, and yet labour to begger the inferior Clergy: This is that they call Reformation, and in truth 'tis the Reformation of *Scotland*, where the Tenths of the Clergy are possessed by the Ruling Elders, above all by the Lords, some of them having the Tenths of whole Provinces. Therefore ye need not wonder they fight with such Zeal for a Reformation which is so profitable.

In *England* ordinarily the great Towns and rich Parishes are impropriated, and in the hands of Lay persons, the rest of the Benefices have but to provide in a Mediocrity for Students in Divinity: Those who Reform the Clergy, are those who possess the Goods of the Church; and besides the Tithes that are alienated, many of them even make use of the Tithes of the Clergy, with which they are lawfully invested, terrifying their poor Ministers with Sequestration, too weak to contend against them, and force them to injurious and damageable contracts. How many Patrons are there who sell their Benefices to them who will give most? And by the infamous Simony of these Gentlemen, who make a noise of Reformation, the door of the Church is shut to the Clergy, unless they have a golden key to open it; and thus they prefer profit before conscience: 'Tis well done of them to mend that which they have marred, and they of all other have reason to take in hand the Reformation of Ministers, because themselves have done what possibly they can to corrupt them.

Of all Liberal Professions, Divinity is the poorest, and have most Thorns in her way; and therefore Parents find it more profitable to put their children to a Trade, than bring them up in the Study of Divinity; and yet after all this, their very poverty seems superfluity in the eyes of envy; and untill these hungry Harpies have caught that little which hath escaped the claws of Sacriledge, they will never leave calling for the Reformation of the Clergy, that is to say, wholly to ruine them.

The devil who hates the Gospel, labours to ruine it by the poverty of those who preach it, knowing well that the indigence of Ministers brings contempt upon the Ministry; And that the Rewards being taken away, the Study of Divinity will be neglected, and then there will be none but the meanest of the people, like
to

to the Priests of *Jeroboam*. Poverty abates the courage, and clips the wings of conception, and oft-times occasions evil designs and Councels in those whose means are too small for their Degree. To do well in Pulpit, and by Writing to build up indeed the Kingdom of Jesus Christ, and to destroy the works of the devil, they ought to have their spirits free, and not oppressed through necessity, *Magna mentis opus, nec de Lodice paranda Attonita*; They that require, and would a man should do well, and yet will not do well to him, 'tis an unjust demand; and many now in *England* pass the unjustice of *Pharaoh*, requiring double the number of Bricks, and yet give to them less straw.

If they alledge to us that Jesus Christ and his Apostles were poor, we answer, that so were their auditors; and the condition of our Lord and his Disciples is a pattern as well for Layicks as the Clergy. And if the Primitive Church of *Hierusalem* spoken of in the *Acts*, ought to be proposed for an example of the Ecclesiastical and Civil Government of all Christendom, the Clergy of *England* humbly beseech the Gentlemen, our Reformers, to imitate these pious souls, who sold their possessions, and brought the price, and laid them down at the Apostles feet. Let them sell their Lands, and bring the mony to their Pastors to dispose of according to their discretion, and the Ministers will part with their Tithes.

If we were now to speak to the Clergy of *England*, we would exhort them to love their Office and their Benefice, and now that God hath called them to the Cross and poverty, to rejoyce in their conformity to Jesus Christ, who made himself poor to enrich us, expecting their reward in Heaven, bearing patiently the spoyling of their goods, accounting themselves rich enough if God be glorified, and his Gospel purely Preached, but these Exhortations have an evil grace in the mouth of them who come to plunder or Sequester them, which is as if a thief in robbing a traveller, should preach a Sermon to him of Christian patience and contempt of the world; 'tis the method of our enemies, who driving their Ministers from their houses and Revenues, read such Lectures of Divinity to them.

For the present, some Ministers who have been the principall instruments of their party, have means and honour, and yet little enough, considering the great service they have done them. *Peters* their great and active agent, had for a recompence given him, but with great glory and ostentation, two hundred pound *per Annum* in Land: But who so considers well the *genius* of the Faction will judge that, that little good they do now to their Ministers, will not long continue. It were a pleasant thing to consider, if there were not greater cause of sorrow in it, how of two Ambitions, the simple serves the Ambition of the crafty; for the Ministers who animated the people against their King, are people impatient of subjection, who would be every one of them Kings and Bishops in their Parishes, and during these agitations, they reign in the Pulpit a time, but they are set a work by those who manage the publique affairs, who raise them up and flatter them to the people, untill they have done their work with them, for when these Gentlemen shal have done to destroy Church and State, and built their Imaginary Throne of Jesus Christ, upon the ruines of the Kingdom, they will have so strict a hand of the Discipline, that the power and the profit shall remain with them, allowing their spiritual Fathers a portion purely spiritual, and will discharge them of those cares which accompany the riches and honours of the world.

Before these Civil Warres, the Bishops were profitable to all Ministers, friends and enemies, for those who submitted themselves freely to them enjoyed
their

their protection, and those who opposed them were respected and secretly maintained by the adversaries of the Episcopal Order, but now the Bishops are cut off, there is neither protection nor opposition, that can gain respect or support to the Clergy. The stubborn and refractory Ministers have struck so violently at the root of that great tree which they have now made to fall, after they had been a long time cover'd under the shadow of it, but they may assure themselves that it will not be long before they themselves be crushed under the fall of it, and draw upon themselves a just punishment: They will then consider too late, that they have been but Instruments to the covetousness and ambition of others, and in the dissipation of the Goods of the Church, they shall be dealt with as the Captain of *Samaria*, to whom the King of *Israel* committed the keeping of the Gate, where the Provision was to enter, then when the people after a long Famine pressed to enter, they shall behold the plenty, but not taste of it; but be trodden under foot.

CHAP. XX.

Of the Corruptions of Religion objected to the English Clergy, and the ways that the Covenanters took to Remedy them.

WEE will answer to the Objections against the King and his Party, and will begin with the most ordinary.

Now they reproach us with corruption in Religion; in such an accusation we must have regard to them

that

that speak it; its those who turn the rising up of the people against their King, into a Doctrine and Article of Faith; its those that have absented themselves from the Lords Supper for these many years, those who summoned their King before them to give account of his actions, those who have committed against his Sacred Person an execrable Paracide, those who will employ the Body and Blood of our Lord to knit up a conspiracy against their King. Those who neither teach the people in the Church, nor their children at home, the ten Commandments, the Creed, nor the Lords Prayer, those who suffer and make use of all damnable Sects, and punish none; but those who teach to suffer for righteousness, and not to resist the Supream Powers, to all these we might add many more hateful Truths; but we will not without necessity publish the evil that may be hid, for we love not to teach evil by representing it: Whosoever shall consider their belief and practice, will never wonder that such kind of People find something to say against our Religion. God be praised that thus opposing us, they make all the world to know that we are not guilty of their evil opinions; amongst men, blame and praise take their force from him that gives them. Those who accuse us of corruption in Religion, should do well to tell us first, amongst the scores of Religions that are, what their Religion is; for there are many Religions which are together with the Covenanters, and live together, as so many wilde beasts in the Ark, who when they are gone out thence, will devour one another, or flee one from another, but at present they all agree to tear us a pieces.

Now to these accusers of Corruption, we present the thirty nine Articles of our Confession, which they and we have sworn and subscribed, and let their Consciences judge between them and us, which of the two Parties have violated and falsified their Oath. How have

have they obſerved the thirty ſixt Article, in which they acknowledged that the conſecration of Arch-Biſhops and Biſhops uſed in *England*, and confirmed by Act of Parliament, contains nothing in it, that is either Superſtitious or Impious; and yet now thunder out againſt this Order as a mark and branch of Antichriſt; Is this to want memory, or conſcience? Can they upbraid us with any thing like unto this, to have oppoſed in a Body, and condemned an Article of our Confeſſion. The corruptions which they alledge againſt us, are falſely ſo named, or at the worſt they are but faults of particulars. But the Body of the Church hath kept and doth keep the Confeſſion of their Faith inviolable. If they produce any we would have brought in any new Doctrines or Cuſtomes, who can produce others that have oppoſed them, and that the Religion ſubſiſted entire, whilſt they ſubſiſted.

Let them not rob thoſe Divines of their due praiſe who in the beginning of the Parliament laboured ſincerely to confirm the Doctrine, and to ſtifle the difference about Diſcipline. We have before repreſented with what Wiſdom, Piety, and Vigor, many Biſhops and Divines choſen by his Majeſty, had lead the two Parties to accord upon a certain number of Propoſitions, which contained the Body of Religion, and what great hope there was, that the point of Diſcipline would be amiably compoſed; and how a Faction, enemies to the peace of the Church, and jealous leaſt any good ſhould come by the means of the Biſhops, broke off that excellent accord, which could never ſince be renewed; perſecuting the Prelates with all rigor, never giving them reſt, until they had impriſoned them as Criminals, although they were not guilty of any other crime, then becauſe they would have terminated the differences of Religion. But this was to ſtifle the Covenant in the cradle, and take away all pretext from this

holy

holy Rebellion. It's not then a wonder if this sin be not pardoned them; it appears by the testimony of the Reverend Pastors of the Church of *Geneva*, in what esteem our Religion was amongst our Neighbours, for in their Epistle to the Assembly at *London*, *They beseech God that he would restore our Church and Kingdome to such a high degree of holineß and glory, as it had shined in until that present*: By this they acquit us of the corruption, which they impute to us, and do obliquely accuse this Assembly, and those that imploy them, that by their means the Kingdom hath lost his glory, and the Church her holiness.

Now put the case that the Corruption were as great amongst us, as they make it, yea put the case also, that even in our Liturgie, composed with so much piety and wisdome, that there were something to mend, as a Freckle in a fair Face, and that the Discipline ought to be over-looked; what could there be more expected of the King and the Clergy, then to submit the Persons and things to be Reformed? How often had the King offered to joyn his Authority to the Advice of Parliament, and a National Synod, to examine and punish the faulty, and correct disorders, yea and even the Laws themselves, if there were need?

To these so reasonable commands, behold here what obedience they yielded: A part of the House of Commons, having driven away the other by violence and popular tumults, and put to flight nine parts of ten of the House of Lords, besides the Bishops who represented the Body of the Clergy; this small rest, in lieu of a National Synod, by lawful deputation of the Church, chose some Ministers of their Faction, for to make use of their Advice so far as it should please them. These Ministers who had no Deputation, nor Representation, nor Authority from

the

the Body of the English Church, and having divers Lay persons joyned with them, who wholly govern them, mould a Religion all new, defame the reputation of the Church and Confession, to which they had sworn Obedience; invite to their aid Forreign Churches, as their brethren, and ordain that which serves the intention of their Masters.

We know that amongst these Divines, there were some men of Merit, Persons which we know, had it been in their power, would have overcome evill with good; but amongst pieces of gold, there is many times a great deal of small money, like unto our clipped half Testors; they are the little heads without learning.

If the two Houses had assembled the body of the Clergy, as was proposed to them by his Majesty, they had found themselves filled with Orthodox Persons, and they cannot complain if those persons whom they had most desire to, received not the publike censure of the Clergy, since they would not permit the Clergy to assemble themselves; neither can they complain, that any guilty hath gone unpunished, for they have taken a sure course, for by the universal ruine of the Deans and Chapiters, they have involved the innocent with the guilty.

Hearken what the King said hereupon: *I was content to accord and render to the Presbyter (that is to say, to the Body of Pastors) all the right which with reason and discretion they could pretend in their conjunction with the Episcopal degree, but to suffer them wholly to invade the Ecclesiastical Power, and to cut off altogether with the sword, the Authority of this ancient Order, for to invest themselves in it, it was that which I accounted neither just, in regard of the Bishops, nor sure nor profitable in regard of the Presbyter himself, neither any way convenient for the Church or State.*

A right and good Reformation might have been easily produced by moderate Councils, and I am perswaded such Councils

Councils would have given more contentment, even to those very Divines, who have been perswaded, with much gravity and formality, to serve the designs of others, which without doubt, many of them now acknowledge, although they dare not make their discontent appear for finding themselves frustrated of their intentions.

I am very well assured, that the true method to reform the Church, cannot subsist with the perturbation of the Civil State, and that Religion cannot justly be advanced in depressing Loyalty; which is one of the principal ingredients and ornaments of true Religion; for after the Precept to fear God, the next following is, to honour the King.

I make no doubt but the Kingdome of Christ may be established, without pulling down mine; and in a time free from partialities, its impossible any should pass for a good Christian, who shews not himself a good Subject.

The Government of Christ serves to confirm mine, and not to overthrow it, for as I acknowledge, I hold my power of him, so I desire to exercise it for his glory, and the good of his Church.

If any one had sincerely proposed the Government of Christ, or understood in their heart what it required, they would never have been so ill governed in their words and actions, as well towards me, as one towards another.

As the good ends cannot justifie the evil wayes, so also the evil beginnings cannot produce good conclusions, unless God by a miracle of mercy make Light to spring out of Darkness, Order out of our Confusion, and Peace from our unruly Passions. This is spoken as a King, as a Phylosopher and as a good Christian.

Our enemies to blind the eyes of their Neighbours, made them believe a long time that they desired such a reformation as theirs, but the hypocrisie of this profession appeared then, when the King offered to assemble a National Synod, and to invite the Neighbour Churches

ches to it, whom these people would seem to imitate. And this the good King would never have named, had he not an intention to defer much to their Judgement. But of this his Majesty could never obtain an answer; for it was that which the Independents feared above all, and we see not that the Presbyterians did any way favour this proposition; the actions both of the one and the other were such, that it was the surest course for them to palliate them with Declarations sent a far off, rather then to have them brought to light here at home in a Synod; and they were very well content to receive their Neighbours to their Society, but not to admit them to their Counsel. They have hereby made it appear, that it was not reformation, but the revenues of the Church they pursued; otherwise they would have imbraced the proposition of his Majesty, and the request of the Clergy, who desired nothing more then to be heard in a lawful Synod, and to reform willingly, that which was displeasing to some. But this had untwisted the designs of their enemies, who then should have had no pretext to ruine the Clergy, and enrich themselves with their spoils, and take from Monarchy the support of the Church, if the Ecclesiasticks had been reformed.

Then let the rage and invective malice of our enemies greaten our faults in quality and number, as much as they can, let them make small spots, imposthumes; Let them paint us out in false colours, and disfigure us like devils to the eyes of all the world; All that the severest Justice can require of us, is to amend and freely to submit our selves to the censure of a lawful Assembly; and then when a great King, who is subject to none but God, shall come to them, and offer to change that which hath been practised or tolerated, and to lend his ear to receive better information. O this was a grace capable to molifie hearts of stone, and to turn the
com-

complaints of his subjects into acclamations of joy and praises.

But they will neither the grace of the King, nor our amendment. To these offers of the King so sincere and frequent, they answered not but by complaints and blowes, and they consulted not of means to correct us, but to destroy us; they will not take the pains to cleanse the Church, they will cut it up by the root, root and branch. 'Tis the Watch-word of the seditious, whereby they pretend to know those that are of the godly party; and they have also put an unnatural maxime in the mouth of the furious and blind people, that the reformation must be made in blood. This they call to renew, or revive the Church; but it's as the Daughters of *Pelias* undertook to make their Father young again, who to that end cut his throat to let his old blood pass out of his body, but after, it was not in their power to put in new. God keep us from them who come to reform the Church their Mother with a Sword, and that would cut our throats to make us young again. Certainly beholding Chyrurgeons coming to let us blood with a Sword in both hands, we have reason to withdraw into some safe quarter, and to fear a healing which will not take away the evil, but in taking away our life.

We dare say for our Clergy, that if it should cost them their lives to redeem the peace of their King and State, they would account them well imployed, and willingly consent to be cast over-board with *Jonas*, that their loss might appease the tempest.

This is of greatest anguish and affliction, to see Murther pass for Piety, then to suffer in their persons, and they cheerfully wish, that a potion of their blood could quench the heat of their bloody zeal.

This zeal appeared in the title of *Sions Plea*, and in the book called, *Christ on his Throne*. The first pleads

for

for the Presbyterian, the other for the Independent. Both of these books have this Text in the Frontispice: *Bring those mine enemies, that would not that I should raign over them, and slay them before me.* By enemies they understand those who will not imbrace their Discipline. And their actions now have, and do make a bloudy commentary upon the Text. That if our Lord Jesus Christ, who poured forth his most precious bloud to spare ours, put not a stop to this flux of bloud, these Zealots will reform *England*, as the Anabaptists reformed *Munster*, and as the *Spaniards* converted the *West-Indies*.

Let all Christian Churches of the World then know, that the English Church confesseth humbly before God, her infirmities, and acknowledgeth her self the defaults which peace and the length of time is wont to bring to the best established order, and hath done her duty to reform, submitting her self to a general Synod, and the States of the Kingdome under the Authority and conduct of her good King, and that a sacrilegious and murthering faction, drunken with the bloud of their Soveraign, and the goods of the Church: Having oppressed the liberty of the Assembly of States, snatched this holy work out of her hands, and would hear of no other reformation, but her total destruction; introducing in the place of ancient and lawful order, a Chaos of prophane and licentious Heresies, destructive to Religion and State.

CHAP.

CHAP. XXI.

An Answer to the Objection, That the King made War against the Parliament.

IT'S the ordinary complaint of the Covenanters, that the King made War against his Parliament, a phrase which seems tacitly to imply, that the King rebelled against his Superiours; and indeed there are many that understood it so in good earnest, conceiving the Parliament to be above the King. And hereupon it was declared by the House of Commons at *Westminster*, That the Kings coming to their House was Treason, as if the Majesty resided in the Commons, but how ridiculous and false this is, hath heretofore been shewed: and yet they could in no other sense call the Houses at *Westminster*, his Parliament, since they had taken up Arms against his Majesty; doubtless those of both Houses, who adhered to the King at *Oxford*, without comparison the more considerable in quality, were rather his Parliament, for these were for him, and the other against him.

Moreover by this frequent expression, they would frequently signifie, that the King was the Aggressour, and he that first assaulted them; a thing which they have much laboured to perswade the world, although it be notoriously known that his enemies had seized upon his Forts, Towns, Magaziens, Ships, Revenues, and Levied Souldiers, before ever the King had so much as one single company of Horse, or Foot. When he first came to *York*, he had not so much as his ordinary guards, whereas his enemies had all the strength of the Kingdom, they wanted only God on their side: and this great
power

power encouraged the seditious in all countries where he passed to entertain him with the same courtesie the *Gergasites* received Christ Jesus, beseeching him to depart out of their quarters, and the good King had then this conformity with his Saviour, that he had not where to lay his head. He was then in a condition to suffer, but his enemies in a posture to oppose.

When he would in a peaceable manner without Arms enter into his Town of *Hull*, he found the gates shut, and the walls garnished with Souldiers, presenting their Muskets against him; upon this his Majesty levied six companies of Foot, and two Cornets of Horse, for the Guard of his Person, but set not up his Standard until four moneths after this prodigious act of hostility and rebellion, having often before endeavoured to reduce his Subjects to their obedience by all reasonable and Christian offers, witness a number of most excellent Declarations composed and written by himself, wherein the world beheld the sincerity of his actions, with the piety and candor of his spirit, worthy so great a Prince.

The Covenanters considering that they could not persuade them who had any remembrance of common sense, that the King began the War, laboured to prove that although they began, yet their Armies were but defensive; affirming, that a War undertaken, upon a just fear, was defensive, yea although they struck the first blow; and that they seized upon the Forts, Magaziens, and Revenues of the King, because they feared he would make War upon them; That is to say, that they made War upon him, least he should make War upon them. A reason much like that of Count *Gondomore*, Ambassador of *Spain* in *England*, who by his cunning and subtilty had wrought so far, as to have a gallant *English* Knight to be condemned and put to death; being demanded what evil he had done

M that

that he so persecuted him: Answered, That it was not for any evil he had done, but for that evil which he might do.

But the Court that did it, had just reasons, far from the *Spanish* interests; but in these mens dealings with the King, were he even a Subject, the injustice is both without reason, and without example. For, was there ever any Court of Justice, which condemned a man to lose both his goods, and his life, not because he had done any evil, but for fear he should.

That which would be most unjust against the meanest Subject, can it possibly be thought, and reputed a work of Piety and Justice against their lawful Soveraign? But leaving these persons, who from the beginning had this Diabolical design, which since they have inhumanely executed; we will believe of many of the Covenanters, that the intent of their Army was not to punish the King for the pretended exorbitancies of his past Government, although they laboured by all means to perpetuate the memory, and to stifle those eminent and signal acts of grace, by which the King had merited the love of his people beyond all his Predecessors. We are willing also to believe that some amongst them condemn the Doctrine of *Goodman*, turned since into sad practice, *That Judges ought to summon Princes before them for their offences, and proceed against them, as against other Criminals and Malefactors.*

If it were not then for the punishing of what was passed, it was for fear of the future, they took up Arms, which indeed is the only reason left them. For after the King had promised to give content to his people, in all their reasonable requests represented to him, and they had taken the power out of his hands, then when he would have accomplished his promises; all the reason they give for so violent a proceeding is, *That they durst not trust the King*; Which verily is a most frivolous

volous and injurious excuse. Which is as if one had a Neighbour that dwelt by him, more mighty then himself, and whose displeasure he feared, it should be permitted him to watch his opportunity to surprize his house, seize upon his revenues, and drive from his possessions, to free and deliver him from fear? But such an action as this from Subjects towards their Prince, is beyond all comparison more unjust. The Question between the King and his Subjects, being not, Whether they may with confidence leave the Sword in the Kings hand? but whether God hath committed the Sword to the King to be born by him?

Now in this their dealings with the King, they give him an evil example, for by the same reason he may take from his subjects the propriety, they have in their estates, because he dares not trust them, and finds by sad experience, they use it for his destruction; And he should have much more reason to do it, since the Subjects hold their Lands of the King; but the King holds not his power of the people; Prudence ought not to seize upon Justice. The care of a mans self cannot give him a right to the goods of another: The duty of a Christian is not to fortifie himself against his fears, but to obey the Commandments of God: But if his fear and forecast carries him beyond his duty, he should above *all fear him that can cast both body and soul into hell. Yea, I say unto you, fear him,* Luke 12. 5. Taking then that which themselves accord, that the Subjects took up Arms to secure themselves against their fears; Had not the King as much reason to take up Arms after their example to provide against his? If he had been their equal, this reason had been sufficient enough, how much more then being their Soveraign, for the sword that they had drawn against him, was his own; those Forts, Towns, Ships, Arms and Revenues, which they imployed against him, were his;

M 2   there-

therefore he had a double reason to take up Arms, one to defend himself, and another to recover his own rights.

By all Laws Divine and Humane, the King alone hath the power of the Sword, whosoever strikes without him is a murtherer. Saint *Bernard* preaching to the Knights Templers of *Hierusalem*; to perswade them from Duells, saith that two things are required to make a combat just and lawful; The defence of a just cause, and obedience to a lawful power. The last of these is the principal, and that alone which gives to Souldiers a just call, for in wars ordinarily the interests of Princes are only known to themselves, and often the right and wrong being of two sides, we esteem it not necessary that every Souldier be perfectly satisfied of the Justice of the Armies of his Soveraign; but as for obedience to a lawful power, its a condition absolutely requisite to justifie the taking up of Arms of a Souldier, and there is no exception, nor modification, that can be brought against it.

Sermon 1. of Duells, to the Templers.

Saint *Augustine* saith, *That a just man bearing Armes under a sacrilegious Prince, may justly obey his commands, if he knowes not the war wherein he serves, is against the Commandment of God, or if he be doubtful of it;* So that the Prince may be faulty in commanding, and the Subject innocent in rendring the duty of his obedience: According to this wise Councel, if it be not palpably manifest that the commandment of the Prince do transgress the Laws of God, whom we must ever obey rather then men, the subject in matter of war, be it forraign or civil, hath but one thing to consider for conscience; namely, where the lawful power

August. lib. 21. Contra Faustum cap. 75.

power is ? Who he is to whom God hath committed the sword, and who hath power to give it to others, and to whom God hath subjected him ? in taking up the sword at his command, we cannot do amiss.

This gives full satisfaction to their consciences who took up Arms and fought for the King, for besides the goodness of his defence which is just and necessary, if ever any were, they learn that it is possibly to fight justly for him, even when his cause may be unjust; but without him it is impossible to draw the sword justly, much less against him, how just soever the complaints and fears of the contrary party that draws the sword be. All lawful demands, religious intentions, specious pretexts, pretended necessities, the publick good (the Masque of all Rebellions) prayers, fastings, Covenanting with God, all this and much more can never make a war just, which receives the sword from him to whom God hath not given it, and draws it against him to whom God hath committed it.

Therefore the principal of the Covenanters well perceiving this, endeavoured from the beginning to make the King either give them, or lend them the power of the Militia. In doing whereof, they did much wrong to their cause, for if they had the lawful power of the sword, why did they then so often demand it of the King? And if they had it not, why did they draw the sword without the lawful power, and against him to whom the power appertained by their own confession? Why else should they ask it of him? They either did injustice to the King to take from him the Militia, or else they did injustice to themselves to demand it: Certainly by their importunity for the Militia, they manifestly condemned themselves, and acknowledged that the Militia belonged to the King, and that they made the war without his authority, and therefore they had great need of many Sermons, fastings, prayers, protestations, Oaths upon Oaths, to bind in many knots this Covenant, which otherwise held by nothing; and to perswade the people, that in stead of the Lawful and Ordinary Power, they had an Extraordinary one, which was conducted by Revelation.

Rebellion is against nature, *Samuel* saith, *Its as the sin of Witchcraft* or Divination, *1 Sam.* 15.23. It is composed of such charms which for a time corrupts the use of reason, but cannot destroy the faculty, but at last the cloud will vanish and they shall retain nought, but the impression of shame and astonishment for their past errors, and an earnest desire of an acknowledgment. This natural notion is imprinted in the hearts of Subjects, *That they ought to obey the King, and that to him pertaines the Power of Peace and War.* The very Name of King will make even Souldiers spring from the ground to serve him, the Plow-shares shall furnish him with Swords, and the Flayls and long Staffes shall fight for his Crown. The Arms which they have ravisht from him, shall acknowledge their Master, and return of themselves to him, as those which were unjustly taken from *Ajax*. It's a very hard thing to fight against nature: This appeared in the Counties of the Covenanters, wherein whilst the King was Master, he raised Ten Thousand men in Eight Daies, but after the Covenanters commanded in them, although they levied Souldiers continually, their Forces ever decreased, and those they listed in the day, disbanded and run away in the night. That if the secret judgment of God which would chastise us, had not rendred the people fearful and dismayed for a time, such was their number and hatred against the Party of the Covenanters, that they had easily dispatched the Countries against the King, though themselves were disarmed: And it must be in the end that Nature surmounts the

constraint

constraint, for the King is the center of the State, whither all parts tend by their own proper weight, and wherein all the lines of the common interests terminate.

Their complaints of violence by the Kings Forces, are of no consideration; the Armies of the King as well as those of the Covenanters were not composed all of Saints, but these complaints sound ill in their mouths, who lifted up their hands against their Soveraign, those who had so often planted their Artilery against the Squadron where the person of the King was, and had shot fifty Cannon shot against the Queen in her bed, and after all this, cut off the Head of their lawful Soveraign, can they assume the impudence to complain of our Souldiers taking away their poultry and killing their sheep? If those who were in actual Rebellion against their King, had been punished by our Souldiers as they deserved, they would never have had the power to complain that their houses were plundered, or that they spoyled and destroyed their Goods: We dare maintain, that those amongst the Covenanters that suffered less than death, have suffered less than they deserved; we do not desire that every one should be punished according to his deserts, for we would not that God should so deal with us, but that our enemies may know, both by the divine Law, and the Law of Nations, every person that rebels against his Prince, is guilty of death, *Josh.*1.18. and loseth his propriety in his Goods and Possessions. Let them know also, that being destitute of lawful Authority for the war, and drawing their swords against him that bears the sword by Divine Authority, every stroak they struck against the faithful Subjects of the King, they committed an execrable Murther, 1 *Sam.* 11.12. And every Penny they levied upon them, they committed Rapine, employing their Robberies to maintain Murther and Rebellion: If the Names of these

these crimes offend their ears, the crimes themselves should much more afflict their Consciences; these terms proceed not from passion, but flow from the necessary consequence of this Truth, *That the war of the Covenanters is destitute of all Authority, lawful and divine.* Oh that every Christian who hath drawn his sword in this sinful cause, would seriously consider how he should answer it before God and man, and that he may have horrour and dread in him for the evil he hath deserved, and yet much more for that which he hath committed.

CHAP. XXII.

Of the Depraved and Evil Faith of the Cove-nanters.

BUT we cannot so slightly let them pass with their fore-alledged excuse for the War, that they durst not trust the King. The cause is evident, which is because they had taken from him all the ground of reason that might be, that he should trust them; nothing being more to be distrusted than a Depraved and Ill Faith: The King permitted them to perpetuate the Parliament as long as they pleased, he committed himself wholly over to their Faith, Affection and Conscience; if any thing obligeth a man to be faithful, it is to repose an entire and free confidence in him, and there is nothing more odious and unworthy the name of man, than to employ that assurance and confidence they have freely committed to us, to deceive and ruine them. They themselves after this

this signal favour, without example, often declared to the world, that if they should abuse so great a trust to the dammage and detriment of his Majesty, they should be unworthy to live upon the earth, but this was before the Loyal Subjects had separated themselves from their company. They are then condemned by their own confession, for that most signal Act of Trust, such as never King gave to his Subjects, they returned him the most infamous and perfidious Acts, and base ingratitude that ever Subjects rendred to their King. He that said, *Fidelem si putaveris, facies,* the means to make men faithful, was to think them so, was never known to these men.

In Conscience can ye believe that when the King committed to them this great power, that he understood it thus, That when he should refuse to do any thing they requested him, he gave them liberty to force him to do it, or to do it without him, to take from him his Children, to seize upon his Revenues, to turn his Armies, Navies, and Forts against him, to make a broad Seal, and to break his, to dispose of all the Offices of the Crown, to levy Forreign Souldiers, and bring them into his Kingdom, to deprive his Subjects of their Goods and possessions, to drive the Ministers of the Gospel from their flocks, to rob the Church of her Revenues, to overthrow the ancient Laws of the Land, and to make a Religion all new? After all this, can any man wonder if they durst not trust the King? For where is the Criminal or Malefactor that dares commit himself to, or trust the Judge? and where is the Cozener and Deceiver, who being discovered, dares trust him whom he hath cozened and deceived?

If by these vile actions they have violated the trust the King reposed in them, and if by the Act for the continuance of the Parliament, the King gave them a

power

power to deal thus with him, we refer our selves to the better part of the Parliament, who withdrew themselves to the King, abhorring such a prodigious violation of the publick faith, and of the duty of Subjects and Christians unfaithfulness; they committed the like to the people, who deputed and committed to them the publick safety: For doubtless in their choice it never enter'd into the Spirits of them who sent them, to invest them with an absolute power over their goods and persons, much less over their King, for they could not give that which they had not, nevertheless they have executed this power, casting their fellow-Citizens out of their houses and possessions, and gather'd together great treasure out of the rents of the King and his Subjects, manifesting themselves very liberal of the goods of others.

But they defend these actions by a new Maxime of State, invented upon this occasion; Some of the principal Citizens of *London* being oppressed by their great and often Taxes, came to the House, and represented to them that it was their duties to maintain the Subjects in the propriety of their goods, and beseeched them, not to fall themselves into that inconvenience which they were bound to remedy. The Gentlemen of the House of Commons answered them, that in truth the Subjects might plead the propriety of their goods against the King, but not against the Parliament, to whom it appertained to dispose of all the goods of the Kingdom; but to perswade the people to believe this, is a very hard task, who rather judged, that the Parliament whom they had chosen, had violated the publick faith and the trust committed to them, and had taken that into their disposing which was never committed them. Let these Gentlemen never hereafter speak so loud of their publick faith, since they have lost it, nor ever attempt to borrow more money upon so sorry a caution. There

There were none in either Houses who had not often taken the Oaths of Allegiance and Supremacy, by which they acknowledge the King their Soveraign, depending of none, and had sworn to him loyalty and obedience. They moreover took the protestation made in the beginning of the Parliament, and imposed upon the whole Kingdome, wherein also they swear the same thing. The Oath of the Covenant which was taken after, renew'd the same promise, and there they swore *to defend the Person and Authority of the King, and cause the world to behold their fidelity, and that they would not in the least thing diminish his just power, and greatnesse.* Consider here (good Reader) Oaths enough to binde them to perform and keep their promise. But this multitude of oaths is a kind of proof of their ill faith, for they that swear often, manifest thereby, that they think themselves unworthy to be believed, and distrust, that every one mistrusts them; It had been better for them to have been faithful to their King without swearing: for as in the Grammar Latine, two Negatives make an Affirmative, these on the contrary in stead thereof, would seem to make two Affirmatives to make one Negative, and that many oaths to be faithful to their Soveraign bound them to do the contrary; for in effect these last oaths were solely imployed to ruine the antient Oath of Allegiance, for if their intentions had been simply to be faithful to their Soveraign, they needed have taken no other oath then the first. Therefore after these two new oaths, came the third, which they called the *Negative Oath,* in which they caused men to swear, *That they should neither directly, nor indirectly assist the King in this war.* And thus behold in fine the mask taken off, and the intention of their former oaths uncover'd.

 There can be no greater symptome of a desperate sick State, then the multiplication of oaths to form parties

ties and factions; and we may say after the Prophet *Jeremy* 23. 10. *The land mourns because of Oaths.*

As for the principals who imposed the Oaths, they made use of them to halter, and intangle the consciences of the people, for to serve their ambition, practising the Doctrine of *Lysander*, who taught that men ought to be amused with oaths, as children with bables; and as for the people upon whom the oaths were imposed, for the most part they took them rather for imitation, then knowledge, or for fear, or from a blind zeal, or an implicit faith. Moreover the multitude of Oaths do imbase the dignity, and a people accustomed to them, respect no more an oath, then their old shoes. Those also that swear often, are often forsworn, overthrowing one oath with another.

But the Oath of the Covenant hath this singular, wherein it surpasseth all *Chymera's*, *Centaurs*, *Hypogriffs*, in extravagance and contradiction; for in taking it in the sense of the Covenanters, they overthrow this Oath by the Oath it self? and they forswear that which they had sworn; for in swearing that they would defend the Person and Authority of the King, and make the world behold their fidelity, according to their opinion they are bound to make war against him, and by virtue of this Oath, they persecuted, rob'd, and after all deposed him. Oh supreme degree of perfidy, and frantick blindness? Have we not whereat to mourn and lament, to behold these illuminated Reformers so plunged in the gall of bitterness, and bonds of iniquity, for to persecute their good King with all rage and violence, because they had sworn to defend him, and to be faithful to him.

This Oath was called Covenant, that is to say, Alliance, or confederation, because those that took it (for at present its forbidden to be taken) pretended to make an Alliance and Covenant with God: This Oath is yet in vogue in *Scotland*. It's their New Covenant,
besides

besides that of the New Testament, and the modern Canonical Scripture, which is Judge in all cases of conscience, and from which there is no appeal.

Their ill-faith is moreover evident in the composition of this Oath, and certainly it's the only thing evident in the third Article, which is a discourse so twisted and interwoven, composed expresly not to be understood: *There they swear to defend the Person and Authority of the King in defence of Religion and the publique Liberty.* It's very hard to say what that signifies, every good soul who suffer'd himself to be perswaded to take this Oath, understood thereby, that to defend the Person of the King, was a necessary point, both to preserve their Religion and Liberty, and that they could not fear God as they ought, without honouring the King; and those that took the Oath in this sense, were bound to fight against the Covenanters for the defence of their Religion and Soveraign.

But the unworthy companions of the Covenant interpreted it thus, that they bind themselves to defend the Person and Authority of the King, so far forth as it is compatible with the defence of Religion and Liberty. Now (say they) we find that the defence of the Person, and Authority of the King is incompatible with the defence of Religion, and the Publique Liberty; and therefore we are bound to oppose and ruine the King for the defence of Liberty and Religion. And thus it appears that this malicious obscurity is a fold of the Serpent, and a lurking hole of the evil spirit, even the rather when we narrowly consider this construction, *to defend one thing in defence of another*, which signifies nothing, and wants both true Logick and common sense.

The Oath being a profession before God, and the strongest affirmation of all, had need to have been clear, and couched in such terms, that every one might have

have understood it in the same sense they took it; but to insert such equivocations, was to abuse the Name of God, whom they took to witness, and the simplicity of the people. He that takes a forked Oath, and understands it not in the sense that he that gives it, or understands it not at all, swears not in Truth, in Righteousness, and Judgement, which are the qualities required in an Oath, for he calls God to witness his hypocrisie, blindness and temerity.

The same Article makes profession *of fidelity to the King, and to diminish nothing of his just Authority and greatness*. It's no new thing for Rebels to take the Oath of Allegiance to their Soveraign, to combine a faction against him. The Mutineers in the time of *Richard* the Second, took an Oath to be faithful to the King and people, and yet nevertheless made use of this Oath to stir up the people to ruine the King: And these did the like; and when hereupon we tax them with unfaithfulness, and breach of their Oath, they answer, and pay us with a distinction betwixt the politick and personal capacity of the King, and they tell us that it was against *Charles* they made the Warre, and not against the King, making the King a pure Idea, an Accident without a Substance. It's very hard for them to say what became of the politick capacity of the King, then when they beheaded him in his personal capacity, for they so long honoured him in Idea, that at last they massacred him in substance.

But they forget that in the same Article they had sworn to be faithful to the Person of the King, and protested to defend *his Person and Authority*; as things conjoyned and inseparable: So strong is truth, and respect due to Soveraignty, so natural to Subjects, that even in the Oath which they formed, to confederate against him, their duty is couched in express terms, which will one day be produced in judgement against them.

But

But in good earnest have we not much to wonder at, and to acknowledge the wrath of God, in the blindness of these men, that so many millions of men should think they were bound to persecute the King to all extremity, and to take away his goods, honour, liberty, safety, and at last his life; because they had sworn *to defend the Person and Authority of the King, and make the world behold their fidelity, and that they would diminish nothing of his just Power and Authority:* Is it possible that their by-got zeal could so dislocate their brains, and a-brutish their spirits, as to make them commit so many crimes and enormities, upon so unreasonable a consequence. *Oh Lord create in us a clean heart, and renew a right spirit within us.*

In the fourth Article of this Oath, they promise to endeavour with all their power, to bring to condigne punishment all those who were the cause of separating the King from his people; and according to this, it was, they made the people believe a long time, that the occasion of their taking up Arms was to bring the King to his Parliament; but the hypocrisie of protestation, is now clearly manifested, for when the King offered to return to his Parliament, they utterly refused to receive him; telling him plainly if he came, he *should come at his peril.* Forbidding all persons whatsoever, under pain of death, to receive or entertain him in their houses. Let all good subjects who have taken this Oath, open now at last their eyes, and acknowledge that the intentions of their Guides, was quite contrary to their professions.

The Sixth Article required every person to swear; *That this cause touched the Glory of God, the happiness of the three Kingdomes, and the Dignity of the King.* Indeed this cause touched the Glory of God with such fowl hands, as have defiled it as much as possible men could, and it touched the happiness of the three Kingdomes

with

with such malignant claws, as have torn them to pieces. But if they will that we take them in their sense, namely, that their cause defends and advanceth the Glory of God, the happiness of the Kingdomes, and the Dignity of the King, we behold and feel the contrary : But grant that this should be true, 'tis not a thing for which we must swear. Oaths are of two sorts; the one sort are to affirm the truth of a thing present or past, the other for to promise and oblige our will for the future; these two sorts of Oaths cannot be taken together.

The Oath of the Covenant is of the latter; and therefore it is very ill done of them to confound it with the first, which is altogether of another nature and usage, and in a promise for the future; to thrust in an affirmation of a thing present, yea, of a thing false, or at least doubtful, and whereof they of their party are not accorded.

But suppose that this Oath were of the first sort, the things which we should affirm upon Oath, are such as require the testimony of the person who swears: Such are all questions of fact. But as for questions of right, they ought not, neither can they be decided by Oath; and it is to want common sense, to make his neighbour judge, to know which is the true Religion, and to judge whether the Cause of the Parliament is better then the Kings. There the Oath loseth his use, for its made to perswade and give Authority to the thing, by the witness of the person. If the Cause of the Covenant be the Cause of God, there is no need to swear it, but to justifie it by reason and practice. And although we should even believe that it searcheth and advanceth the Glory of God, the happiness of the Kingdome, and dignity of the King, it were unjust and ridiculous, to press us to swear it; for moral truths, and even also Theological, ought to be believed, not sworn. Civil things

things only, and those amongst them which are matters of fact, ought only to be affirmed by oath; we have a very firm belief of the truth of many points of Religion, and of the honesty of divers persons, and yet nevertheless, for all the world, we would not swear to them; all who have any ingenuity, or good sense acknowledge, that to force us to affirm the goodness of the Covenant by Oath, is an extreme tyranny, and full of ignorance and absurdities. And also seeing we are very ill satisfied of the goodness thereof, its another tyranny to make us swear to defend it; and a most barbarous cruelty, to confiscate our possessions, and sequester our Ministers of their benefices, because they refuse to take so unreasonable an Oath, and yet all this was practised during the Presbyterian Reign.

The Articles of the Covenant were assisted with a Religious Prologue and Epilogue, full of protestations of zeal and repentance, and therefore it was almost impossible, but the most part of them that took it should be perjured, considering the generality of the people are evil. And this should have prevented the Gentlemen to impose the Covenant indifferently upon all, under such great penalties. For as they will not suffer the Sacrament of the Lords Supper to be administred to the people, for fear to encrease their condemnation: They should have by the same reason, according to their principles, have withheld to administer these protestations of zeal and repentance, to their consciences, whose disposition they were ignorant of.

Now a great evidence of their depraved and evil Faith, consists in their protestations of sanctity and superlative expressions of zeal; in which the Independent party who rejected the Covenant, without comparison, fly higher then their Predecessors; All their Ordinances, and Declarations, yea even their Letters of News, were sallies of zeal. All their murthers and robberies were to establish the purity of the Gospel, to conquer a Kingdome for Jesus Christ, and that godliness might reign and flourish.

If they speak of the abominable parricide committed against their Soveraign, they say that God made bare the Arm of his Holiness, that the Lord is on their right hand, that he hath smote Kings in the day of his wrath, and that they may wash their feet in the blood of the ungodly. Thus they made their horrible crimes march disguised in terms of Scripture, and the devil borrowed the language of the Spirit of God.

Whosoever shall well consider the use they made of the Scripture, and whereto they imployed their great shew of holiness, shall find an Answer to the Question in the 50 *Psal.* 16. *But to the wicked God saith, what hast thou to do to declare my Statutes, or that thou shouldest take my Covenant in thy mouth.* Behold here the work of the Covenanters; they declare the Statutes of God, and take his Covenant into their mouths, to put on rebellion, the mask of Religion, and to invest themselves without trouble, of the Authority and Revenues of the Crown, the goods of the Church, and without suspition to grope the purses of the people; for the outward shew of devotion, doth much amuse the assistants, and gain their belief; for who can fear any evil from those who so piously invite them to repentance, and the advancement of the Glory of God? who would not confide and trust in them that declare the Statutes of God, and take his Covenant in their mouth? Satan in all forms is dangerous, but he is never so pernicious as when he clothes himself as an Angel of Light, and it is ill going Procession when the Devil carries the Cross.

Moreover by their fruits ye shall know them. How often abused they the credulity of the people, when they *conjured them to help to fetch the King from his evil Coun-*

Conncellors, and to bring him gloriously to his great and faithful Counsel, that is to say, to themselves; but their faithfulness appeared then when he departed from them whom they called his evil Conncellors, to yeeld himself up to them; for then their terrible mennaces against him, and all those who should dare to receive him, forced this poor Prince to travel disguised in great danger of his life through their Armies which besieged *Oxford*, and to go and cast himself into the arms of the *Scots*, as a chased Boar casts himself into the toils.

He found by sad experience in this his miserable refuge, that the Covenanters were of the same Genius in other Nations, and of the same evil Faith. It imports not much whether it be true or false, which was said of the *Scots*, that they had secretly invited him, and promised to expose both their goods and lives for his defence and safety; but how ever it was, they were bound by their natural duty to do so: But instead of rendring him the duties of faithful subjects, as crafty Merchants they made their profit of him; for after they had kept him captive some moneths, at length they drew two great benefits by him; the one upon their promise to imploy their Armies for his service, they made use of his Authority, to make that Miracle of Valour and Fidelity, the Marquess of *Montrosse*, the Kings Lieutenant in their Country, and the terrour of the Rebels, to disband, and lay down his Armes; the other, in making sale of his Majesty, to the Gentlemen at *Westminster*, for two hundred thousand pounds sterling in ready money, obliging them to pay the like summe ●●e two years after. Upon which this most wise ●●nce, being demanded whether he had rather continue with his Scottish Subjects, or go to his Subjects in *England*, answered with an excellent grace and serenity, *Without question, I must be with those who have bought me, and not with those who have sold me:* And in his

medi-

meditation upon this subject, *Since I am thus sold by them, I am only afflicted for the evil they have done, and to behold my self valued at a higher price then my Saviour.* These words proceeding from a quick and well governed Spirit, a King of his passions, and so conforming himself to the passion and obedience of the Sonne of God, cannot be heard, nor read by good Christians with the same moderation they were pronounced; but this magnanimous patience, should produce in every pious soul, a most just execration of this the most base and barbarous treachery, that hath been committed since that of *Judas*, and which in iniquity yields only to the abominable paracide, to whom he was deliver'd by this infamous sale.

It matters not much what is said hereupon, that the *Scots* in delivering up the person of the K. to the Gent. at *Westmin.* drew from them a promise to treat him with safety, liberty and honor; for they ought not impose upon other then themselves, this duty which was natural to them. Neither could they expect that the *English* should render him that safety, liberty and honor, which themselves refused him, or that the buyers should not as well search to make their profit by him, as the sellers, and to reimburse themselves with usury by his ruine.

But for their care they took of the K. when they deliver'd him, let us do them the favour to pass by their perfidiousness, and behold how the Gent. at *Westm.* performed their promise to treat the K. with safety, liberty and honor. Behold how they led him captive to *Holmby* house, where they set a guard of souldiers, his enemies upon him, denied him his Revenues, Rights, liberty, children, servants, and (that which with greatest earnestness he desired) his Chaplins, and the free exercise of his conscience, extremely misusing him with insolent threatnings and injurious demands,

And for all this the *Scots* never seemed to be moved or trou-

troubled, whilst the K. was in the Presbyterian parties custody. But when the Independents had seised vpon his person, although his captivity was a little sweetned over it was before, the *Scotch* began to demand aloud the accomplishment of their promises for his liberty, whereupon the Gent. at *West.* made a Declaration, to break and null all their former promises of loyalty, and respect made to his Majesty by this Parl. *Telling the Scots, that these promises were formed, published, and imploid according as the state of affairs then stood, but they might now be altered, and yet nevertheless these promises to preserve the person and authority of the K. had been made with the solemnest and sublimest protestations, we protest* (say they) *in the presence of Almighty God, which is the strongest bond of a Christian, and the publick faith, the most solemn that any State can give, that neither adversity nor success shall ever cause us to change our resolutions.* Now at this day it sadly appears how much they respect the presence of Almighty God, and how much they find themselves obliged by the strongest obligation of a Christian, and the Publick Faith, the most solemn that the body of an estate can give. It is to be doubted, whether they believe there is a God, or that he is Almighty, or so just as to call them before him in Judgment for the prophanation of his most Holy Name.

Husbands in his book of Declarations, p. 557. and 663.

Before these Gentlemen did openly manifest that they would not grant the King neither liberty, honour, nor safety, they set awork their hypocrisie and treachery. The Independent Army having taken away the person of the King from the Presbyterians, began to use him more Honorably, but not out of love to him, but in hatred to his former Goalers, and to flatter and lull asleep the Royal Party, and for this effect this Army made some Declarations in favour of his Majesty. See here some of their expressions.

Forasmuch as a scandalous information hath been presented to the two Houses, importing that his Majesty is kept prisoner amongst us, and uncivilly and barbarously dealt with, we judge our selves bound to declare that this suggestion, and all other of the same nature, are most false and absolutely contrary, not only to our requests, but also to our principles. And a little after, *we profess openly that we see not how there can be any firm or durable peace in the Kingdome, without a due consideration and provision for the rights, repose and immunities of his Majesty and his Royal Family.* And in another place they promise, *that until such time as there be made a settlement, his Majesty shall find amongst them all civil and personal respect, with all reasonable Freedome.*

But let us next see how they performed this promise, after they found this great Prince inflexible to all their unjust and dishonourable propositions, and especially to those which concerned the ruine of the Church, they restrained his liberty, and set over him more insolent guards in his house at *Hampton* Court; at which nevertheless *Oliver Cromwell*, who was then in effect chief of the league, seemed to be much troubled, and very careful of the life of his Majesty, and therefore perswaded him to escape by night, and to save himself out of such wicked hands into the Isle of *Wight*; for being resolved to charge the King with a criminal process, which was the way as he thought most proper for the designs of his ambition, then privately to make him away; but he durst not proceed thus far, whilst the King was so neer the gates of *London*, and in the heart of his Kingdome, the hearts whereof he possessed. I will not undertake to sound the mysteries of iniquity of this Agent of Satan, but shew you a piece of his perfidiousness, and profound hypocrisie.

The night before the King stole from *Hampton* Court, *Cromwell* came to visit him, causing all persons to withdraw

draw out of the Chamber, except Major *Huntington*, in whom he only confided, and taking the King aside, had a long discourse with him, which *Huntington* could not hear, but could well behold his passionate gesture, which witnessed a singular freedome and affection. *Cromwell* at his departure cast himself upon his knees, and took the King by the hand, kissing it many times, wetting it with his tears, and at length lifting up his voice, said to him: *Sir, so God bless me and my children, as I am resolved to endeavour to place you and your children in your rights and dignities*; after this, approaching to *Huntington*, Major (saith he) *tarry with the King, and if there happen any thing new this night, take a good horse, and come with all speed and acquaint me.* This night then the King passed secretly the Thames, and taking post, cast himself into the trap they had laid for him in that retired place: So soon as *Huntington* knew of the departure of the King, and whether he was gone, he went in all hast to give advice to *Cromwell*, that the King had escaped into the Isle of *Wight*, who beholding him astonished and amazed at this sudden change, laughed at him, telling him, *That the King was there where he desired, and that there wanted nothing now to the satisfying of his desires, but that all his children were there with him.* This history is attested by *Huntington* himself, a person of credit and repute, whose eyes this action and the like hath opened, and turned his heart towards the King his Soveraign.

Now the King being confined into this little Island, where all the avenues might easily be kept by the Creatures of *Cromwell*, and the other Gentlemen of the Covenant; the Mask was presently taken off at *Westminster*, and in the Army, and all their oaths and protestations to maintain the person and authority of the King, were changed into loud cries, in calling for Justice against him, to which the Gentlemen at *Westminster* easily com-condescended, and for this effect declared him incapable to govern; charged him with all the crimes malice could devise, forbidding all persons to make any more addresses to him: But in this fair way, they had some disturbance, by those Parties that in the year 1648. rose for the King, but God justly provoked against this sinful Nation, suffered injustice to triumph through the disloyaly of persons, who having until that time born Arms against the King, took part with him expresly to betray and ruine him.

And thus from the beginning to the end of this Tragedy, falshood hath plaid his part, and at length this just Prince lost his life by the hand of those his Subjects, who had called Heaven and Earth to witness their Loyalty and Affection; and this is very admirable and memorable to all ages, how the Conscience and constancy of the King took a way altogether contrary to that of the Covenanters, for whilst the Covenanters swore themselves to destroy him, he would do neither the one, nor the other to save his life, or Crown; for its manifest that there was a time, wherein if the King would have promised that which he was resolved not to have kept, he had in a short time been put into such a condition (according to all humane appearances) as would have put him out of the power of all the discontented to constrain him to have kept his promise.

I cannot pass the last Act of this hideous Treason, without letting the world behold another piece of the damnable Hipocrisie of *Oliver Cromwel*. The day assigned for the Execution of the King being come, the Councel of War sate, which was then the Great Councel of the Kingdom: A Letter without Name was addressed to this Councel to represent to them by Reasons of Conscience and Prudence, the formidable consequences of so strange and hateful an Execution.

-cution. *Cromwel* seemed to be much touched at it, (which caused some suspicions, as though he himself underhand had procured it) and proposed it to the consideration of the Councel, part of this company began to yeeld to the force of Justice, and their duty, and to lean towards compassion: *Cromwel* beholding this made a turn to the door, and sent one of his confidence to those to whom the Execution was committed, to command them to dispatch the business: Then returning to the Councel Table, made a long Discourse shewing the inconvenience of this execution, and advised them so to secure the person of the King for the time to come, that he might neither do nor receive hurt. This Discouse was seconded by others, and then again re-assumed by himself with a great many words to lengthen the Consultation, until that one briskly entring into the Chamber told them, Gentlemen, You may cease to consult, the work is done, the King is executed: Upon this *Cromwel* suddenly fell upon his knees with signs of great devotion, crying out, That this was the work of God, and a true stroak of heaven, the Councel being disposed to save his life, but the Divine justice would not suffer so much innocent blood shed by this Tyrant to pass unpunished, and hereupon made an eloquent Prayer to give glory to God, and acknowledge his providence.

And from this History I leave the Reader to draw a Character of this Person, whose perpetual method was to make his Impostures to pass for miraculous and divine managements. When he would make his Inventions pass into publike resolutions, he would suborn a Prophet or Prophetess, who should come and find him in full Councel, or in the head of his Army, for to enjoyn him on the behalf of God, that which before he had resolved; he caused all the Councels he proposed to pass for motions of the blessed Spirit, therefore if

his

his Councels and Actions did ill accord with his preceding professions, his inspirations from above excused all, and he laid all the fault upon God; when any minded him of his Protestations made to preserve the person of the King, and restore him to his Dignities: He would Answer, That it was indeed his Intention, but that when he sought God to open him a way for the performance, God had silenced him, and shewed that it would not be acceptable to him. His partie seriously give him this commendation, *That he was so affected with the glory of God, that if he had promised any thing with the most solemn and holy adjurations, and that afterward God should put it into his spirit, That the contrary to what he had promised was most expedient for his glory, he presently forgot all his Promises.*

Therefore when he had the K. in his power at *Hampt. Court*, and often conferred with him; his Majesty expressed his perplexity to persons of Honour, telling them, *I cannot* (saith he) *treat with these people upon any foundation, who refer me to their inspirations, for that which they promise me to day, they contradict too morrow, if the Spirit dictate to them;* but you must note that the Spirit never dictates any thing to them but for their profit.

The wrath of God is great against us in suffering us to be ruined and destroyed by fraud and hypocrisie, but verily his indignation is yet greater against those who are seduced; for it is a lesser evil to be persecuted by the Devil, then to mistake him for the Spirit of God.

But let us consider other Acts of the evil faith of the Covenanters. How have the Members of Parliament answered the intentions of those that sent them? Was it the desire of those Countries and places for which they served, that the Divine Service so much loved by the people should be taken away, and their Ministers driven from their Benefices, and

Anabaptists

Anabaptists and such like, without knowledge and call, established in their places? Did they give them Commission to levy and make War against their King, to cut off his head? And were they not sent and deputed to councel and advise the King, and to succour their Counties? and have not they done the contrary? When their fellow Citizens chose them, did they chuse them to be their Soveraigns? Was it their intentions that they should sit in Parliament to perpetuity, and place in their children to perpetuate their Raign in their Families? whereby they have gained more in a few years then the house of *Austria*, which hardly in two hundred years of an Elective Empire, have made one Successive; for these people have in a few years turned into succession an Empire, in which they have no Election. And it would be very hard to tell, who gave them the power to dispose of the goods and lives of the people, and to govern the Kingdome by an Army, of which *England* hath never hope to be delivered, but by an absolute victory obtained by the King. Of these high actions of Presumption and Tyranny, warranted by no Authority, and upheld onely by the strength of Arms, they must render account to God, and since they maintain that the Soveraignty resides in the people, they must also one day give an account to the people of their administration.

<small>This was written during the sitting of the long Parliament in *Anno* 1650.</small>

They made an Ordinance, That no Member of Parliament should exercise any Office in the State, but how well did they keep it? Did they not make amongst themselves a Monopoly of all the gainful Offices? They gave out they would give an account of the Treasure expended of the State, but in the mean while they followed the Councel of *Pericles*, which was to studie how never to give any.

They

They invited the people to present their plaints against their own Members, but those who dared to do it were ruined in the prosecution, and served as a sad example to all others to beware and keep themselves from so dangerous an enterprise for the future.

They have also forced the Consciences of men to break their Faith, witness the breach of Articles subscribed in the Counties of *York* and *Chester*, whereby the Gentlemen engaged on both parties, were mutually obliged to lay down their Arms and live in peace, but the Gentlemen at *Westminster*, frighted with this *Hideous* name of Peace, declared this accord *Null*, as destructive to their affairs; for both the Devil and the Covenanters maintain themselves by dissention.

They forced the *Londoners*, taken and released by the King at the Battel of *Brainsford*, to take up Arms against him the second time, against their Faith sworn to his Majesty, who most graciously gave them both their Lives and Liberty, releasing them without any ransome.

But as for them they wickedly massacred those who yielded themselves upon their promise of life, and liberty, as Duke *Hamilton*, the Earl of *Holland*, and the gallant and noble Lord *Capel*, Sir *Charles Lucas*, Sir *George Lisle*, and many others.

They being thus habituated in disloyalty and unfaithfulness, their great quarrel against the late King of blessed and glorious memory was, That he would not break his Faith, nor falsifie his Oath he took at his Coronation, to maintain the Rights and Priviledges of the Church, and to defend the Laws of the Land.

And as they were perfidious to us, so were they also to one another, they falsified their faith to their Army, which had too well fought for them, under the Command of the Earl of *Essex*, and disbanded them without their pay.

But

But another Army paid them for this perfidiousness by another. The Independent Troops were those which professed to them fidelity with the greatest zeal: And these were they which unroofted them at *Westminster*, and pull the Gentlemen out of their Thrones, leaving there, only such as pleased them.

And in passing, let us mark another feat of activity, of *Cromwel*, he perswaded the House of Commons to casheer this Army, promising them that he would lay down his Arms at their feet, but he gave them this counsel only for to provoke and irritate the Army against them, and to ruine them, as indeed it did.

Then when the Army began to present criminal informations against the King, they sent an Embassie of six Collonels to the House of Lords to keep them quiet, promising to maintain their priviledge of Peerage, but as soon as the King was beheaded, they casheered the House of Lords, and those Lords having basely abandoned their Head to the slaughter, presently lost the Life of Honour, which flowed from thence upon them, and were most justly laid aside as dead and unprofitable members.

The *Scots* also for having been too faithful to their Brethren in Rebellion, were paid with the like treachery, for all that power aud interest which they ought to have had in the affairs of both Kingdoms, according to the Articles of their League, was denied them with scorn and insultation.

Amongst our miseries, this is a recreative spectacle to us, to behold the Thieves who pillaged us, to pillage and rob one another, and to deal treacherously amongst themselves after they betray'd us.

To their disloyalty let us joyn their falshood, wherein consisted the Foundation and Building of all their Fabrick. This appeared singularly in the beginnings

ginnings of the Covenant. Then the Gentlemen discovered daily some Treason or other, with as much facility as the Labourer finds his work.

News of *England*, written from *Spain*, *France*, *Italy*, *Denmark*, Politick Discourses of a *Dutch* Mariner, to an *English* Hostler, of Armies kept under ground by the King, to cut the Throats of all the Protestants in a night; and the greatest danger of all, which caused the chiefest fear to the subtle spirits of *London*, was a design laid for a mine of Powder under the *Thames*, to cause the River to drown the City; but this dangerous enterprise was discovered a little before the Execution, whereupon the devout people very conscientiously gave thanks to God, and they took special order for the future that the *Thames* should not be blown up. In two or three moneths these Treasons amounted to the number of nine and thirty, according to the account of a venerable Member of the House of Commons, in one of his Speeches. This indeed was the time they had most need of them to form a Party.

They made use of the same path according to their occasions; after a defeat, they used to keep a day of Thanksgiving for a victory; if the King offered peace to his Subjects, they gave out amongst the people that he refused it, and would have none; and the Ministers told God of it in their publick Prayers, with all the news of the times, that he might have no cause to pretend ignorance. To draw money from the people, a plot would be discovered, for which publick Thanks was to be given to God, and afterwards the *Londoners* must pay a hundred thousand pound Sterling in acknowledgment of so great a Benefit. By these plots which were only against their Purses, the people were often pillaged, yet they had not the wisdom to beware of them, the Devil having sent amongst them such strong delusions, that they should believe a Lie. Certainly

this

this Device or Motto should have been written upon the Standards of the Covenanters, *Possuimus in fallacia Latibulum nostrum, & mendacio protecti sumus. We have made Lies our Refuge, and under falshood have we hid our selves*, Isa. 28. 15. But this covering will not long continue, *For the hail shall sweep away the refuge of Lies*, saith the Prophet, *v.*17. And that which is builded thereon, shall fall as an House built upon the Sand.

And thus much for them who boast of their *Publick Faith*, and say they dare not trust their King.

CHAP. XXIII.

Of the Instruments both Parties made use of, and of the Irish *Affairs.*

LET us now come to the accusation which made the lowdest noise: Our enemies reproached the King, that he made use of wicked Instruments. For beholding to their great regret, that the person of the King was without blame, they cast all the sins of his Court and Armies upon him. But we will see what Instruments the two Parties served themselves with, and whether the consideration of the Instruments can alter the nature of the cause.

But first of all let us make our advantage of that which our enemies are forced to yield us, for envy which tare a pieces those which served the King, found nothing to fasten on, in his person, yea though continually endeavoured, even after his death, when the Covenanters entertained, and yet do, Writers in pay,

pay, to write sandalous and defamatory Libels against his sacred Majesty.

There was never Rebel which called not his Prince unjust, otherwise they would condemn their own party of injustice: But the open conversation of the King was a subject very improper, either for the detracter or flatterer; he lived not obscure and hidden as the Kings of *China*, but made appear to the eyes of all the world what he was, as the Sun makes himself seen to the Universe by his own proper light.

This Prince whom the Covenanters persecuted under colour of Piety and Reformation, was four times a day upon his knees at his devotion, was guided by the fear of God, and comforted by his Love, made his Word the Rule of his Belief and Actions, humbled himself in his adversities under his mighty hand, and reposed himself with a firm Faith upon the same hand which smote him. His discourses were honest, religious, pertinent and judicious, and his Writings were the same; wherein shined forth a Vigor and Majesty truly Royal. And the sanctity of his retired Meditations, which are now publick, will for ever fill all good souls with consolation and instruction, and his enemies with confusion. He was a Prince sober, continent, temperate, a spirit composed by singular Geometry, so equal in all his inclinations, that it is hard to say, to which passion he was most enclined.

Greatness arms vices with power, and tempts the desires by the facility; and the Devil hath his Agents in the Courts of Princes, who observe and watch their humours, and advertise them of all the evil they may do; for to resist such trials, one had need of a Soul wherein Nature and Grace had contributed to strengthen against such temptation; this our Prince shewed by his behaviour, that he believed there could be no pleasure where there was sin, *Abhorring that which was evil,*

cleaving

cleaving to that which was good, Rom. 12. 9. The councellours of vice had here assayed in vain, all which might move youth or power: If in any thing he manifested passion, it was in favouring Vertue, Knowledge and Arts, which he loved by judgment and experience.

The injustice they are able to reproach him with, is that which he committed against himself, having taken from his own Rights to preserve and augment those of his Subjects. It were to be wished for their good, that he had less loved them, and himself a little more; for if he had given them less, they would have had more than they have at this day.

Of his Clemency, none can speak more than his enemies, for his greatest adversaries were those who were the principal subjects of it. He preserved the lives of those who purchased his destruction: He restored the Inheritances to the children of them, which ravisht and took from him his own, and who died with their swords in their hands against him, he offered a free pardon to them who would not pardon him. But if this way hath not gained their affections, doubtless it hath Gods.

Certainly since they have rejected and destroyed their good King, they deserve God should give them such Masters, like the King of the Frogs in the Fable, Storks and Herons which should devour them and consume them one after another; but if he doth not, I fear there will be such good order amongst them, that they will mutually devour one another, there being no tyranny so cruel as that of a multitude, nor worse servitude than to want a Master.

Behold here then a great point gained, That the King was a just and good Prince! Those who so much complain of his evil Counsellors or Instruments, ought to love him so much the more, and to acknowledge that he

could

could find no Instruments like himself; there is no Malady in the body of State which is not curable, whilst the head is sound: In all Kingdoms, the injustice committed in the Courts of Judicature, is done in the Name of the King; and there is no Government so just and prudent, no, even that which is governed by a prophetical conduct, as that of *Davids*, which have not faults enough, to give occasion to an *Absolom* to say, *Oh that I were made Judge in the Land, that every man which hath any suit or cause, might come unto me, and I would do him justice,* 2 Sam. 15.4.

In publick grievances, good Subjects are wont to cast the blame upon the Ministers of State, and rest satisfied in seeing some of them punished, accounting it their principal interest to preserve the honour of their Soveraign; and good Princes when they are informed that the Ministers of State have abused their Authority to the damage of their Subjects, which is theirs, are wont to examine them, and judge them according to the Laws. And in this, the King did as much as possible they could require of him, having submitted the persons of those whom the Covenanters complained against, to be judged, and tried by lawful and ordinary waies: But whilst they tread under foot the Royal Authority, the Power of Parliament, and the Majesty of the Laws, and that they were in open war against him, what reason had he to submit his Servants and Ministers to the judgment of his enemies? Being certain that whilst the War continued, they would aim most at them who served him best.

Then when the Parliament was whole and entire, there passed a Vote worthy the gravity of that great Court, That the King could do no wrong, and that his Officers, and not he were guilty of the evil which was done in the publick Government: But since those who loved the King departed, and withdrew themselves

to

to him, those which remained at *Westminster*, followed a way quite contrary, for they cast upon the King all the faults of his Servants, and made use of them against him, whom they ought & should have punished for having ill served him. Then when they took in hand to examine the Ministers of State, in stead of punishing them which were guilty, they received them into favour, yea, after their faults proved against them, and turned all the discontent of the people upon the King; What a great noise was there in the House of Commons against the forgers of Monopolies? One would have thought that hardly any should have escaped with their lives, but there happened altogether the contrary: For because the Monopolists and other accused persons, made a considerable number in Parliament, they made use of their faults, to make a strong faction against the King, terrifying and making them understand, there was no way left to preserve them from utter ruine, but to joyn with the new party which was forming, and hereupon they were promised impunity for what evils they had done, on condition they should do greater.

Some of these were sent to the King to *Newmarket*, in the behalf of their companions, to whom his Majesty said these words, capable to convert them, or to make their Inditement at the day of Judgment.

Gentlemen, lay your hands upon your Consciences, Who are they which invented those Taxes by which you have so provoked my people against me? For whose advantage and profit were these Imposts levied? Were my Revenues encreased by them? It was you that induced and moved me to them, for your own particular profit, and now you return me a worthy recompence.

Other Parliament men, guilty of many crimes, were kept in the Parliament in hope of impunity, the holy Covenant was a Garment which covered a multitude of sins, even to the violating of a great Lady, and abusing her by own of their Members, almost in the sight of the Parliament: Behold these, the Reformers of Church and State! Others which were not of the Parliament, but under censure, for having been Councellours, or Instruments in the Imposts and Taxes of the people, were released by them, and employed for the same business, as persons who well understood the Trade, who pillaged then with a good Conscience, for the advancement of the Kingdom of Jesus Christ. Those whose infamous life was the shame of the Royal Court, were the honour of the Court at *Westminster*, and the Pillars of the Covenant. Likewise the Judges accused of corruption, and the Ministers of a scandalous life, in taking the Covenant, obtained a plenary indulgence of all their sins, for after that, there was no more to say to them, for those who washed themselves in this water, returned as white as if they had been washed with Ink, or with the second Baptism the Anabaptists use at this day.

But now let us look upon the Armies: Our enemies cry aloud, that the King made use of those of the Church of *Rome*, to serve him in his Wars. Upon which, an excellent Writer makes this gentle Question to them, How many were in their Armies, or how many they would have had? For if the common report do not much wrong them, they employed divers persons of that Religion, there were persons of Honour and Quality, who assured us, that they Prisoners of the same Religion, served the Covenanters. We refer our selves to their own Consciences, if they gave not a Commission to my Lord *Aston* to levy Forces.

The Relation in notable, the King being at *York*, this gallant man, accounted the most experienced, and best Commander of War of his time, came to present

present his Service to his Majesty, the King gave him thanks, and withal told him, he was resolved to employ none of his Religion in his Army. Well (saith he) I will go then to those who will employ me, and indeed went presently to *Westminster*, where he was received with open Arms, and a Commission given him written and signed, which he carried to the King; Ye cannot wonder then, that the King made use of him, and others of his Religion, whom before he was resolv'd not to employ, although he had, to take away all shadow of occasion from his enemies, who sought something whereat to quarrel with him, made a Proclamation that none professing the Religion of the Church of *Rome* should come neer his Court.

After this, the Covenanters used all their power to make them draw to the Kings Party, well considering, their party being so small, would bring more hatred than help to the King; and for this effect, they treated them with great inhumanity, forcing them to forsake their Houses, and Lands, and run and hide themselves under the Kings Protection, and this the King could not refuse them, for as they owed him their Subjection, the King owed them his Protection, so long as they governed themselves according to the Laws, and accomplished the Conditions whereby they were permitted by Act of Parliament to live in the Kingdom.

By this reason of Reciprocal duty, the King protecting them as his Subjects, they were bound to defend him as their King, and ye shall not find in all the Statutes which concern them, that they are exempted to serve the King in his Armies, neither is it reasonable that they only should be free from the perils of war, whilst their fellow Subjects venture their lives, and are shedding their bloud for the defence of their Country.

O 3   The

The Covenanters made it appear sufficiently to the world, that they judged that Religion ought not to exclude any from bearing Arms in the publick danger, for in their Armies they made use of all Religions, yea that of the Church of *Rome*, as we shall shew hereafter. If it were lawful for them to make use of those who denied the Incarnation of Jesus Christ, and of others that denied his Divinity, and those who were re-baptized and denied Baptism to Infants, and the Blessed Sacrament of the whole Church, it were not less lawful for the King to make use of Souldiers of the *Roman* Religion; and if those whom they now call Reformed, embrace the Doctrine of the Jesuits, touching the deposing and murdering of Kings, and that persons of the *Roman* Religion reject this, and joyn themselves with the Reformed Church in this point, the King had reason to serve himself of the Last as well as of the First.

Moreover the King had but two Religions in his Armies, which were too many: And although the *Roman* is not tolerated by the Laws, yet the Statutes give protection to the persons which make profession of it, but the Covenanters Motly Army consisted of many Religions, there can be no certain number of them, for they multiplied and subdivided daily; and these Religions had no tolleration by the Laws, nor the persons which made profession of them.

But put the case that the Covenanters were a party Reformed, uniform and illuminated, since they have destroyed their King, what Law Divine or Humane, doth hinder him for using all means that God gives him to defend himself? And if amongst his Loyal Subjects, there be some who are blinded in matter of Religion, why should he not make use of those who are blind to repress those who are illuminated; and maintain his Life and Crown?

'Tis

'Tis then a ridiculous Question, which they demand of the King, whether he will defend the reformed Religion with Souldiers of the *Roman* Religion? for he makes not use of them to defend his Religion, but his Person and Scepter, which those whom they call Reformed, would wickedly pluck out of his hands. 'Tis foolishly and unjustly done of them to complain that the King made them to kill the Protestants, a name which they make a great noise with, when they have lost the thing; they were not Protestants but Rebels, whom the King killed in his just defence. The King was not to enquire of what Religion they were that made War upon him; the true Religion gives not license to Malefactors to do evil, and to binde the hands of the Judge, that he should not punish them; chiefly, when the Malefactor fights against the Judge, and he to whom God hath committed the sword to execute vengeance in wrath, is constrained to make use of it to defend his life and authority; the Malefactor who is instructed in a holy Religion is doubly guilty, he is the evil servant in the Gospel, who knows his Masters will, but does it not, and therefore he shall be beaten with many stripes.

This above written serves as an Answer to the exclamations of our enemies, That the King caused an Armie of *Irish* Papists to come over to kill the Protestants in *England*, for it matters not what Religion the *English* be of, if they be Rebels, and who can blame him for employing Rebels converted, against Rebels obstinate, but onely those that perish by them: But that which gives occasion of laughter in this Objection is, that there were none, and the *Irish* have not yet sent over their Army into *England*, according to their promise to help the King. We grant that the *English* are far more considerable to the King then the *Irish*; suppose the difference be as great as betwixt a Son and a servant, but if the Son prove unnatural and draws his sword against his Father, who can blame the Father if he arms his servant, were he a *Barbary* slave, to defend his life? 'Tis not to purpose then for them so often to object to us, that the *Irish* were the Executioners to cut the throats of a multitude of Protestants in *Ireland*, and that it's a horrible thing to bring them over into *England* to do as much here; for at the worst they were but Executioners of Rebels: Certainly civil War is a horrible thing, where one destruction draws on another, *Abyssus abyssum advocat*; but since the enraged and implacable obstinacy of the Covenanters, brought the King to this extremity, that he could not quench the fire that they had kindled in his Kingdom, but by ruine; like those who would quench a Town all in flames with Cannon-shot, what could we do other then call in the *Irish* to his succours? having rebellions then on all sides? Was it not wisely done of him to make an agreement with the most tractable and pliant, and to serve himself with their Forces to make head against the others? If the *English* would not have had the King made peace with the *Irish*, why did they then refuse the peace and pardon which the King so often, and so graciously tendred them? And did he enter into Treaty with his *Irish* Subjects, before he had a long time in vain sollicited his *English* to their duty? Should he rather willingly have lost two Kingdoms to help his enemies to render themselves Masters of the third?

But say they, the *Irish* shed abundance of Protestants blood in *Ireland*, which should have been revenged in stead of granting them peace. Its true, they committed many fearful and strange cruelties, but this blood hath been sufficiently revenged; For, for one which they put to death, five of theirs have been killed since the beginning of the War; And more moreover this reason sounds ill in the mouthes of Christians, who ought to leave vengeance to God. We could not expect that the Covenanters would ever commend this peace, which might have been so disadvantagious to them, and might have supplied the King with many Souldiers, if the *Irish* had kept their word.

The principal reason of their complaint was, because the *Londoners* lost much hereby, for they had advanced great sums of monies to the two Houses, for which they were to have had the *Irish* Rebels Lands, after they were extirpated; which was to buy the Bears skin before he was killed; and this partly was the cause of breaking up of the Treaty at *Uxbridge*, for the Citizens of *London* would by no means hear of Peace, unless the King would break his faith with the *Irish*, and root them out; for the quarrel that the *English* Covenanters had with them was not for their Religion, or Rebellion, but because they would not suffer themselves to be killed in a peaceable and quiet manner, that thereby the Merchant Adventurers of *London* might have their Bargain. And thus the Covenanters as much as in them lay, justified the unjust arms of the *Irish*, since they would by no means have peace with them: And after all, the King hath the sole power of Peace and War, and if he will receive into grace, and pardon his Subjects who have offended him, he is to give account to none. Yet nevertheless that it may appear to all the Reformed Churches how much our good King departed, loved his Religion, he would not grant peace to his *Irish* Subjects on the conditions they demanded, advantagious to their Religion; which if he had accorded, he might have had Legions in stead of Regiments, and not wanted neither the help of his Subjects, nor their neighbours; but rather then he would buy their assistance at that price, he chose to sink and fall

under

under the oppression of the Covenanters; after this piety or humanity ought to have converted the enemies of the King, if he had had to do with persons who had either the one or the other. But if the Gentlemen at *London* lost their monies which they advanced upon the *Irish* affairs, they have cause to complain of the Gentlemen at *Westminster*, who made use of this money, not to reconquer *Ireland*, but to make war upon the King, who had a great desire to terminate that business, and would have gone in Person, but not to serve the avaritious and barbarous intentions of these Merchants of blood, but to recover his Rights, and to restore a number of his exiled Subjects to their possessions; Those ruined and remaining Families of the generall Massacre, cried aloud in the ears of the King and Parliament. For to help them there was a generall Collection through the Kingdom, and the Ministers by Order of Parliament were to excite the charity of the people to a liberal contribution, which was done, and great sums of money were raised for the *Irish* War. But to what was the charity of many pious souls imployed? to make War against the King; The Armies which the cries of the poor exiled *Irish* had raised, and were ready at their Port to be shipped, were called back, and conducted against his sacred Majesty; and although many in those Troops had their Interests in *Ireland*, they were constrained to forsake them, for unknown Interests, and an open Hostillity against their Soveraign. 'Tis no wonder then, if part of those Troops at the battel of *Keinton*, turned to the King; and took a bloody revenge of so great injustice. For what a most horrible tyranny was this, to make them fight against their King in *England*, whilest the throats of their wives and children were cutting in *Ireland*?

We earnestly beseech the Covenanters, that whensoever they curse the *Irish* Rebellion, they would remember

ber these two things; the one, that the *Scots* shewed them the way, having before made a Covenant for Religion, and levied Arms to maintain it, and obtained by this way, all that they desired. The *Irish* seeing this was the way to obtain the liberty of their Religion, presently followed the example of their Neighbours, and as a judicious Writer saith pleasantly, That if the *Scots* had not piped, the *Irish* had never danced.

Let them remember also, that the *Irish* as wicked as they were, had without comparison more reason for their rising, then either the *English* or *Scotch*, for it's most certain that the *Irish* were held in with a bridle, which had a ruder bit then the other Subjects of the King. Many of the *Irish* for their former Rebellions were dispossessed of their Lands; and although the sentence was just, the loss nevertheless was sensible; moreover they had not the free exercise nor liberty of their Religion, the *English* nor *Scotch* cannot alledge any thing like these. Hardly shall you find in any History a raign of fifteen years more flourishing, peaceable, and mild, then the fifteen first years of the Reign of the late King, notwithstanding all the grievances the Covenanters reckon up to his disadvantage: There never shined more happy days upon *England* and *Scotland*; In effect, they were Nations sick of too much ease. When Subjects undertake to criticise upon mysteries of State, and come to quarrel amongst themselves for subtilties of Religion, or points of Discipline, its a symptome of an easie yoke, and of excess of ease and prosperity.

Moreover the *Irish* fought against men of another Religion, and of another Nation, they fought not against the Person of their King, cut not the throats of their Brethren, nor ruined those of their profession; imposed not necessity of Conscience upon others; but only demanded publick Liberty of Conscience for themselves, although many amongst them contented themselves
with

with lesse; for by the Articles of peace in *Septemb*. 1646. the King gave them no Toleration for the publike exercise of their Religion; Certainly therefore as those of *Niniveh* shall rise up in judgment against the *Scribes* and *Pharisees*, so shall the *Irish* against the *English* and *Scotch* Covenanters.

Further, our enemies are very unjust to complain, that the King assailed to bring over *Irish* Armies into *England*, since they in effect a year and half before had brought Armies of *Scotch* into *England* to serve them. If they take the boldness to entertain the Armies of strangers within the Kingdome of their Soveraign, shall it not be lawful for the King to defend his person and Kingdom with his own Subjects, which in this quality are not strangers in respect of him, but the *Scotch* are strangers in regard of the *English*. Histories furnish nought parallel to this crime, to have brought the *Scots* into *England*, and to move them to come, gave them part of the Kingdom of *Ireland*; but its easie for them to give that which was none of theirs; with the same right the Devil offered to Jesus Christ all the Kingdoms of the world, for they can produce their Authority no other where.

This Nation abounding in men, living in a barren Countrey, will be easily induced to plant Colonies in a more fertile soil, and who will believe that having their weapons in their hands, and being in *England*, backed with their forces from *Scotland*, they will govern themselves at the devotion of those that sent for them, and go no further then they are comanded; there is danger least it happen as to the fountain of *Lucian*, which a student in Magick, with certain words he had learn'd of his Master sent to fetch water, to which the fountain obeyed, but the poor apprentise knew not the words to make it stay, which in the mean while went and fetched water without ceasing, till it filled the house up to the windowes.

windows. Certainly our Mutineers had the wit to make the *Scotch* come to their help, and there needed no great charm to perswade a people which had nothing, and had nothing to do, to come and fish in troubled waters, in their neighbours pond: But I have great fear, that those which caused them to enter upon their March, were ignorant of the charm, to stay them that they should go no further, and that the *Scotch* will not have done, when the *English* have done with them.

It was not then an action of judgment to cause the *Scots* to enter *England*, without having power to make them return, and to hinder their coming again, much less an action of piety, for God needs not the wickedness of men to advance his Kingdom, it was an action purely of spight and stomack, a stroak of despair, proceeding from persons resolved to destroy their Country with them, rather than to suffer the insultation of a Conqueror, or the reproach of their treachery: But in doing this, they have rather augmented their reproach, and drawn upon themselves perpetual infamy: For as long as there is a God in Heaven, and Conscience in the world, the memory of those, who had but a finger in so base an action, will be hateful to all good men, their names will offend their ears, and their posterity will be forced (if any remain) to change their Names, for fear of being stoned by the publick.

But lets return to *Ireland*, and poure into the bosom of our enemies the Objection they have so often pressed against his Majesty, that he invited *Irish* Papists over to his party; and shew to the world, that it was the Covenanters, and not the King, who really employed them.

For to unwind this intangled and intricate business, we must take the thred of the affair higher; ye must then

then know, that there are two sorts of *Irish* Papists; the one, ancient Inhabitants of the Country, who since the Conquest of *Ireland* bear an hereditary and irreconcilable hatred to the *English*; the other, the posterity of those *English* Colonies which were planted in *Ireland* about four hundred years since, to preserve the Conquest for the *English*, and are accounted as *English*, by the ancient Inhabitants, for they yet preserve the Language, manners and inclination of the Country from whence they issued; the *English* and *Scotch* Protestants in *Ireland* are new Colonies, which during these forty years of peace, have encreased in number almost equal to the others.

When the Rebellion brake out in *Ireland*, soon after that in *Scotland*, being encouraged by their example, the old *Irish* and the old *English* Colonies joyned together in one common design to establish the *Roman* Religion, whereupon the Gentlemen at *Westminster* in stead of suppressing them speedily by Arms, (which his Majesty desired, and offered to go in person) made an Ordinance wholly to extirpate them, to which the King would never consent, alledging that it would be a means to cause the Colony of Protestants in *Ireland*, who were without defence, to be extirpated; as it came to pass, for the *Irish* being provoked by that bloody Ordinance, did what they at *Westminster* had taught them, and extirpated the most part of the Protestant Colonies, killing man, woman and child, with most horrible barbarousness. I leave to the just Judgment of God to decide against whom this Sea of innocent bloud cries.

In this Butchery, the old *Irish* were the most active and cruel, the others went along with them only for company; and besides, their interests were different, for the intention of the old *English* Colonies went little further than the design of freeing themselves in matter

ter of Religion, but the native *Irish* would as well be freed of the Nation, as have the freedom of their Religion, and would shake off the yoke of the *English* Monarchy, take possession in the name of the Pope, of the Abbies which were all in the hands of Lay men, recover all that they had lost by Confiscation, for their former Rebellions, and for this effect, null all Titles which held of the Crown.

This Intention was contrary to the old *English*, who held all their Estates of the Crown, and possessed divers Abbies by Pattent Royal, and besides this, had an hereditary affection towards their King and ancient Country; and therefore they had reason to fear, that after the extirpation of the *English* Protestants, their throats should be cut, and upon this consideration they listned to the overtures of an accord the King made to them, in the year 1643. And although they brake not off suddenly with the old *Irish*, yet they loosed themselves by little and little, and in the end, declared themselves for the King; but it was not until a long while after they did him any Service, having been amused and abused a long time by the subtilties of *Rome*, who upheld and instructed the old *Irish*, for to pass into *England* and serve the King, if ever they had promised it, the same subtilties and their dissentions would never permit them to do.

No man of understanding or sense can blame the King to receive from them the service they owed him, neither did he ever make any profession to the contrary, as they at *Westminster*, who passed a Vote of extirpation against them, and stirred up the people against the King by this pretext, that he made use of persons of the *Roman* Religion; now after this, if they themselves shall make use of them, they are inexcusable before God and man.

But now let us see how their actions agree with their
words

words and looks. The Royal party being greatly encreased in *Ireland*, especially by the conversion of the Protestant Forces which before served the Parliament: The Gentlemen of the Covenant finding themselves very low in that Kingdom, found no better expedient to repair their languishing affairs there, than to joyn their interest with the Popes, and the old *Irishes*, for it's most notoriously known, that before the death of the King these *Irish* Papists took pay of the Parliament, and served them in the warre, and have since rendred many good Services to the holy Covenant, above all, before *Derry*, which the Covenanters held, but was besieged by the *Scotch* Royalists, and had been taken without the coming of the *Irish*, conducted by *Owen Row O Neal*, who forced the *Scotch* to raise the siege with a signal loss, when the besieged were in great distress, and ready to yield up the Town. And this conjunction endured near a year, for it was not till after *October* 1649. that these *Irish* returned to the obedience of their King.

And indeed we have not here any thing to wonder at and be astonished, if two sorts of Rebels who agreed together to cast off their King, joyn themselves together in one party, and if their temporal interest which binds them be preferred before the spiritual, which both in the one and the other League served but as a pretext to their covetousness and ambition, the Gentlemen at *Westminster* judged right, that the advancement of the Pope in *Ireland*, was less disadvantagious to them, than the whole reduction of that Kingdom under the obedience of his Majesty.

This scandalous conjunction having much exasperated the spirits of the by-got people, whom they had taught to hate the King, because he had made peace with the Papists, and murderers of *Ireland*, the Gentlemen at *Westminster*, after they had a long time denied ed it, and seeing they could not any longer dissemble this infamous action, publickly called before them in examination Colonel *Monk*, who was employed in this agreement, and demanded of him, who caused him to make it? he being instructed beforehand, answered, that he had done it of himself, of his proper motion; then being enquired why he durst make such an accord without a Commission, he answered, that he judged his agreement then profitable for the interests of his party; and hereupon he was dismissed and sent away without any punishment, and these Gentlemen condemned this accord and allyance by a publick Act.

But where is the man that is so simple as to be deceived by so sottish a force? But to undecive the abused, and to shew that these Gentlemen gave no orders for to break this agreement; they had news a while after, that great succours were put into this Garrison of *Derry*, (then the Covenanters) by the Troops of his Holiness; and then all the Jugling was discovered; and there rested then no other answer for them to give, but that of the *Italian*, who being exceedingly pained with the Gout, and having prayed to God and all the Saints, and yet found no ease, began to call and pray to the Devil for help, and gave this Reason to them that rebuked him for it, *Ogni adjuto e bono*, all help is good from whomsoever it come.

Now every man who shall compare their Protestations with their Actions, may demand these Questions with astonishment and horror. Are these the men who have so cried out against the murtherers, which massacred so many thousand Protestants? Are these they who before and after the Massacre, did so press the King to sign their utter extirpation? Are these those who rendred the King odious, only for offering them peace and pardon? Are these the men that stirred up the people against their King, because he had

P

some

some few Souldiers of the *Roman* Religion scattered here and there in his Armies (for he never had an entire company of that Religion) and yet behold they themselves, entertain a great Body of an Army of the most refined Papists, and the most violent enemies of the Reformed Religion, to whom (when the King treated with them) he refused to give them any toleration. Behold the Army of the Popes become the Parliaments, behold the Murderers whom they would have rooted out, become their Souldiers; Behold the revenge of the blood of their Brethren, which they made such a noise of! The Massacre of the Protestants is pardoned the Murderers, provided they massacre those that remain of them. Is it to pay the Armies of his Holiness, that such great Summes of Money are raised of the Protestants? and that they suck the poor Families even to the very Marrow? Is this the effect of so many solemn Professions, of so many Fasts and publick Humiliations for the establishment of the Gospel in *Ireland*? Where is their shame? Where is their Ingenuity? Where is their Conscience? Be confounded Infamous Hypocrites, and since ye cannot hereafter avoid the execration of men, endeavour to prevent by your repentance the Judgment of God upon your Impostures.

CHAP. XXIV

How the different Factions of the Covenant agreed to ruine the King, and contributed to put him to death.

WE will not undertake to deprive the Independants of the glory to have been the last Actors

Actors in that execrable paracide, committed upon the Sacred Majesty of their King; an action which being the shame of the Nation, and reproach of Religion, was neverthelefs set forth to the eyes of the world, with the oftentation of Juftice and Piety; and for this horrible execution, there was a folemn Thankfgiving enjoyned to be rendered to God by a publick Ordinance. It's true, this Ordinance was ill obeyed, and many Minifters cryed out againft it, which did fo provoke their new Mafters, that they appointed a Committee, to eject the Minifters out of their Benefices, and to place in Lay perfons.

Now becaufe the Presbyterians thunder aloud againft this action, we will fee whether they have not contributed to it, and if their behaviour to their good King gave him occafion to hope for better dealing at their hands.

And for this purpofe we may do well to confider the Propofitions which they prefented to the King at *Beverly*, and fince at *Uxbridge*, and at *New-Caftle*, then when the Presbyterians held the better end of the ftaffe; they required of him in fubftance, that he fhould not difpofe, neither of the Militia, nor of the civil Government, nor of his Townes and Revenues, nor of his Children, nor of his Court, nor of Honours, nor of the Offices of the Crown; and that he fhould hold no power in the Treaties of peace, of War, and of Commerce with his Neighbours: That his Councel fhould no more depend upon him, that he fhould have no Negative voice in Parliament, and fhould be bound to grant whatfoever the Parliament would demand of him; that he fhould fhew no Acts of Grace, nor execute Juftice, and not have the power to do either good or evil; that he fhould confent that his party fhould be for ever ruined, and deliver up all thofe who had ferved him to their rage and Butchery: That he should utterly overthrow both the Civil and Ecclesiastical Government, cut all the Nerves of Government, and dispossess himself and his posterity without resource: In brief, that he should betray all the trusts God had committed to him, and render himself the most miserable and guilty creature in the whole Universe: All the choice left this poor Prince, was, whether he would be destroyed by his enemies, or by his own proper Act, for if he condescended not to these demands, being then in their hands that made them, the least he could expect, was to be deposed; and if he granted them, he deposed himself: Every man that hath either prudence, or Conscience, will chuse rather to be executed by another hand, than be his own proper Executioner: Read the Articles, which are too long to be inserted here, and if there were any thing that was his, or which God had given him to keep, that these Gentlemen demanded not of him, except his life, and if he could assure himself of his life, after he had given his enemies the Sword of Justice, and had by consequence acknowledged them his Superiours, before whom he was Justiciable: The Sequel of Affairs have shewed the truth of this consequence, for it was upon the Presbyterian Principles, that the Independants built their Conclusions.

Let them weigh well this reasoning, Saint *Paul* teacheth us, *Rom.* 13. that the Supream Magistrate beareth the Sword by God, he is his Minister; upon this ground the Supream Magistrate exerciseth Authority in the earth, by way of force: Observe that the Apostle saith not, he beareth *Swords*, he assignes him but one, and this sword, both executes Justice, and the Militia by one and the same power. Now the Presbyterians have a long time taught, that the Sword of the Militia appertained of right and originally to the people,

ple, of whom the Parliament is the Representative, and if this Doctrine be not true, their Arms were unjust; but if it be true, the sword of Justice also belongs to them; for if upon these grounds it was lawful for them to wrest out of the hand of the King, the Sword of the Militia, to make use of it against him, it was no less lawful for them to employ the Sword of Justice against him; all their Philosophy cannot divide these two Powers, which have the same foundation both in Scripture and reason, and which have been equally violated in beheading him, and making war against him.

Therefore the Presbyterians who now cry so loud, that the Person of the King was inviolable, and not subject to the sword of Justice, condemns by this all their past actions; for if it were an execrable paracide, to cut off his Head upon a Scaffold, it could not be the action of a good Subject to take off his Head by a Cannon Bullet in the field, as they many times assayed. And in employing the Militia against the King, they gave the Independants the Sword of Justice, who unhappily massacred him: After they took from him, his Sword, his Crown, his Revenues, his Servants, his Children, the Liberty of his Person, and which is much more, of his Conscience, they left the Independants but a step to go further, which was to take away his life. And all wherein these last surpass them, was that they gave the last blow to the King; the Presbyterians laid his head on the Block, and the Independants cut it off.

The name Independant was hardly known then, when his Majesty complained in one of his Declarations, that divers persons to the number of seventeen, had been accused to have said, they would kill the King, and how the Accusers could obtain no Justice against them; if the Members of Parliament who now abhor

this

this murder, had then had any care of the safety of his sacred person, they would never have stayed the course of Justice against these crimes. They had not entertained in pay *Mercurius Britannicus*, and such Rascals, by horrible Libels to defame his Majesty, and enflame the rage of a foolish and seditious people against him. If the quarrel had been only against his evil Counsellours, (which is the old and super-annuated pretext of all Rebels) they would never have cashiered the Army of the Earl of *Essex*, for to employ a————and a medly of pestilent Anabaptists, whom they knew to be mortal and sworn enemies to the King and Monarchy.

    Certainly we have so much Charity as to believe, they had not an intention to put him to death, when they began the war against him, no not even when they imprisoned him; as *Judas* according to all appearance, had no intention to cause his Master to be crucified, when he sold him to the Council of the *Jews*, and never thought that the Priests would proceed so far; for when he heard they had condemned him to dy, this unexpected blow so surprized him, and moved him in such a manner, that he presently brought back again the reward of iniquity, and rendred witness to the Truth, and to his Conscience before the Council, *I have sinned in betraying innocent blood*: 'Tis more than the Presbyterians have declared, beholding their K. condemned and beheaded by their practises, although it was beyond their intention, neither have they been so smitten with remorse of conscience, to bring back again that which they have got by sacriledge and rebellion, and yet notwithstanding, Jesus saith of *Judas*, much more penitent then some of them, *That it had been better for him he had never been born*.

    In speaking thus, we have no design to lead them to despair, but to repentance, to which the mercy of God is ever open, since we speak of the party, and not of
parti-

particulars; many whereof deteſt their Councels and paſt actions, and we do not doubt but that of ſuch, the King ſhall yet receive moſt ſignal ſervices: Its that whereof his wiſe and glorious Father aſſured him in his laſt inſtructions: *Be aſſured* (ſaith he) *as I am, that the moſt part of thoſe who have injured me, have done it, not through malice, but through miſinformation, and a ſiniſter apprehenſion of the affairs. None will be more loyal and faithful both to me and you, then thoſe ſubjects, who being ſenſible of their errors, and of the wrongs we have received, ſhall feel in their ſouls moſt vehement ſtirrings to repentance, and ardent deſires to do us ſome reparation for their paſt offences.*

Without queſtion there are many that yet ſerve the Covenanters, eſpecially thoſe in civil imployments, and even ſome in the Parliament, who groan under the yoke of impiety, and ſigh after Religion, peace, their King, and their duty: But alas 'tis but to think of liberty when they are in chains; although ſo afflicted as we are, we have great compaſſion on them, and eſteem their condition worſe then ours. Its a great miſery to be obliged to evil, becauſe they have done evil, and to do the work of the devil, and to know it, and cannot retire. Behold the fruits of affranchiſing themſelves in the beginning to do evil, to the end that good might come of it; flattering themſelves with a good intention (which pretext cannot be wanting to any injuſtice) and with a vain hope to return to their duty when they ſhould ſee it expedient, and to amend when they would, what they had marred; they offended God with gladneſs of heart, but now they find themſelves fettred in a cruel neceſſity, continually to offend him, or to caſt themſelves into our condition; they were better to come and keep us company, and generouſly to be ruined for the love of God, then to be perpetual Actors in the ruine of their King, their Country, their Church, and their Conſcience;

ence; and by *their hardness and impenitent heart, treasure up wrath against the day of wrath, and the declaration of the righteous judgement of God, who will render to every one according to his works.*

CHAP. XXV.

Of the cruelty of the Covenanters towards the good Subjects of the King.

FRom the oppression of the King, let us cast our eyes upon that of his subjects; to begin this discourse, is to enter into a gulf without bottom, of misery and impiety; for the Covenant is the den of Cyclops paved with blood, hung with spoils; 'tis the Cave of Radamanth, where is heard the noise of whips, the clattering of chains, the menaces of furies, and the pitiful shrieks of those whom the Vultures tear a pieces, and who are flead alive; there you shall behold thousands massacred, stretched upon the ground, the Flower of the Church and State cut off, the grandure of the Kingdome reduced into a heap of ruines, upon which set some petit Gentlemen, enriched by the general wrack, and fatted by the blood and bowels of their miserable country, there you shall behold the Grandees of the Kingdome a foot, begging the favour of their inferiours a horseback, and beholding their offices and revenues distributed among common persons, and their enemies.

Against them and all the Nobility is the great quarrel, the Covenanters hate them, because they are persons of honour, and acknowledged the King for the Fountain of Honor, and as such for the most part, they have followed and served him; thus almost all the rich and wealthy families of the Kingdome were wholly ruined,

ned, not by the insolent souldiers pillaging in hot blood, but by the extorsion of a new Committee, and robbery, which was done upon the carpet, and in cool blood.

Of these grand revenues, they accommodated themselves in the first place, and then those who have served them, assigning for a recompence to their instruments, persons of no worth, and newly raised from the dust, the antient rights and revenues of Lords and Gentlemen, they wanting nothing to be such but blood and generosity. The Covenanters party often celebrate the feasts of *Saturn*, where the servants sit at the upper end of the table, and are served by the Masters, and this fanatick insolence proceeded so far, that these spoilers esteemed themselves as lawfully invested in the inheritances of their superiours, and country-men, as the *Israelites* were of the lands of the *Amorites*: There is but this difference, the *Israelites* took possession by the command of God, these against his command.

Now by the special favour of the Gentlemen at *Westminster*, it was ordered that the fifth part of the revenues should be for provision for the wives and children of Delinquents, (such they call them, who so little respected the Majesty of the House of Commons, that they were faithful to their Soveraign.) Thus their wives sometimes were admitted to be Farmers of their husbands estates, and reserving themselves the fifth part, paid the rest to the State. But at last, even the Delinquents were admitted to compound for their estates; those who were best dealt with, paid two years value of their rents, others this double; if such be their compassions, what is their severity? Is not this for them to comment upon the saying of *Solomon*, which saith, *The mercies of the wicked are cruel*.

But moreover these favours were not granted to all, there being many who were never admitted to farm their estates, no neither to redeem them by compositi-

on,

on, and whose wives and children have scarce bread, nevertheless, the confiscation of their estates, their perpetual banishment, the sentence of death pronounced against them, are honorable marks of their great and loyal services to their Soveraign.

Of all those who suffered in this quarrel, the Ministers of the Gospel were the most barbarously dealt with, and for the least cause, very few amongst them, who ingaged themselves in the war. The Bishops whom the Laws gave the precedency in the House of Lords, have wholly lost their places, through the violence of the House of Commons, assisted with the seditious multitude; their Houses and Ecclesiastical revenues have been sold, and are torn from the Church for ever, their persons a long time imprisoned, and the most eminent of them had his head cut off upon a Scaffold.

This cruelty executed upon the heads, descended upon the members, all the revenues of the Dean and Chapiters through the Kingdome are become the prey of sacriledge, and of lazy bellies, which cram and fill themselves with the patrimony of the Church; the lawful possessors, without any distinction good or bad, were dispossessed: whereby the gentlemen of the Covenant clearly shew, that it was not the amendment of the Clergy, but their own enriching with the spoils of the Church, was the mark and scope of this Reformation.

In the ninety seven Parishes within the walls of *London*, there were found upon account, that there were fourscore and five Ministers driven by violence from their Churches and houses; and to number the Suburbs and Parishes adjoyning to *London*, the number of the Ministers, were a hundred and fifteen, without comprising those of S. *Pauls* and *Westminster*, where the Deans and Prebends ran the same fortune; of this number, twenty were imprisoned, and of those who are dead

Note that this book in the French was printed in the year 1650.

by

by distress, and anguish in divers prisons, in the holds of ships and banishment, they reckoned five years since twenty two; but this number is almost doubled since, and the others dispersed and fled into strange countries, or otherwise oppressed and ruined, are left to meditate upon this of the Psalmist, *The Lord is the portion of mine inheritance, he shall maintain me,* for any other of the Church its denied them. In the other parts of the Kingdom, many faithful Ministers to the King had the like usage, especially those who possessed the fairest and best benefices, for this was an unpardonable crime, and some of them were massacred by the furious Anabaptists, as a Sacrifice well pleasing to God.

Now whereas some other Delinquents have liberty to dwell in their houses, to farm their rents, and to compound for the principal; to the Clergy nothing like this is accorded, but they are turned out in their shirts, condemned to a total ruine without resource. There is indeed an Ordinance of Parliament, that the wives and children of ejected Ministers, should have the fifth part of the revenues of their benefices, but it is very ill observed, for the new incumbents into these benefices, carry themselves with such pride, and inhumanity to these poor women, refusing to obey the Ordinance, constraining them to plead before Judges, their adversaries; who instead of speedily relieving them, delay them with length of time, and make them consume in Suits that which they borrowed to plead their Cause.

So that these poor desolate persons, through the greatness of the expence, and tediousness of delays are constrained to desist their prosecution; and many being ejected out of small benefices, dare not present their petitions for the fifths, because the expences will amount higher then the principal: Certainly if there were any charity or sincerity in the Authors of this Ordinance, they would cause it to be strictly observed, they would
not

not permit that the poor wives and children whom they have ruined, should be shuffled off with litigious and crafty tricks, and oppressed with charges, when they come to demand that small alms which is granted them out of their husbands estates, they should not deny them that in retail which they have accorded them in gross.

Moreover you must know that this pretended gratuity is but for the wives and children, but as for the Ministers, who have neither the one nor the other, they are accounted unworthy to live, and not any part of their Estates is given to them; and thus they have rendered the Ministers of the Gospel conformable to their Master, who had not where to lay his head, and Jesus Christ is yet persecuted in his servants.

But the persecution staid not at those whom they Ejected. Behold a new invention, to root out at one stroak, all those who remained loyal, or Orthodox in the Church and State. It was ordered that all who had any office either in Church or State, should subscribe to be faithful to the present constitution of Government, by the House of Commons, without King or Lords, but the principal aim was to pick a quarrel with the Ministers of the Gospel upon their refusing, and to abolish the Ministry, for which they had already prepared the people, having appointed a Committee, *to displace disobedient Ministers, and to put those in their places, who condemned their vocation:* these are the terms of the instruction given the *Committee*, this horrible menace should give to all faithful Pastors, cause rather of hope then fear, for he that said to his Disciples, *He that refuseth you, refuseth me,* finds himself refused, and rejected in the persons of his servants, and yet more in their Ministry; without doubt he is provoked to jealousie, and will take upon him the cause of the Ministry of his Word.

Whosoever shall seriously consider all that hideous spectacle of devastation of the Church, the abolition of
Go-

Government, the ruine of the Pastors, the corruption of Religion, the profanation of the service of God, and shall compare this persecution with that the Greek Churches suffer at this day, shall find that all the ravages of the *Turks* since the taking of *Constantinople*, have not so disfigured the Church in two hundred years, as these Reformers did in six or seven years in their own country, and amongst their brethren in the faith.

But pass we from the Ecclesiastical to the Civil, the new Courts erected to hear complaints, and to receive the compositions of Delinquents, were as so many Butchers Shambles, and Flaying-houses, where they tore off the skin, and pulled out the bowels, and where they dismembred, and cut in pieces many antient and good houses; our miserable party had to do with worser Judges, then he spoken of in the eighteenth of S. *Luke, which feared not God, neither regarded man*; and yet he suffered himself to be overcome by the importunity of the afflicted Widdow, and said, *I will avenge her*, or I will do her Justice; *We propose him for an example to these cruel souls, and say after our Saviour*, Hear what the unjust Judge saith; *And shall not God avenge his own Elect, which cry day and night unto him, though he bear long with them, I tell you that he will avenge them speedily.*

There could be expected no juster sequel of iniquity from their beginnings, then when it was commanded for every person through the Kingdom to bring in their Plate and Jewels, which the seditious Zealots contributed as freely as the idolatrous *Israelites* to make a Golden Calf, but those who did not bring their Plate, they plundred their houses, and took it away by force; at the same time they commanded the people to take up arms under the penalty of being hanged, and this sentence was executed in the Counties of *Essex*, *Suffolk*, and *Cambridge*; the principal actor of this tyranny, was the Earl of *Manchester*, who caused some to be hanged, who

nor

not being well learned in the Catechifme of fedition, refufed openly to take up arms againft the King, others for the fame reafon were tyed neck and heels, unreafonably mifufed, and caft into prifons until they had learned Rebellion, and the reft of the people affrighted hereby, went peaceably to commit treafon againft his Majefty.

Therefore the greateft cruelty of the Covenanters, was not in rendring their country miferable, but in having rendred it wicked, and forced fo many fimple people to be inftruments of their ambition, and partakers of their crimes. How will they anfwer for the blood and the confciences of their Souldiers killed in the act of paracide, then when they difcharged their Muskets againft the Squadron where the perfon of the King was? How will they anfwer for them who were actually imployed in the maffacre of the King, and who have fince felt a hell in their confciences? we muft confefs that they have been more cruel towards their own party, then towards ours, fince they have only made us to fuffer evil, but they have forced their adherents, both to fuffer and do evil, which are the two principal things wherein all the work of the devil confifts.

After this execrable murther of their excellent Soveraign, how many murthers did they heap upon this? Duke *Hamilton*, the Earl of *Holland*, the truly Noble and loyal Lord *Capel*; many others killed in their armies in divers places, many in every County condemned to death by partial Judges, who received all accufations againft thofe who had ferved their King, and many thoufands good fubjects murthered in *Ireland* by thefe Sanguinary Zealots.

It would be infinite to reckon up all their crimes againft God, their Religion, their Church, their King, and their Country, and all that can be fpoken, is nothing in comparifon to that prodigious mafs of iniquity, which ftricks heaven with its height, and makes even the earth

to

to sink with the weight which draws from the bottom of our wounded souls, these ardent sighs.

Oh our good God, art thou so wrathfully displeased against these Nations, as to give them over to a reprobate sense, and abandoned to do the will of the devil, and establish his Kingdome? Oh Religion, Conscience, King, Church, State, Order, Peace, Justice, Laws, all are violated, defaced, disfigured and melted into a horrible Chaos of obscurity and confusion! Alas how can it be that this people enlightened with the knowledge of God, abounding with the riches of heaven and earth, should fall into such a diabolical frenzy, as to trample under their feet their Religion, cut off the head of their King, pluck out the throat of their Mother, the Church, and deal with their Fellow-countrymen, and Brethren in Jesus Christ, more cruelly then the *Mahumetans* deal with the Christians, who drives them not from their houses and patrimonies in *Turky*, nor reduce them to the fift part of their Revenues, *How is the faithful City become an Harlot! it was full of Judgement, righteousness lodged in it, but now murtherers*, Isa. 1.21. Certainly although the evil they do unto us, should not force us to go out of our Country and leave it, yet the evil that we behold in it, is capable to make us forsake it, and to imbrace the Prophet *Jeremies* choice, Jer. 9. 2, 3. *Oh that I had in the wilderness a lodging place for way-faring men, that I might leave my people, and go from them, for they be adulterers, an assembly of treacherous men, and they bend their tongues like their bow for lies, but are not valiant for the truth, for they proceed from evil to evil, and they know not me, saith the Lord.*

Ha people frantick? whose eyes the God of this world have darkned, and exasperated your passions with a seditious rage, cruelly and bloodily to persecute your Church and Soveraign? Miserable people who do the work of their enemies, and execute upon themselves the malediction pronounced to *Hierusalem* in Rebellion, *Sion shall tear her self with her own hands*, ridding and casting their crown and glory upon the ground, cutting their own sinews, and breaking their bones, and by their weakness and disunion, invite the enemy to come and make an end of them. Blind Zealots, who stirred you up so disorderly to pull down Antichrist? you will find in doing thus, you have contributed to raise him up, and having drawn an horrible scandal upon our most Holy Religion, by your impious actions, and infamous Doctrines, have healed the mortal wound of the beast, and hardned the consciences of men against the Sword of the Gospel, which rarely penetrates with efficacy, when its welded with wicked hands.

That which comforts us in beholding you take such courses as to make faith cease from being in the earth, is, that hereby you advance the desired coming of Jesus Christ, who hath marked that time for his return, when he will deliver his Church, from the bondage of seduction, vanity, blindness, and misery, for to invest her with liberty, holiness, and glory, which he hath purchased for her by his blood.

In waiting for this happy deliverance, if we must still behold Rebellion proudly domineer, over the Supreme Powers ordained by God, and sacriledge make havock in the Church, and crimes turned into Laws and Doctrines of Religion, we shall preserve our selves by the grace of God, from murmuring at his Justice, and the conduct of his Providence, remembring that God punisheth us justly by instruments which are unjust, and that he will assuredly manifest his just judgements upon them, when he shall see it most expedient for his glory, which he is used to advance by wayes contrary, in appearance, and makes, as in the Creation, light to shine out of darkness; we will endeavour to learn in our calamity, this divine wisdome of *Solomon*, Eccles. 5. 8. *If thou seest the oppression of the poor, and violent perverting of Judgement, and Justice in a Province, marvel not at the matter, for he that is higher then the highest, regardeth, and there be higher then they.*

Being persecuted by a people who in destroying us, pretend they do God service, and who palliate their cruelty with zeal of his glory, we comfort our selves in this holy promise, as made expresly for our condition. Isa. 66. 5. *Hear the word of the Lord ye that tremble at his word, your brethren that hated you, that cast you out for my name sake, said, let the Lord be glorified, but he shall appear to your joy, and they shall be ashamed.*

O our God we beseech thee forgive our enemies, confound their pernicious designs, and convert their erring consciences, repair the hedge broken down of thy vine, whereby the Wildboar out of the woods break down the branches, and root up the tender plants, *wherefore shall they say amongst the heathen, where is now their God.*

Soli Deo Gloria.

El poder malamente adquirido, no suele ser duradero.

FINIS.

www.ingramcontent.com/pod-product-compliance
Lightning Source LLC
Chambersburg PA
CBHW031342230426
43670CB00006B/415